Guardians of the Nation?

RECENT TITLES FROM THE HELEN KELLOGG INSTITUTE FOR INTERNATIONAL STUDIES

Scott Mainwaring, *general editor*

Michael Fleet and Brian H. Smith, eds.
The Catholic Church and Democracy in Chile and Peru (1997)

A. James McAdams, ed.
Transitional Justice and the Rule of Law in New Democracies (1997)

Carol Ann Drogus
Women, Religion, and Social Change in Brazil's Popular Church (1997)

Víctor E. Tokman and Guillermo O'Donnell, eds.
Poverty and Inequality in Latin America: Issues and New Challenges (1998)

Brian H. Smith
Religious Politics in Latin America, Pentecostal vs. Catholic (1998)

Tristan Anne Borer
Challenging the State: Churches as Political Actors in South Africa, 1980–1994 (1998)

Juan E. Méndez, Guillermo O'Donnell, and Paulo Sérgio Pinheiro, eds.
The (Un)Rule of Law and the Underprivileged in Latin America (1999)

Guillermo O'Donnell
Counterpoints: Selected Essays on Authoritarianism and Democratization (1999)

Howard Handelman and Mark Tessler, eds.
Democracy and Its Limits: Lessons from Asia, Latin America, and the Middle East (1999)

Larissa Adler Lomnitz and Ana Melnick
Chile's Political Culture and Parties: An Anthropological Explanation (2000)

Kevin Healy
Llamas, Weavings, and Organic Chocolate: Multicultural Grassroots Development in the Andes and Amazon of Bolivia (2000)

Ernest J. Bartell, C.S.C., and Alejandro O'Donnell
The Child in Latin America: Health, Development, and Rights (2000)

Vikram K. Chand
Mexico's Political Awakening (2001)

Collier and Collier
Shaping the Political Arena (2002)

For a complete list of titles from the Helen Kellogg Institute for International Studies, see http:www.undpress.nd.edu

GUARDIANS OF THE NATION?

Economists, Generals, and Economic Reform in Latin America

GLEN BIGLAISER

UNIVERSITY OF NOTRE DAME PRESS
Notre Dame, Indiana

Manufactured in the United States of America

Library of Congress Cataloging-in-Publication Data
Biglaiser, Glen, 1963–
    Guardians of the nation? : economists, generals, and economic reform
in Latin America / Glen Biglaiser.
        p.   cm.
    "From the Helen Kellogg Institute for International Studies."
    Includes bibliographical references and index.
    ISBN 0-268-03874-0 (cloth : alk. paper)
    ISBN 0-268-03875-9 (pbk. : alk. paper)
    1. Southern Cone of South America—Economic Policy.
    2. Southern Cone of South America—Politics and government—
20th century.   3. Military government—Southern Cone of
South America   I. Helen Kellogg Institute for International Studies.
II. Title.
HC167.S67 B54   2002
338.98-dc21

                        2002003991

    ∞ *This book is printed on acid-free paper.*

CONTENTS

TABLES, CHARTS, AND DIAGRAMS

ACKNOWLEDGMENTS

A main tenet of architect Frank Lloyd Wright is that form and function should be one, joined in a spiritual union. Wright introduced the term "organic" into his philosophy, showing the harmonious relationship between the form and function of a building. Wright's work complements research in the economic development literature. For years, development theorists claimed that the form of government and the functioning of the economy went together. Authoritarian governments, so the story went, possessed advantages over their democratic counterparts in the pursuit of economic development. This book shows that military regimes may not possess advantages for economic performance. The findings in this study indicate that military regimes rarely achieve their economic goals. Indeed, fragile democracies in Latin America and elsewhere should take note of the lack of economic success under military or authoritarian rule.

Many scholars and friends have stimulated my interest in political and economic development in Latin America. Among the academic circle, I owe my greatest debt to Barbara Geddes. One of the most generous persons in the profession, Barbara helped me to uncover a puzzle that melded with my interests in politics and economic development. Her detailed and helpful comments on multiple drafts of this project made this work far better than it might otherwise have been. I am also deeply indebted to Jeff Frieden. Through course work at UCLA, Jeff nurtured my interest in Latin American political economy issues. His challenging criticisms and good-humored retorts also forced me to rethink arguments, instilling greater clarity and rigor in the work. My debt to Arnold Harberger is no less great. Access to firsthand information on economic policy choice by someone with a strong commitment to promoting economic prosperity in the developing world made Al an invaluable resource. Al opened doors to information and connections in Latin America that field researchers treasure. His contacts, and his own personal experiences, enabled me to gain a better understanding of the politics under military rule. Michael Wallerstein and Jose Moya also offered their expert suggestions in the early stages of this project. A number of other scholars also read portions of this manuscript and provided useful comments. They include Jonathan Hartlyn, Ron King, Veronica Montecinos, Paul Sum, Nicolas Van de Walle, and Kurt Weyland.

Many others have also contributed to this study, often more than they might realize. My gratitude goes out to my good friends and peers at UCLA—David Brown, David D'Lugo, Tony Gill, Carlos Juárez, Steve Kay, and Nancy Lapp. David Brown and Tony Gill, in particular, deserve special mention for critically reading the entire manuscript and offering informed and reasonable suggestions. Their camaraderie and banter also made work on this project more rewarding and fun. I also cannot forget my new colleagues at Bowling Green State University, who have provided encouragement and support.

Field work in Latin America would not have been possible without the support of several people and agencies. In Argentina, I owe thanks to Carlos Rodríguez, who provided research affiliation for me at the Centro de Estudios Macroeconómicos de Argentina (CEMA). I benefitted immensely from the discussions at CEMA with Carola Pessino, who offered useful ideas and was a great friend. My sincere appreciation also goes out to the Sturzenegger family, who put me up in their home for a few weeks and helped me to find permanent housing accommodations. Adolfo Sturzenegger also assisted me in establishing contacts and made my stay in Buenos Aires very comfortable. In Chile, I am grateful to many members of the economics department at the Pontificia Universidad de Católica. Economists Rolf Lüders, Alvaro Donoso, and other Chileans trained at the University of Chicago contributed more than they can imagine through their time, patience, and information. In Uruguay, my thanks go out to Juan Rial and Carina Perelli at the Sociedad de Análisis Político (PEI-THO) for providing research affiliation. I extend my warmest regards to the late Daniel Vaz, the general manager at the Uruguayan Central Bank. Daniel and his support staff arranged interviews with nearly everyone in Montevideo. His untimely death is a loss to his family and to the Uruguayan educational and financial community. I received material help for this project through several grants from UCLA's International Studies and Overseas Programs, the Latin American Center, and the Center for Business Education and Research.

Finally, and most important, I cannot forget my debts closest to home. It is hard to imagine undertaking this project without the support of my family and loved ones. My parents and siblings have always backed my efforts. Since I have known her, Najma Bashar has not only supported my research, she has also improved my tables and graphs, lending her artistic touch. She has also tolerated my various travels. For her love, caring, and warmth, I thank her.

ONE

The Effects of Institutions and Ideas on Policy Choice

Cities will have no respite from evil, my dear Glaucon, nor will the human race, I think, unless philosophers rule as kings in the cities, or those whom we now call kings and rulers genuinely and adequately study philosophy, until, that is, political power and philosophy coalesce, and the various natures of those who now pursue the one to the exclusion of the other are forcibly debarred from doing so.

—Plato, *The Republic*

The great philosopher Plato once argued that the wisest of citizens—the philosophers—should govern nations. He assumed these philosophers would have the interests of the common good in mind when making policy and could overcome deleterious appeals to self-interest—from individuals and particularistic groups—that might rip the commonwealth asunder. In Plato's time, populations were smaller and economies simpler. Today, the need for a division of labor in governing makes it unlikely that philosophers could rule as kings. Obtaining and retaining office requires skills that are often different than those needed for policy making. Nonetheless, it is widely believed that rulers (kings) should govern on the advice of experts (philosophers) in specific areas of policy, be it national defense, public health, or economics. The more insulated these policy experts are from the pressure of self-serving interest groups, the more leeway they have in crafting policy that benefits the common good.

Of course, all this assumes that the wisest people are immune from self-interested behavior. This may very well be the fatal flaw in Plato's theory. Some of the most intelligent humans have proven to be disastrous governors.

In the realm of economic development, scholars have often debated the virtues that various forms of government have on the prosperity of a nation. For centuries, scholars have extolled the virtues of democratic governance, but are cautious about its prospects for economic development. Tension arises from the fact that electoral challenges force democracies to pursue policies that satisfy short-term goals. Policies that foster economic development require patience. Only more centralized forms of government operate under long enough time horizons to implement and sustain such policies.[1] As Alexis de Tocqueville (1945, 243) wrote, "Democracy favors the growth of the state's internal resources; it extends comfort and develops public spirit, strengthens respect for law in the various classes of society, . . . But a democracy finds it difficult to coordinate the details of a great undertaking and to fix on some plan and carry it through with determination in spite of obstacles. It has little capacity for combining measures in secret and waiting patiently for the result."[2] Tocqueville's observation reaches to the heart of a central debate in contemporary political economy—to what extent are democracies superior in implementing policies than more centralized forms of government?

Among the more centralized kinds of government, military regimes are expected to hold advantages, especially in the developing world. As the more modern elements, militaries can do everything which needs organization and technical know-how. The goal of national security requires that the military receives training and develops skills that provide it with greater initial political capacity in comparison with other civilian groups (Janowitz 1977, 103–4).

The anticipated advantage of military regimes is not lost on economic development analysts. Conventional wisdom suggests that military regimes provide the ideal circumstances for the attainment of high rates of economic growth in the medium and long run.[3] This wisdom evolved, in part, because of the maintenance of state-led, inward-oriented economic policies under democracy. Import substitution industrialization (ISI)—a development strategy based on the replacement of previously imported goods by local production—dominated the policy agendas in much of the democratic developing world from the 1940s through the 1970s. During these years, policy makers who identified with the dependency school and nonaligned movement divided the world's economic system into an industrial center in the developed world and primary-product export periphery in the developing world. In this division, the developing world produced goods that experienced declining terms of trade and erratic prices relative to the industrial goods they imported. Policy makers proposed having the state subsidize the domestic manufacture of industrialized goods to solve this imbalance.

However, by the late 1960s, democracies that continued to back protectionist ISI policies experienced serious economic decay. Many policy makers knew the inherent limits of ISI by the early to mid-1960s. Hence, the stillborn attempts to create free-trade zones. But societal interests dictated otherwise. Indeed, analysts explained the inability of democracies to change policy direction based on the state's limited autonomy from societal interests. Democratic governments, tied to the necessity of winning elections in order to maintain power, served the interests of powerful pluralist groups that favored ISI policies. The high frequency of elections combined with the need by incumbents to look good before elections also compelled politicians to take a short-term, redistributionist approach to economic problems.

Unable to withstand political pressures and impose costs on large parts of the population, democracies continued to initiate policies that produced worsening economic results. Over time, as economic disorder and political conflict grew, military leaders mounted coups. The prevailing wisdom suggested that military regimes, insulated from most societal groups, would institute economic measures necessary for economic development (Huntington 1968).[4] Since military regimes do not seek reelection or popularity, so the story goes, they are able to ignore societal interests, and impose their policy preferences.[5] These preferences may include market-oriented, neoliberal policies that cause economic dislocation in the short term but are expected to promote long-term economic growth. Military governments also have less rapid turnover at staff levels, which facilitates the implementation of long-run plans. Unlike democracies, where presidents face elections on regular intervals and where policy makers are replaced after each succession, military leaders rule indefinitely and can maintain their staffs for a long time.

Much of the debate over regime type and economic policy choice has focused on Latin America. Politically independent since the 1820s, Latin America has a long history of political instability based on economic crisis. Despite having ample natural and human resources, skilled and entrepreneurial immigrants, and substantial foreign capital, Latin America's economy has stagnated for much of the past two centuries

(Frieden 1991, 3). The enigma of poverty combined with favorable factor endowments has frequently contributed to military coups. Once installed, authoritarian or military rulers are expected to do what democratic leaders cannot, that is, to initiate economic policies that use Latin America's abundant resources to promote economic growth and development.

For many pundits, Chile is the perfect case in point.[6] In the 1970s, with state ownership and protectionism dominating policy agendas in most developing countries, Chile under the military regime of General Augusto Pinochet became the first Latin American state to orient its economy towards the market. Despite economic inequalities and severe military repression, some argue that Chile's high rate of growth in the mid- to late 1980s makes it an ideal model for others to imitate.[7]

What supporters of this argument fail to notice, however, is that military regimes have initiated different economic policies and have varied widely in their economic results.[8] In fact, many military regimes did worse than the democratic regimes they replaced.[9] As Remmer (1990) points out, military regimes may not perform better under crisis conditions either.

This study intends to fill a gap in the development literature by identifying the larger historical processes underlying policy choice in military regimes. Most studies on economic policy choice have relied on single case studies, compared democratic and authoritarian regimes, or examined democracies exclusively.[10] Although these studies have provided us with detailed and rich information, few of them have compared policy choice under military regimes.[11]

Using a comparative framework, this book examines the economic policy choices of military regimes in the Southern Cone: Chile (1973–89), Argentina (1966–73, 1976–83), and Uruguay (1973–84). These countries offer a unique opportunity to compare the economic performance of military regimes under similar circumstances. During the 1970s and 1980s, military regimes in the Southern Cone faced nearly identical international conditions, had similar cultural and historical legacies, and were at comparable levels of economic development (Stepan 1985). Many of the finance ministers and government leaders in Argentina and Uruguay mimicked Chile in declaring their support for market-oriented orthodox policies. In the end these regimes failed to follow the Chilean model. In fact, it has been democratic regimes that have embraced the Chilean model, counter to many expectations.[12]

Rather than seeing Chile's experience as a model for others to follow, the evidence presented in this study demonstrates that its experience represents an anomaly among military regimes. The circumstances under which Chile initiated and sustained market-oriented economic policies are fairly uncommon, as shown by the policies chosen by other military regimes. Indeed, the notion that Pinochet, who previously rejected neo-liberal reforms, is an exemplar for market-oriented policies is an oddity in itself. This study suggests that the path to economic development does not follow automatically from a military regime, as some supporters of the Chilean model would have us believe. In order to evaluate the applicability of the Chilean model to other states we must first understand the unique aspects of military rule in Chile. By comparing the economic policies of military regimes in Argentina, Chile, and Uruguay, this study shows how stringent are the conditions under which military regimes achieve economic growth.

A study about the reputed success of Chile's military regime takes on greater significance as developing democratic countries face mounting economic difficulties. Despite the success in calming inflationary pressures, the rewards of operating under an open-market system have not been shared equally in many countries. Pressures are building from many disenchanted voters about growing income and wealth disparities. In Latin America, for instance, political competitors upholding "populist" messages have sprung up in Venezuela, Ecuador, Paraguay, and elsewhere in response to the challenge of economic globalism. This has led to fears that people in these states may be tempted to turn to "the man on horseback" to solve their economic problems (Finer 1962).

The potential return of military rule makes it imperative to examine the economic policy results of past military governments.[13] The economic performance of military regimes in the Southern Cone demonstrates that such regimes do not always provide a sure path toward economic development. In fact, military regimes often experience poorer economic results than their democratic predecessors do, which hopefully will discourage future military interventions.

Theoretical Perspectives on
Economic Policy Choice under Military Rule

The principal goal of this book is to answer the following question: Why do military regimes that claim to favor the same policies vary widely in their policy choices? If, as it is often claimed, military regimes can insulate themselves from the pressures that inhibit democratic governments, why don't military regimes adopt similar policies to produce high economic growth rates?

The appropriate policy to produce high growth rates is a heated topic. There are some who argue that economic growth rates are not important unless there is equitable distribution of the benefits of growth. Although equitable distribution and social improvements for the entire population are important long-term goals, as Frieden (1991, 4) contends, it is "impossible to undertake an equitable distribution of the fruits of economic growth if there is no economic growth to start with."[14] Moreover, a near consensus has emerged in the economics profession in favor of stable macroeconomic policy and market-oriented reforms for stimulating economic growth.[15] Indeed, many economists have returned to the classical liberal ideas tied to Adam Smith, David Ricardo, and others to explain differences in development among countries. This book does not intend to enter the debate about whether one set of policies is more likely to support growth and development. Instead, the goal of this research is to explain why military regimes, presumably insulated from popular pressures, and which claim to back the same market-oriented reforms, are unable to initiate and sustain their policy preferences.

Although differences exist over the best strategy to foster economic growth and development, nearly all agree that policies chosen by domestic policy makers affect economic performance (Frieden 1991; Bates 1981). This was not the case in the 1960s, when many theorists claimed that international factors largely determined policy choice. Today, however, scholars of economic development using such diverse approaches as pluralist arguments, state autonomy concepts, and even international theories agree that domestic policy choice affects economic performance. If economic performance is in large part a result of domestic economic policies, the next step is to determine how these policies are chosen.

Economic policy choices under military rule have received less attention than in democratic systems. The difficulty in obtaining information about the internal workings of policy making in military regimes may be one explanation for this. Another may be that analysts find transitions to (and consolidations of) democracy inherently more interesting than studies of military regimes. The few studies of economic policy making in military regimes have focused almost exclusively on four general explanations: (1) the influence of international financial organizations, (2) the "left threat," (3) economic interest groups, and (4) ideas and institutions.

Some contend that international financial organizations such as the International Monetary Fund (IMF), the World Bank, or the "Washington consensus" influence policy choices. It is argued that the higher the debt level accumulated by debtor countries to international organizations, the greater the likelihood that international factors will affect policy choice (Haggard 1990; Lancaster 1988, 1990; Stallings 1990, 1992). Others assert that class elements like a high "left" threat in democratic regimes preceding military coups increases the likelihood of orthodox market-oriented policies and makes it more likely that the policies will be sustained. As orthodox policies have negative effects for the societal groups from which leftist organizations draw support, military governments promote these policies to reduce left threats (O'Donnell 1988; Frieden 1991; Stepan 1988). Some argue that pressures of powerful economic interests lead to a particular set of economic policies. Domestic class alliances or domestic and international class alliances determine economic policy choices (Cardoso and Faletto 1979; Frieden 1991; O'Donnell 1973, 1978; Silva 1991, 1993). Others examine the effect of ideas and institutions to explain the adoption, implementation, and consolidation of policy choices. The ideas and ideology of policy makers and the president—who are aware of international and domestic constraints and opportunities— influence the adoption of economic policies (Sikkink 1991; Hall 1989; Goldstein and Keohane 1993). This study tests these hypotheses of policy choice under military rule on a comparative basis.

In addition to testing these four previous hypotheses, I advance a new explanation that builds on the domestic institutions and ideational literatures and the work of Karen Remmer, among others. According to Remmer (1991), Chile's ability to apply more orthodox policies than the other Southern Cone countries depended on the concentration of political power achieved by Pinochet. Remmer asserts that political power concentrated in a single individual rather than by the military as an institution provided state technocrats with autonomy from social forces and from the military itself. The history of professionalism in Chile's military enabled Pinochet to limit the influence of outside pressures without politicizing the military. Since neoliberal policies threaten many interests, including inefficient producers, who are the most likely candidates to lobby for the policy status quo, a concentration of authority helps leaders resist these pressures (Nelson 1990).

This study also stresses the importance of institutions and state technocrats—insulated from interest-group pressures—for the initiation of orthodox policies. However, it goes a step further by detailing when ortho-dox policies are most likely to be initiated. The study also complements pluralist arguments in that it shows under what circumstances interest groups will influence economic policy choice. In addition, the study helps reveal how among a preexisting menu of ideas, some are chosen while oth-ers are not, which builds a stronger foundation for the ideational literature.

To understand why military regimes choose different economic poli-cies, this work stresses the importance of ideas and professional socializa-tion. For centuries, scholars have pointed to the role of ideas, especially when other explanations failed to account for different policy decisions. Ideational explanations have made a comeback. Recent studies have at-tempted to explain big exogenous structural changes, such as the shift from Keynesianism to monetarism (Hall 1989, 370). Despite the revival of interest in the importance of ideas in making policy choices, no one quite knows how to use them. Efforts have been made to show that ideas inform policy choices, but the difficulty in building theoretically sound arguments around ideas has led some to suggest ending the revival. In-deed, how ideas are used under normal circumstances, as compared to times of crisis, has eluded scholarly attention. This raises the question of how do ideas matter?

This study proposes an anchor for the ideational literature: an ap-proach to the influence of ideas on policy choice based on the strategic interests of government officials. In specific, it focuses on the appoint-ment strategies of military leaders to understand the interplay between ideas and institutions. The keystone of the argument is that differences in long-standing characteristics of the military and in the kinds of gov-erning institutions installed by military leaders shape the appointment of ideational entrepreneurs (namely, economic policy makers). A leader under one-man rule, whose military has little experience with factions, provides leaders with more autonomy in their appointments than colle-gial governments or factionalized militaries that require consensual agree-ment. This also provides greater opportunity for ideational entrepreneurs to turn their thoughts into real policy.

Whom military rulers appoint as their economic policy makers shows how ideas matter in a strategic sense. Institutional structures that pro-mote autonomy provide rulers with better opportunities to select ideo-logically committed economists as their policy makers. The evidence pre-sented shows that the decision to appoint ideologically committed policy makers affects policy choice. Specifically, the selection of a high propor-

tion of neoliberal economists in economic policy-making positions—
most of whom received their graduate training in economics in the United
States or studied under others trained in the U. S.—contributes to the
initiation and maintenance of orthodox economic policies.[16] Based on
their training, neoliberal economists hold similar economic ideas. Their
ideas enable them to create a buffer against societal interests, which helps
them to implement their policy preferences.

Policy Choices and Political Survival

The argument presented here suggests that the educational background
of economic policy makers helps to explain policy choices. The general
line of this argument claims that a high proportion of neoliberal economists in economic policy-making positions produces more orthodox
economic policy choices. Economists who have been taught that the free
market and minimal government intervention are key ingredients for
economic growth and development are more likely to initiate these types
of policies than policy makers without such training. Thus, to understand
the selection of economic policies we must first understand how economic
policy makers are chosen. Although a variety of means are used to select
economic policy makers in military regimes, in nearly every case the military itself has the final say in determining who is selected.

Few studies, however, have addressed which economic policy makers
the military will choose. Instead, much of the literature has focused on
democratic governments and the goals of democratic leaders.[17] A central
assumption of this literature is that politicians seek reelection or what
some have called political survival (Ames 1987). Geddes (1994) and Mayhew (1974), for example, argue that politicians are motivated by the desire
for political survival and success and offer arguments to persuade read-
ers that the assumption is plausible.[18] Political leaders in democratic governments are perceived as "single-minded seekers of reelection" who make
decisions to bolster their opportunities for victory in the next election
(Mayhew 1974, 5). Whatever additional interests they may have, the prime
interest of political leaders focuses on their attempts to maximize their
career success (Geddes 1994, 7).[19]

Some leaders, of course, retire after serving one term in office and
are not interested in political survival. But as the long service records of
most members of the United States Congress clearly demonstrate, most

politicians desire to remain in power and enhance their political careers. Decisions ratified recently in the legislatures in Argentina, Brazil, Peru, and Venezuela—made at the request of the executives—that have enabled their presidents to serve consecutive terms without stepping down from power also suggest that executives are interested in maintaining their political survival.

The desire for political survival is not just held by politicians in democratic governments. In one of the few works to discuss the role of military leaders on policy choice, Ames (1987) argues that like democratic leaders, military leaders often want to survive in political office and increase their own power.[20] Although most professional officers "detest politics, engage in governance reluctantly, and extricate themselves institutionally from direct political rule without regret once the armed forces' corporate interests safely allow disengagement," (Loveman 1998, 122), achieving the presidency takes a lot of effort.[21] Without denying that they have additional interests, we can assume that those who achieve the presidency and their rivals want to achieve high office and remain there.[22] The long history of dictatorship without time limitations attests to this.

In attempting to extend their political careers, one of the most common but least-studied survival strategies involves appointments to economic policy-making positions.[23] Appointments of policy makers in areas related to the economy are especially important, as economic performance often has important effects on the military leader's likelihood to survive. Unlike democratic governments that acquire legitimacy through elections, military regimes need good economic results to legitimate their rule. As Haggard and Kaufman (1995, 11) write, authoritarian regimes "are arguably more dependent than democracies on their capacity to deliver material resources to key supporters, and it is for this reason that economic performance can be pivotal in dislodging them."[24]

In selecting economic policy makers, military rulers usually consider three appointment strategies to extend their political careers: patronage, co-optation, or technical merit. In the first scenario, military leaders may use appointments as forms of patronage to reward fellow officers and others who have supported them. In providing jobs for their friends and supporters, however, military leaders may forgo potential economic benefits that they would have earned if they had hired technocrats who best understood the policies that needed to be implemented in order to achieve economic success.

Alternatively, military leaders may adopt co-optive appointment strategies that promote consensus among rival leaders. Fear of a counter-coup by military rivals weighs into appointment strategies chosen by leaders. Because military governments have no official unbiased body or document to enforce agreements among junta members, consensual arrangements among leaders on the choice of economic policy makers is even more critical. Like the patronage option, the need for consensus works against the appointment of technocrats. Most officers favor appointees who back protectionist policies and a large state, as these policies provide jobs for officers and subsidies for military enterprises that might not survive without the state's support.

Alternatively, leaders may make appointments that appear to be based more on technical merit than on issues of political patronage or coalition building. Leaders may appoint technocrats who, on the basis of their training, the leaders believe are best qualified to manage the economy. If these policy makers, who "rule as kings" of economic decisions, can produce strong economic growth and improve economic development, they may serve the career goals of their leaders in office.[25]

The approach proposed here thus explains the choice of ideologically committed policy makers based on the behavior of military leaders. This approach suggests that military rulers have different appointment strategies that they can choose from depending on which will best promote their political careers. Rulers need good economic performance and political support mainly from the military to remain in office. As these scenarios suggest, the need for short-term political support may prevent rulers from achieving good economic results in the medium and long run. It may be the case that military leaders are constrained politically in their appointment strategies.

The Military, Governing Institutions, and Economic Appointments

Although military regimes in the Southern Cone shared many similar regime characteristics and economic goals, leaders in these regimes followed different appointment strategies. To understand why military leaders make different policy-making appointments, we need to focus on the political conditions and constraints that shape their decisions. Differences in long-standing characteristics of the military and in the kinds of governing institutions established by military rulers help to explain appointment strategies chosen by survival-minded military leaders.

The specifics of this argument are more fully detailed in chapter 3, but the general line of causation is straightforward. Some nations' military forces tend to experience much greater inter-service rivalry than those of others. The reasons for this are often complemented and embedded in the historical experience of various nations' military forces. Military forces with strong histories of inter-service rivalry are often referred to as being factionalized, while military forces with lesser experiences of inter-service rivalry are simply "less factionalized."

An important characteristic of factionalized military forces is their tendency toward politicization. Three historical factors can contribute to factionalization and are, at minimum, good indicators of the presence of factionalization within the military. These factors include: (1) the frequency of political interventions by the military, (2) the experience of the military with politicized promotions, and (3) the history of competition among the armed services for scarce resources. These historical circumstances promote dissension and disagreement among the forces, as officers become directly involved in political and distributive decisions. Such decisions increase ideological dissension and lead to the creation of proto-parties within the officer corps. The formation of proto-parties contributes to struggles over policy and control in the military that may, in extreme cases, give rise to armed confrontation among the forces. These struggles among officers promote factions in militaries.

Less factionalized militaries, in contrast, have had little experience in political matters. These military forces have rarely wrested power from democratic forces, or been exposed to politicized promotions. Officers in these militaries generally focus on strictly professional issues such as national security and defense, areas where they are more likely to find consensus. In addition, the "senior" service, most often the army, holds the greatest proportion of resources and manpower, which limits the intensity of competitive political struggles among services for their share of the defense budget.[26]

These differences in long-standing characteristics of the military have implications for the political survival strategies and appointment decisions made by military leaders. I contend that military leaders backed by factionalized military forces are more likely to make explicit agreements for power sharing and consensus building among the services in order to discourage counter-coups. Attempts at power sharing among the services prompt rulers to make patronage appointments that serve their short-term interest in political survival, but which come at the expense of their medium-term interest in economic performance. Political contenders from within the military induce rulers to offer appointments, jobs, and favors to military loyalists and competitors in return for short-term political support.

The need to appease interests within the military and among their civilian allies also works against the appointment of ideational entrepreneurs of a particular ideological coloration, namely neoliberal economists. Contrary to popular belief, an important common denominator among most military officers in the developing world is their intense opposition to policies supported by neoliberal economists.[27] Through their training, officers learn about the important role played by the state in promoting economic development and insuring the security of the nation (Stepan 1971). Officers back measures to insulate the country from the vagaries of international markets and to protect "national treasures," such as copper mines and oil interests, from international capitalists. Neoliberal economists, by contrast, want to shrink the state and foster economic growth and development through market forces.

Since factionalized militaries struggle to reach agreements in order to satisfy a broad range of interests within the officer corps, and most officers oppose neoliberal policies, factionalized militaries are expected to restrict the appointment of neoliberal economists. Rather than satisfying factional interests, the appointment of neoliberal economists and their policy choices would exacerbate divisions in factionalized military forces. Military governments often use profits and employment opportunities from state-owned enterprises to distribute benefits among officers and reduce factional pressures. These governments also use subsidies and protection for goods produced in military industries to satisfy officers. Neoliberal economists, however, favor market-oriented policies, which limit sources of patronage and access to state resources. Privatization and economic opening, cornerstones of market-oriented policies, reduce opportunities for rent seeking (Krueger 1974). Since neoliberal economists threaten access to state resources used by leaders to build their support, officers are not expected to favor the appointment of these economists in cases where the political position of military leaders is less secure.

Factions also attract interest-group pressures. Since the military serves as the most effective channel for exercising influence over military leaders, interest groups lobby officers. As many interest groups benefit from protectionist policies, these groups are likely to solicit officers to put up fierce resistance to the appointment of policy makers who support neoliberal policies, which further influences policy-making appointments.

In less factionalized forces, military leaders face a less pressing threat of counter-coups. A history of military professionalism reduces the likelihood that officers will engage in political intrigue. Less factionalized militaries, however, do not by themselves assure the appointment of neoliberal economists. While less factionalized militaries reduce the likelihood of counter-coups and provide leaders with fewer incentives to satisfy a broad range of interests within the military, governing institutions installed under military rule also affect appointments. Chapter 3 will break down the different kinds of governing institutions into more specific categories, but broadly speaking, military regimes are usually managed under one-man rule or junta governments. These institutions provide military leaders with varying degrees of autonomy from societal and military interests.

In less factionalized militaries governing as juntas, the service chiefs from each branch of the military, or officers from the "senior" branch, hold prominent positions in the government. In their positions, the service chiefs are actively involved in decision making. Before making important decisions, service chiefs attempt to reach a consensus, with conciliation and compromise being trademarks of junta rule. Each service usually controls appointments for several ministries, but no one service controls all economic policy-making appointments. The parceling-out of influence to each service and intra-institutional bargaining in turn influence appointments. Consensual agreement among mostly protectionist officers impedes the appointment of neoliberal economists. Each member of the junta may also have the power to veto appointments, which contributes to compromise. In addition, the fact that service chiefs and many officers are involved in policy decisions increases access points for protectionist interest groups.[28] Moreover, as leaders struggle for prominence in a junta government, they may try to mobilize support for themselves by promoting protectionist policies favored by most civilian groups.

Different types of military and governmental institutions thus have important consequences for economic policy-making appointments. Military rulers have a choice of using appointments for short-term political considerations or medium-term economic goals (Geddes 1994). Political constraints under these kinds of governmental or military institutions, however, force rulers to make appointments that satisfy immediate short-term goals. Fear of counter-coups, responsiveness to powerful interest groups, and satisfying a broad range of societal and military interests force rulers to adopt appointment strategies that serve their short-term goal of political survival, but which may come at the expense of medium-term economic success.

One-man rule with a less factionalized military (from now on referred to as consolidated one-man rule), by contrast, may be critical for rulers' medium-term interest in economic performance to supersede their short-term interest in political survival. Under consolidated one-man rule, the leader has less need to consult with other officers prior to making important decisions. Consensual agreement and compromise, which are mainstays in oligarchical systems, are less critical under one-man rule. The use of veto powers to derail appointment strategies and undermine attempts to initiate orthodox policies—a familiar feature of junta governments—is also less common under one-man rule. Because less factionalized forces are in turn less politicized, military leaders have less fear of military counter-coups. This suggests that leaders have fewer incentives to placate other officers and greater autonomy from the military than leaders whose military governments are teeming with factions.

One-man rule also limits access points for interest groups, who have one access point to lobby for change, namely the military leader. Leaders, of course, cannot wholly ignore societal or military interests, as they can be overthrown. Consolidated one-man rule, however, confers greater autonomy on leaders in their appointment strategies.[29] Greater autonomy in economic policy-making appointments does not insure that leaders will appoint neoliberal economists.[30] But, in contrast to situations which compel leaders to expend political capital to satisfy immediate political considerations, leaders under consolidated one-man rule and efforts to achieve such rule can follow medium-term survival strategies.

The appointment of ideologically committed neoliberal economists may be a part of a medium-term strategy to promote survival and consolidate power. As neoliberal economists are considered knowledgeable in economic policy making, they may have a greater understanding of the policies necessary to obtain long-term economic growth.[31] Through their similar educational backgrounds, neoliberal economists and external financial representatives also speak the same economic language (Pion-Berlin 1986, 323).[32] These connections increase credibility between lenders and debtors that aid in the securing of loans for investments. Policies endorsed by neoliberal economists, such as the reduction of the role of the state in the economy, also contribute to the decline and fragmentation of many powerful interest groups who depend on the state for their survival (Weyland 1994, 8). Their decline makes the leader less beholden to any one group, which helps to consolidate his power (Garretón 1986, 155).

Economists, Ideas, and Policy Outcomes

Attempts to understand why military leaders appoint neoliberal economists to economic policy-making positions in one country and not in others leads to a consideration of the effect neoliberal economists have on policy choice. In the past decade, scholars have focused less on policy makers and more on the impact of ideas to explain policy choice (Grindle and Thomas 1991; Sikkink 1991). While many theorists agree that ideas influence policy making, many question why, out of all the ideas available, certain ones are chosen. When and why in an intensely competitive market for ideas some reach the political agenda and affect policy makers continues to puzzle.

In the epistemic community literature, a subfield of the ideational literature, theorists examine the role of experts in terms of their ability to frame, develop, and clarify ideas and information and thereby either limit the range of policy options or create a middle ground among choices.[33] This literature argues for the importance of experts for policy decisions, but experts appear like any other group who attempt to influence policy decisions. The literature does not articulate the mechanism by which the ideas of experts are converted into policy choice. This study explains how regimes implement unpopular policy choices and helps extend and revise the ideational literature. It examines the black box through which the ideas of experts translate into policy decisions. I argue that when similarly trained and ideologically committed experts come to dominate decision-making positions, the mechanism by which ideas shape policy, and perhaps even public opinion, becomes clearer. When a large number of like-minded economists serve as the actual policy makers, they form an "epistemic community of knowledge" (Ikenberry 1992). The training and economic ideology of policy makers make them a cohesive team with a commitment to similar ideas (Kaufman 1990).[34]

This does not suggest that economists will all share the same beliefs. On the contrary, various economic schools of thought exist, which provide competing explanations for the role of the state and market forces in national economies. The training of economists over the past forty years in American universities and/or by local academics who were themselves trained in U.S. universities, however, has promoted an ideology that mainly backs free-market reforms.[35] Once these U.S.-trained economists come to dominate economic policy-making positions, their commitment to orthodox ideas propels them to initiate orthodox policies.[36] This commitment is complemented by their awareness of the country's history with policy failures, such as populist ideas and import substitution industrialization (ISI) policies in the cases under study, which reinforces this commitment to their ideas and their resistance to outside pressures.

Based on their similar ideas, these policy makers form a coherent team that not only contributes to a strong commitment to their policy choices but also helps to insulate them from outside pressures.[37] Given their expertise in economic policy making, economists do not solicit or believe that they need advice from individuals outside their community, enhancing their autonomy (Hirschman 1989). In effect, economists construct a barrier to ideas seeking to penetrate from outside, which is critical in military governments where pressures arise from interest groups and from within the military itself. As economic policy makers stonewall interest groups, these groups may turn to military officers in an effort to counter the policies advocated by neoliberal economists. Military officers, though, are unlikely to influence economic policies as the professional culture of the economic team becomes nearly impenetrable. This leaves the replacement of economic team members as the most promising method to cause policy change. However, as long as policy makers support the leader's survival, the leader is expected to have fewer incentives to replace them.[38] The stability of the economic team thus provides interest groups with fewer access points to affect policy making.

Economists in a coherent team also use the power of persuasion to reduce demands for policy changes and thus sustain their policies. Economists who make up the team tirelessly champion the cause of neoliberal policies by educating, cajoling, and persuading the military and its leaders of the benefits that should result from these policies. Without competition from other economic officials and with nearly identical messages, these economic experts are often able to convince military leaders of the advantages of neoliberal policies (Cortázar 1989).[39] This contrasts with an economic policy-making team composed of individuals from various occupational backgrounds who advocate different ideas on economic policy decisions. Policy makers whose studies have focused on law, economics, or military security, not surprisingly, hold dissimilar economic ideas. The ability of disparate policy makers to persuade military leaders to support neoliberal policies decreases as these policy makers struggle with each other over policy choices.

Data Analysis

A combination of quantitative and qualitative data analysis is used to test the thesis advanced here. Statistical data are gathered on the proportion of neoliberal economists in economic policy-making positions under military rule to test the central hypothesis of this work. Statistical variables, however, can only indicate correlation between the variables, not causation. To establish causal linkages, I refer to a number of personal interviews with the main political and economic actors from the Southern Cone's military governments, including former military rulers and finance ministers. I also interviewed heads of business and labor organizations, and retired military officers, to understand pluralist influences.

Where available, primary sources, including documents produced by the military governments, were also consulted. Much of this information reveals the reasoning behind decisions made by military rulers. Unfortunately, documents rarely provide a complete and accurate view of the motivations and self-interest that are often involved in political decisions. To correct for this, I used secondary sources documenting the actual decisions taken by military rulers, and interviews with several officials, to understand the rulers' motivations.

Some may question whether a case-study approach with so few cases is limited in its generalizability. The issue of whether, and to what extent, the findings drawn from the case studies are generalizable is addressed by supplementing the findings with military examples from Brazil and Peru. In the final chapter, democratic cases are also examined to show the applicability of the work. Another potential limitation is that this research attributes too much significance to the role of neoliberal economists in economic policy-making positions. Some may argue that economists represent an intervening variable that serves as a proxy for the interests of the executive. However, the preferences of executives do not always determine policy choice. Prior opposition to orthodox policies by leaders in

Chile (Augusto Pinochet), Argentina (Carlos Menem), Colombia (Virgilio Barco), and Mexico (Miguel de la Madrid), who later introduced orthodox policies, and the inability of leaders in Argentina (Jorge Videla) and Uruguay (Juan María Bordaberry and Luis Alberto Lacalle), who favored orthodox policies but failed to initiate these policies, suggest the importance of neoliberal economists for policy choices. While leaders possess policy preferences that affect policy choices, their ability to initiate these policies also depends on institutional structures that influence cabinet appointments.

Plan of the Book

Economic policy outcomes and development are the result of economic policies chosen by policy makers. The selection of economic policy makers, the policies they select, and their relative insulation from interest groups help to explain differences in policy choice. In order to understand how policy makers are selected, we need to examine the survival strategies of military leaders and how these strategies are constrained by historical characteristics of the military and governing institutions installed under military rule.

The following chapters elaborate on themes expressed in this chapter. Chapter 2 details differences in policy choices and the maintenance of policies in Argentina, Chile, and Uruguay. It documents how Chile (1973–89) initiated and sustained the most orthodox, market-oriented program while Argentina (1966–73, 1976–83) and Uruguay (1973–84) initiated more gradual neoliberal policies, which they abandoned. Chapter 3 explores the effect of differences in long-held characteristics of the military, such as factionalism, and in the kinds of governing institutions installed by military leaders on economic policy choices. These differences shape the political survival strategies of military leaders, including their appointment decisions, which in turn affect economic policy-making appointments. Chapter 4 examines the importance of neoliberal economists for the initiation and maintenance of orthodox policies. This chapter suggests that the commitment to and coherence of ideas held by policy makers help to insulate them from interest groups and affects their ability to initiate and sustain their policy choices. Chapter 5 discusses one type of orthodox policy, namely privatization, to emphasize the importance of economic policy makers for the initiation of orthodox policies, and the influence of officers who hold governmental positions in state enterprises for blocking this movement. Chapter 6 examines the training of economists in Chile relative to the other countries. This chapter presents more concrete evidence about the economists' ability to insulate themselves from pressures. The final chapter restates the arguments and reviews their implications for democratic regimes.

TWO

Economic Policy Choices
in the Southern Cone

*My dear friend: Give to the people, especially to the workers, all that is
possible. When it seems to you that already you are giving them too
much, give them more. You will see the results. Everyone will try to scare
you with the specter of an economic collapse. But all of this is a lie. There
is nothing more elastic than the economy which everyone fears so much
because no one understands it.*

—Juan Perón[1]

The cases of Argentina, Chile, and Uruguay from the 1960s through the
1980s provide an excellent opportunity to explain economic policy choice
and development under military regimes, as several crucial variables can
be held constant. All three countries witnessed many similarities before
and during military rule. Prior to the military coups, these countries followed industrial development strategies based on import substitution
industrialization (ISI) for more than thirty years that contributed to declining economic growth rates. The countries also faced nearly identical
external financial conditions, had similar cultural and historical legacies, and were at comparable levels of economic development. Moreover, the newly installed, repressive military governments in all three
attempted to dismantle and disarticulate working-class organizations,
restructure capitalism, emasculate the institutions of civil society, and
enhance the state's ability to pursue its own goals (Stepan 1985, 318). Despite these many similarities, the choice of economic policies differed
among the cases.

This chapter sets the basis for the investigation that follows by describing the economic policies pursued under military rule in the Southern Cone. It begins by providing a thumbnail sketch of the economic policy histories of the Southern Cone countries to reveal their many similarities at the onset of military rule. It then demonstrates the variation in economic policies chosen under military rule. The chapter shows that Chile initiated and sustained orthodox policies, while Argentina and Uruguay initiated gradualist policies that they abandoned.[2]

History of Economic Policy Choices in the Southern Cone

From the nineteenth century through the early 1930s, liberal economic theory with its bias toward open-market policies and export promotion influenced much of Latin America.[3] In Argentina, Chile, and Uruguay, this bias contributed to the growth of primary product exports.[4] Because of their fertile land and rich soil, Argentina and Uruguay developed profitable sectors related to agriculture. Wheat, cattle, and sheep and many of their by-products provided these countries with abundant export opportunities (Díaz-Alejandro 1970, ch. 1). Like Argentina and Uruguay, Chile exported agricultural products, including wheat and wine. Nitrate, Chile's most important export, commanded high market prices because of its use in the production of high-quality fertilizers and explosives (Falcoff 1989, 3). These rural-based exports contributed to comparable national income levels among the Southern Cone cases that differed from the rest of the continent.[5]

The Great Depression in the early 1930s and its effects on policy choices further magnified their similarities. Although the Depression negatively impacted countries throughout the world, it hit the Southern Cone especially hard.[6] These countries not only saw the terms of trade on their exports worsen, but they also experienced a fall in export volume. As markets for exports closed, Argentina, Chile, and Uruguay responded by looking inward economically, in an attempt to insulate themselves from the vagaries of world economic conditions (Thorp 1984).[7] As part of this insulation, state ownership of basic industries began to grow.[8]

Chile took action toward increasing the role of the state in production in the late 1930s (Cortés Douglas, et al. 1981, 143). Chile created CORFO (Corporación de Fomento de la Producción)—a state-owned holding corporation and development bank—in 1939, which facilitated state control in heavy industry and intermediate production (Vergara 1986, 86).

Uruguay's initial efforts to promote state control over the economy pre-dated the Depression. In the 1900s and 1910s, President José Batlle y Or-dóñez advocated state ownership of the largest industries, including natu-ral monopolies, in order to build a safety net for Uruguayans and to reduce the influence of British companies (Finch 1981, 12, 193). In the 1930s, state involvement in Uruguay's economy expanded, as evidenced by central-government employment increases from 30,100 in 1924–25, to 32,500 in 1931–32, to 39,400 in 1937 (Finch 1989, 23). The state also developed basic industries in oil refining and cement production. State development in Argentina began in the early 1940s with the creation of Fabricaciones Militares (Lewis 1992, 93). Fabricaciones Militares provided the military with control over many industries, including mining and steel production. Once Juan Perón won the presidency in 1946, he broadened the state's role by nationalizing public services and German companies, and purchasing industries formerly owned by the British (Schvarzer 1981, 35).

The Southern Cone countries also designed an industrialization strategy based on import substitution of manufactured goods. Existing manufacturing firms in Argentina, Chile, and Uruguay expanded plants and established new small firms to produce primarily for the domestic market (R. Kaufman 1979, 196–97). Shortages of manufactured goods during World War II reinforced interest in local production of previously imported goods (Baer 1972, 97). Supporters of import substitution indus-trialization (ISI) policies argued that manufactured products imported by developing countries had a higher value added and better terms of trade than primary goods imported by developed nations (Prébisch 1947). By adopting ISI measures, it was claimed that developing countries could obtain the benefits of industrialization for themselves.

The shift toward ISI and state involvement in the economy created powerful import-competing sectors. Producers that depended on pro-tection from foreign competitors extended their power and influence. The manufacturing component of most import-competing sectors also reflected an urban bias. Rural interests that flexed their muscles from the late nineteenth century through the early 1930s, and provided the engine for export promotion, no longer played such powerful roles. New em-ployment opportunities sprang up in the cities. As more workers left the countryside, politicians attempted to unionize workers in order to at-tract urban voters.[9] Argentina, Chile, and Uruguay's choice of ISI policies adversely affected their economies.[10] Policies designed to subsidize fledg-ling domestic industries led to import-intensive production.[11] However, in order to "compete," import-competing industries relied on overvalued

Table 2.1   Annual Growth Indicators for Latin America, 1945–1975 (%)

Indicator	Chile	Argentina	Uruguay	Rest of Latin America
Gross national product	3.6	2.1	3.7	6.2
Gross national product per capita	1.5	0.7	2.0	3.2
Manufacturing product	4.4	3.3	4.6	7.8
Agricultural product per capita	0.2	−0.2	−0.1	0.9
Volume of exports per capita	0.2	−2.3	−1.2	1.3
Consumer prices	30.0	29.0	24.0	8.0

Source: Ramos (1986, 2).

exchange rates, thereby creating a bias against exports and stimulating balance of payments problems (Bates 1981; Hirschman 1968). These problems, in combination with worsening terms of trade, contributed to hyper-inflations in Chile and Argentina and high inflation for all.

Although nearly all Latin American countries adopted an inward-oriented economic strategy, and suffered economically as a result, the Southern Cone's problems were worse than most. As table 2.1 indicates, Argentina, Chile, and Uruguay witnessed lower levels of growth in gross national product, gross national product per capita, manufacturing product, agricultural product per capita, and volume of exports per capita compared to the rest of Latin America between 1945 and 1975. The Southern Cone countries also experienced higher inflation.

In summary, prior to the 1960s, Argentina, Chile, and Uruguay adopted nearly the same economic policies, which produced similar results.[12] Each country shifted from an export-oriented growth model to import substitution. They protected import-competing industries, saw unions activated, and increased the role of the public sector. Their choice of ISI policies also contributed to similar economic problems.

Policy Choices under Military Regimes in the Southern Cone

Military forces committed coups in the Southern Cone, in part, to over-come economic problems faced by democratic governments. Military leaders claimed that under democratic rule, politicians needed the support of interest groups tied to the maintenance of uncompetitive industries. Activated workers and their unions, public employees in state-owned enterprises, and manufacturers in import-competing industries aggressively lobbied democratic governments to maintain subsidies, protection, and, in the case of public employees and workers, pressed for higher wages. Their ability to block market-oriented reforms contributed to severe fiscal and balance of payments deficits, and high inflation. Military rule could supposedly break the ISI/low-economic-growth cycle by repressing labor's wage demands and ignoring pressures from import-competing sectors and public employees.

Similarities among the Southern Cone countries also made it appear that they would initiate the same kinds of policies. In fact, many Southern Cone military rulers and their policy makers pledged their support for orthodox neoliberal reforms. Although Argentina, Chile, and Uruguay initiated neoliberal policies, the intensity of the policies varied greatly. Argentina and Uruguay initiated gradualist policies, while Chile adopted more orthodox reforms.

Variation in policy choices suggests that it is necessary to design a measure to differentiate policy intensity of neoliberal programs. Six factors are commonly associated with neoliberalism: (1) stabilization,[13] (2) liberalization of capital markets, (3) liberalization of trade, (4) privatization of state enterprises, (5) elimination of price controls, and (6) reduction in industrial promotion programs. When a majority (four or more) of these factors are present and widely implemented, I treat the neoliberal experiment as orthodox. If less than four factors are adopted, I count that country as having initiated a more gradualist neoliberal experiment. Of course, if none of these measures are adopted, the country is not following a neoliberal experiment.

This study also requires a measure to assess the maintenance of neoliberal programs. When neoliberal policies are replaced by heterodox policies (i.e., increases in protection, price controls, and subsidies, and an expanded role of the state in the economy) for more than one year, I treat the neoliberal experiment as having been abandoned. Using these measures, the next sections detail the economic policy choices in the Southern Cone and assess their intensity.

Chile

Economic Turmoil, 1970–73

Economic chaos best describes the Chilean economy prior to the military's intervention. In 1970, Salvador Allende became the first democratically elected socialist president in the world. In one of his earliest moves, Allende increased the state's role in the economy in order to increase production and equalize income distribution. Allende's measures included the expropriation and forced sale of private firms and banks to the state, an increase in the number of social programs, intensification of agrarian reform, introduction of multiple exchange rates, and imposition of price controls and protection (Larraín and Meller 1991). These policies contributed to financial collapse in 1973, culminating in a balance of payments crisis and hyperinflation.

When military forces deposed Allende on September 11, 1973, they faced little opposition. Indeed, the Christian Democratic and Conservative parties initially supported the coup (Spooner 1999, 92). Following the intervention, no one knew for certain what kinds of economic policies the military would adopt. The eventual economic policy choices during military rule are divided into four phases.[14]

Stabilization, 1973–74

In the first phase (September 1973 through April 1975), policy makers attempted to "correct the most serious economic distortions introduced during the Allende regime" (Edwards and Edwards 1991, 17). Facing runaway inflation and huge budget and payments deficits, the government initiated macroeconomic measures to reduce inflation and structural reforms to shrink the state's role in the economy. It decontrolled most prices, cut government spending, tightened monetary policy, demobilized labor unions, and devalued the exchange rate (Ramos 1986, 16). In contrast to its market reforms, the military regime took over failing private firms, which inflated the size of the state. The government wanted to stabilize the situation politically and economically, not promote a liberal economic revolution (Lavín 1988).

Despite these reforms, economic problems persisted. Inflation remained at more than 300 percent in 1975 (Edwards and Edwards 1991, 32). Terms of trade for Chilean exports also fell sharply (see table 2.2 at the end of this chapter for Chile's basic economic indicators). The decline in the price of copper, Chile's main export, and the rise in the price of oil, its main import, caused a balance of payments crisis. In fact, the country's earnings from copper plummeted from $1,623 million in 1974 to $868.2 million in 1975 (Spooner 1999, 105).

Orthodoxy, 1975–83

In April 1975, a second phase began following several new cabinet appointments including Jorge Cauas as minister of finance. During this phase, Chile initiated orthodox policies. In mid-1975, the government introduced privatization reforms that helped to reduce fiscal deficits by 28 percent in real terms (Ramos 1986, 18). The government sold off or liquidated hundreds of firms operating at a loss, many of which Allende had expropriated. Firms that the state continued to hold used marginal-cost pricing—managing firms as if they operated in a competitive market—to promote efficient production.

Policy makers also embarked on a reform of the nearly bankrupt social security system. The government instituted the first private social security system in the world in 1981 (Piñera 1991b). The government also partially privatized the education and health systems and reformed the tax system. It imposed a surcharge on income tax and eliminated exemptions in the value-added tax, which increased the state coffers (Foxley 1986, 23).

The government carried out radical changes with respect to trade policies as well. In contrast with the Allende period when tariff rates reached as high as 750 percent, tariffs fell rapidly under the military. From a maximum of 220 percent in December 1973, tariffs declined sharply through 1979. By 1976, the maximum tariff rate stood at 65 percent. By 1979, a 10 percent across-the-board tariff covered all imports (except for cars), and the government eliminated quantitative restrictions on trade. This tariff rate remained at the same level until 1983, despite massive bankruptcies and economic chaos in 1982 (Corbo 1983, 71–73).

The government also applied more orthodox macroeconomic policies. It instituted stabilization policies and provided access for foreign finance to enter the market. The government also virtually eliminated price controls and industrial promotion programs, and used exchange rate policy in an attempt to combat inflation.[15] It temporarily interrupted crawling peg devaluations of the exchange rate and revalued the currency in 1976 and 1977, as a signal to authorities and investors that inflation would be reduced. As Frieden (1991, 158–59) notes, "Since currency devaluations were widely watched by economic agents as signals of probable future inflation, the authorities felt that the best way to break inflationary expectations was to manipulate the peso's nominal exchange rate to imply that Chilean inflation would fall rapidly." Despite the improvement in many economic indicators, inflation levels around 40 percent continued to plague the Chilean economy in 1978 (Corbo 1985, 897). The government attempted to address inflationary pressures by implementing the *tablita*—a preannounced devaluation of the exchange rate that would decline over time—in February 1978. The *tablita* set the rate of devaluation at a lower rate than ongoing inflation. In June 1979, the government also set a fixed exchange rate of thirty-nine pesos to the dollar, a rate it maintained until June 1982. Policy makers argued that the *tablita* and the fixed exchange rate would reduce inflation by shaping expectations about inflation and by influencing prices on tradable goods (Corbo and Fischer 1994, 46). The domestic level of inflation was supposed to converge to the world inflation level plus the rate of devaluation of the peso (Edwards and Edwards 1991, 36).

Because of many factors, including the 1979 Labor Law, which indexed wages to prior inflation, the high rates of real interest, the real appreciation of the peso against other currencies, the plummeting of asset prices, and the world recession, the boom phase turned bust in 1982. The danger signals first appeared in 1981, when the Viña del Mar Sugar Refining Company, a food-processing firm connected to a medium-sized conglomerate, went bankrupt (Edwards and Edwards 1991, 78). In 1982, Chile encountered a fall in the value of the peso, a sharp cutback of new lending, and the collapse of the financial and private sectors. Manufacturing output fell 21 percent, per capita GDP dropped by 19 percent, and unemployment climbed above 30 percent (counting the 12 percent employed in emergency work programs) (Ramos 1986, 23).

Despite these difficulties, Chile attempted to maintain its overall program until mid- to late 1983.[16] Tariff rates rose across the board to 20 percent, but still remained at a lower level than any other country in the region. However, the state did take over many failed businesses. In the 1970s, conglomerates known as *grupos* purchased many privatized enterprises (Dahse 1979). By 1978, nine conglomerates controlled 82 percent of the assets in the Chilean banking system (Foxley 1983, 80). When the crisis struck, many of the *grupos* were highly leveraged with high debt-to-asset ratios. Once foreign lenders refused to provide more loans, some conglomerates filed for bankruptcy. This led to government intervention of many financial institutions, including those held by conglomerates, with the government taking control of the assets of the holding companies within the conglomerates. But the finance minister who intervened these enterprises claimed that there was never any doubt that the enterprises would be reprivatized shortly (Lüders 1992a). As Stallings (1990, 130) puts it, "Rather than allow them to go bankrupt, the government 'intervened' the large banks (i.e., took them over on a temporary basis), while several small banks were scheduled for liquidation." Moreover, and unlike others in the region, Chile did not default on loan payments. It maintained close relations with the IMF and other international financing organizations (Corbo and Fischer 1994, 40). The government initiated austerity policies to reduce the current account and public-sector deficit, and curb inflation.

Gradualism, 1984

The third phase began in early 1984 and ended late in the year, when policy makers loosened neoliberal policies. Tariff rates no longer were uniform, and the maximum rate climbed to 35 percent. The number of goods with surcharges above the maximum tariff allowed also expanded from 68 in April to 272 in July (Gómez-Lobo and Lehmann 1991, 8). Policy makers also imposed price controls and an aggressive fiscal stimulus package, and increased concessions to debtors. For the first time under military rule, business interests played active roles in decision making. Business owners encouraged stimulus and industrial promotion programs to resurrect the economy.

Orthodoxy Returns, 1985–89

Within a year, the final phase began (1985–89) with the return of orthodox policies initiated in a more pragmatic way. Some policy makers who served in the government during the most orthodox period also came back. In 1985, Chile reintroduced intense liberal economic policies and consolidated and deepened free-market reforms. Policy makers expanded the privatization process, first begun in the mid-1970s, to include large state-owned enterprises. Uniform tariff rates also returned, and tariffs declined from 30 percent in March 1985, to 20 percent by June 1985, and 15 percent by January 1988. Products receiving additional tariff protection via surcharges also fell rapidly in 1985 and continued to drop throughout the military period (Gómez-Lobo and Lehmann 1991, 8–9). The reduction in tariff rates in combination with a sharp devaluation in the

Table 2.3   Economic Policies in Chile, 1973–1989

Policy	1973–1974	1975–1983	1984	1985–1989
Stabilization	Yes (2)	Yes (2)	Yes (2)	Yes (2)
Capital Reform	Yes (2)	Yes (2)	Yes (2)	Yes (2)
Tariffs	High (0)	Reduced Extensively (2)	Higher (1)	Reduced (2)
Privatization	None (0)	Extensive (2)	None (0)	Extensive (2)
Price Controls	Some (1)	None (2)	Some (1)	None (2)
Industrial Promotion	Some (1)	None (2)	Some (1)	None (2)
Total	6	12	7	12

2 = Strong Neoliberal Policies; 1 = Gradual Neoliberal Policies; 0 = Nonliberal Policies

exchange rate served as incentives for the tradeable sector of the economy (Corbo and Fischer 1994, 41). Industrial promotion programs and price controls also disappeared. The government maintained these policies until the end of military rule.

Table 2.3 shows the intensity and longevity of economic liberalization during Chile's military rule. From 1975 through 1983 and from 1985 through 1989, the government drastically reduced tariffs, promoted financial liberalization, and privatized extensively. It also eliminated price controls and industrial promotion subsidies, both often used to support uncompetitive, import-competing firms. With the exception of 1984, Chile sustained the program.

Argentina

Economic Decay, 1963–66

Prior to the military's intervention in 1966, Argentina experienced economic difficulties. Despite the implementation of severe fiscal and monetary policies, inflation accelerated to 38 percent in 1965, not high by today's standards, but high for the time. Powerful unions in the state sector made sure that workers obtained salary increases of between 25 and 30 percent, well in excess of a proposed wage increase of 15 percent (Guadagni 1989, 159). Workers in the private sector also demanded higher salaries. The fact that President Arturo Illia garnered only 25 percent of the vote in a 1963 election that banned the most popular candidate and mobilizer of the union movement, Juan Perón, made it difficult for Illia to refuse union demands. These economic demands, combined with the military's goal to preempt Peronists from winning the upcoming election, led to the military coup in June 1966.

Gradualism, 1967–69

Although problems such as high inflation and wage demands heated up the economy, many economic indicators appeared positive. Indeed, between 1963 and 1966, real GDP grew at 6 percent, the balance of trade showed a surplus, and external payments provided little or no constraint (Maynard 1989, 166). The economic policies instituted during the first six months of the military government, however, exacerbated Argentina's economic difficulties. The first finance minister, Jorge Nestor Salimei, imposed price controls, inhibited capital liberalization, devalued the peso, and made little headway with regard to a stabilization program (O'Donnell 1988, 66–67).

By late 1966, these economic policies led to economic stagnation, accelerating inflation, an increasing fiscal deficit, and a deteriorating balance of payments position (Krieger Vasena 1990, 85). These economic woes resulted in the sacking of Salimei and the creation of an economic normalization program. From 1967 through 1970, the military government implemented a moderate neoliberal program, as shown by its adoption of a stabilization program, its gradual reduction in trade protection, and financial liberalization.

As part of the "Grand Transformation" announced by new Finance Minister Adalbert Krieger Vasena in March 1967, the government initiated a stabilization program based on exchange rate policy. It devalued the exchange rate 40 percent, as part of a one-time-only decision designed to end speculation about future devaluations. The government also reduced tariff rates from a maximum of 325 percent to 140 percent (Krieger Vasena 1990, 88). It liberalized capital and foreign currency markets and worked closely with international banks and organizations to encourage capital inflows. The fact that Finance Minister Krieger Vasena formerly worked for the World Bank and received acclaim from internationally respected organizations also attracted capital from abroad. In fact, Krieger Vasena invited international organizations to offer Argentina assistance (Krieger Vasena 1988, 13).

However, the government did not create a completely open market. Tariffs remained at fairly high levels, and special duty exemptions, preferential import regimes, nonuniform tariff rates, and prohibitive import restrictions made the trade policy less liberal (Schydlowsky 1989, 177–78). Privatization of state-owned enterprises also received little consideration. According to Krieger Vasena (1992), most policy makers did not envision the benefits from privatization. The government instead attempted to restructure public enterprises in order to reduce public sector deficits. The government also increased the role of the state in the economy through the setting of income policies and prices. Workers in the public and private sectors received a 15 percent wage and salary increase in 1967, after which the government froze wages for twenty-one months. The actual size of salary increases in the private sector varied somewhat, depending on when salary contracts expired (Krieger Vasena 1990, 90). The government also worked with employers to set prices. Employers voluntarily agreed to freeze prices for six months in exchange for special access to bank credit and state contracts (O'Donnell 1988, 86). In addition, the government controlled the price of exportable goods through the use of a withholding tax, and subsidized the price of fuel and public services through revenue collected from the withholding tax.

From 1967 through mid-1969, the economic program brought about a recovery. As table 2.4 at the end of this chapter indicates, the program promoted price stability and sustained an average growth rate of 5 percent, with the highest rate achieved in 1969 (Krieger Vasena 1988, 9). Inflation reached single digit figures in late 1968, and foreign exchange reserves increased sharply (O'Donnell 1988, 108). Wage levels, however, declined for workers and lower-level employees, especially in nonindustrial production. Many farmers and urban entrepreneurs also balked at the policies (Wynia 1978, 179). Lowered tariffs, taxes on exports, and greater access to domestic markets by foreign companies frustrated urban and rural groups.

Partly as a result of wage declines, workers struck in Córdoba, Argentina's second-largest city. In alliance with student demonstrators, autoworkers launched a massive uprising that came to be known as the *cordobazo* in May 1969. Fearing for his political life, military leader General

Juan Carlos Onganía sacked several high officials, including his finance minister, and proposed policy changes to appease worker demands. However, the economic goals of newly appointed Finance Minister José María Dagnino Pastore differed little from his predecessor. In fact, he liberalized even further than Krieger Vasena. Dagnino Pastore gradually reduced tariffs on a sectoral basis, imposed a new wage policy to keep inflation in check, increased financial liberalization, and proposed additional measures to reduce fiscal deficits (Dagnino Pastore 1990, 106–9).

Structuralism, 1970–73

By mid-1970, mounting political pressures forced Onganía to resign. His successor, General Roberto Levingston, sacked most of Onganía's cabinet and replaced them with policy makers favored by workers and import-competing capitalists. Levingston's new finance minister, Carlos Moyano Llerena, tried to imitate Krieger Vasena's economic program. Moyano Llerena devalued the exchange rate, subjected exports to a withholding tax, lowered import duties, and proposed a voluntary agreement on prices (O'Donnell 1988, 201). The need for labor's support, however, impeded wage freezes, a fundamental part of Krieger Vasena's anti-inflationary policy. Moyano Llerena's devaluation also was not seen as a one-time affair, which increased peso speculation.

In October, nationalist Aldo Ferrer replaced Moyano Llerena as finance minister and instituted non-market-oriented policies. As Ferrer (1990, 111) later wrote, he intended: "(1) to strengthen Argentine firms, capital and technology, and to give them a leading role in national economic development; (2) to defend the standard of living of the majority and to achieve a constant increase in real wages; and (3) to consolidate the country's territorial integration." Ferrer's concern for territorial integration and national economic development prompted the creation of the National Development Bank. The bank mobilized internal resources necessary for industrial promotion programs. Ferrer also expanded price controls, opposed privatizations, and increased protection for financial and trade markets. As a result of these policies, inflation rose from 6.6 percent under Krieger Vasena to 29.6 percent under Ferrer (Wynia 1978, 190).[17]

Under economic distress and with renewed riots in Córdoba, the military replaced Levingston with General Alejandro Lanusse—seen by most as responsible for Onganía's removal from power—in March 1971. Two months later, Lanusse replaced Ferrer. Over the next two years,

Lanusse frequently changed finance ministers, though all of them maintained Ferrer's nationalistic policies. The finance ministers used selective price controls, expanded wage rates, and liberally distributed central bank credits to finance a growing budget deficit (Wynia 1978, 191). The government also extended industrial promotion programs and increased tariff protection. These policies boosted inflation to 59 percent by 1972.

By early 1973, Lanusse called for democratic elections. Lanusse believed that the public would support his candidacy for president. He even allowed a Peronist candidate to run against him. Lanusse, however, miscalculated his popularity. Through an arranged agreement in the Peronist Party, Juan Perón took over the presidency in October 1973.

Economic Chaos, 1974–75

Once in office, Perón left little doubt that he favored populism and social justice to help build on his power base (Gabriel Leyba 1990).[18] His policies included a social pact between business and labor to freeze prices and increase wages; the return of state marketing boards for exports; and the "nationalization" of bank deposits (Di Tella 1989, 216–18). Less than a year after taking office, Perón died, leaving his vice president and wife, Isabel Perón, to succeed him as president. In no time, political and economic chaos confronted Argentina. In an attempt to deal with societal pressures, Mrs. Perón increased salaries of workers, restricted foreign capital, expanded the role of the state, raised tariffs, and devalued the peso (Epstein 1985, 14–16). Over the next two years, salaries increased while the peso continued to be devalued, resulting in an exorbitant rate of inflation and a dwindling trade balance. The economic and political crisis culminated in the military's intervention in March 1976.

Stabilization, 1976–80

Following the reimposition of military rule, Argentina's economy suffered a hyperinflation and a shortage of available foreign reserves.[19] The primary concern of new Finance Minister José Alfredo Martínez de Hoz was to liberalize, modernize, and stabilize the economy, and streamline the state (Martínez de Hoz 1990, 151). During his tenure, Martínez de Hoz liberalized financial markets, applied a stabilization plan, eliminated nearly all price controls, and privatized some small firms (Ministerio de Economía 1981). In contrast to an orthodox program, however, he privatized none of the larger firms. Tariffs also remained high and nonuniform, and industrial promotion programs expanded.[20]

In the first year, the government initiated a stabilization program and liberalized parts of the economy. The stabilization program attempted to lower inflation through a reduction in aggregate demand and an adjustment of relative prices (Wynia 1978, 228). The government wanted to reduce demand by decreasing wages and salaries and increasing consumption taxes. It unified the multiple exchange rates, cut export taxes, removed some import controls, and reduced barriers to import financing, all in the hope of increasing incentives for exporters (Frieden 1991, 211). The deregulation of financial markets and freeing of interest rates also helped to expand the financial sector and attract foreign capital. These policies promoted spectacular growth in 1977 and somewhat stabilized Argentina's economy. However, the annual rate of inflation remained very high. From its peak of 444 percent in 1976, inflation fell to 176 percent in 1977, but persisted at 175 percent in 1978 (see table 2.4 at the end of this chapter).

Stubborn inflation and the drop in GDP prompted efforts to intensify the neoliberal program in late 1978. As part of this intensification, policy makers put into effect a schedule to decrease tariffs. In January 1979, tariffs would be reduced quarterly over a five-year period until they reached a maximum level of 20 percent and an average of 18 percent (Martínez de Hoz 1990, 154). Prior to this, trade liberalization consisted of policies designed to reduce or eliminate export taxes and multiple exchange rates, while import duties remained high.

Like Chile, Argentina attempted to use exchange rate management through the *tablita*—the preannounced devaluation of the exchange rate based on a declining rate of devaluation—to decrease inflationary expectations. As part of the 20 December 1978 Plan, the *tablita* achieved some success in fighting inflation. The rate of inflation fell from 150 percent at the end of 1978 to 40 percent during the fourth quarter of 1980 (Sjaastad 1989, 260). The reduction in inflation, however, "was too slow to avoid real exchange rate appreciation" (Frieden 1991, 213). High real interest rates and open capital markets attracted funds from abroad, which raised the level of appreciation.

The real exchange rate appreciation led to a serious crisis in 1980. The overvalued exchange rate and ease with which the private sector borrowed from foreign lenders created a frenzy for imports. Imports rose from $1.2 billion in the first quarter of 1979 to $3.2 billion in the last quarter of 1980. Reserves in the current account fell from $10.7 billion in the first quarter of 1980 to $7.7 billion at the end of the year, and then collapsed to $4.7 billion in the first quarter of 1981 (Epstein 1985, 28). According to Ramos (1986, 42), "The current account shifted from a surplus in 1978 equivalent to 25 percent of the value of exports to deficits of more than 40 percent in 1980 and 1981. These deficits implied a heavy volume of imports at the expense of domestic industry, leading to a 4 percent fall in industrial output and an even greater one in 1981."

Not only had the current account experienced a massive deterioration, but local financial institutions also began to collapse. In March 1980, the government closed the country's largest bank, and intervened four more banks over the next few months. The combination of the current account plummeting, bank failures, and expected policies by the incoming administration in early 1981 fueled capital flight (Dornbusch 1989, 296).[21]

Economic Crisis, 1981–83

Economic disaster faced new President General Roberto Viola. In March 1981, Viola abandoned many neoliberal policies. He canceled the tariff reduction program, instituted an extensive devaluation of the currency, and increased industrial promotion programs in order to protect domestic industry. Viola also instituted multiple exchange rates for commercial and financial transactions, reintroduced price controls, and nearly eliminated stabilization and financial liberalization (Ramos 1986, 43). Within nine months, inflation soared to nearly 150 percent, which precipitated another presidential succession.

In December 1981, newly installed President General Leopoldo Galtieri claimed to favor more orthodox, market-oriented policies. During his first three months, Galtieri's economic team headed by Roberto Alemann attempted to initiate policies to disinflate, denationalize, and deregulate the economy (Dornbusch 1989, 299). The team, however, had no time to implement its market-oriented reforms. Within months of taking over, Galtieri invaded the Malvinas/Falkland Islands. The tremendous economic cost of the war made it impossible to control fiscal deficits or initiate orthodox policies (Solanet 1992). In little time, the British defeated the Argentine forces, and the transition to democratic rule began. The economic policies pursued during the year-and-a-half transition resembled policies introduced during Lanusse's campaign for popularity ten years earlier. Real wages increased, industrial promotion programs spread to nearly all provinces, price controls reappeared, and the govern-

Table 2.5   Economic Policies in Argentina, 1966–1983

Policy	1966–1970	1971–1973	1976–1980	1981–1983
Stabilization	Yes (2)	No (1)	Yes (2)	No (1)
Capital Reform	Yes (2)	Minimal (1)	Yes (2)	Minimal (1)
Tariffs	Reduced (1)	High (0)	Reduced (1)	No Change (1)
Privatization	None (0)	None (0)	Little (0)[a]	None (0)
Price Controls	Extensive (0)	Extensive (0)	Few (2)	Extensive (0)
Industrial Promotion	Minimal (1)	Raised (0)	Raised (0)	Raised (0)
Total	6	2	7	3

2 = Strong Neoliberal Policies; 1 = Gradual Neoliberal Policies; 0 = Nonliberal Policies
a. While the government privatized some small firms, it also nationalized others.

ment restructured private debt, providing producers with massive sub-sidies (Frieden 1991, 226).

Table 2.5 summarizes Argentina's economic policies during the periods of military rule. From 1966 through 1970, Argentina initiated a mild neoliberal program, which it later reversed. From 1971 through 1973, industrial promotion programs and tariffs rose, financial markets closed, and stabilization received little attention. The period from 1976 through 1980 marked another gradualist neoliberal program that was reversed in the early 1980s with the reemergence of price controls, expansion of an industrial promotion program, closure of capital markets, and loosening of fiscal and monetary policy.

Uruguay

Economic Decline, 1966–73

Economic and political paralysis plagued Uruguay in the 1960s and early 1970s. Like Argentina and Chile, economic difficulties beset Uruguay's economy. At the same time that public spending climbed, in part because of inefficient production based on ISI and a growing public sector, world prices for Uruguay's principal exports—wool and meat—fell.

Uruguay's political system promoted increased public spending. Building on its history of compromise between the main political parties, the Colorados and Blancos, Uruguay created a collegial executive in the 1920s that divided executive responsibility between the president and the National Council of Administration. Both parties and their respective factions would have representatives on the popularly elected National Council, which controlled several ministries including public finance, industry, labor, public works, and welfare. Modeled on Switzerland's plural presidency, President José Batlle y Ordóñez developed the collegial executive to reduce the possibility of an authoritarian leader ruling as a strongman (Alisky 1969, 29).

In 1934, a constituent assembly wrote a new constitution that restored the traditional one-man presidency, only to have a 1951 plebiscite approve the return of the collegial executive. The plebiscite actually led to a new constitution that made no mention of an executive. Instead, the chairman of the nine-member National Council would be rotated annually. By the late 1950s, declining prices for Uruguay's main exports made it imperative that the country cut public expenses. But the spirit of cooperation engendered by the collegial executive impeded efforts to reduce public spending. No member of the council wanted his party faction to lose jobs in the bloated public sector or welfare benefits. The council's inability to shrink public expenses brought about the revival of the presidency in 1966 amidst economic crisis (Alisky 1969, 42). These negative economic conditions prevailed into the 1970s.

Terrorist groups also paralyzed Uruguay. In the 1960s and early 1970s, a guerrilla group called the Tupamaros set off bombs, committed robberies, and kidnapped and assassinated police officers and military personnel. Despite Uruguay's long history with democratic institutions that dated back nearly 150 years, the combination of civil unrest and economic stagnation prompted the military takeover in 1973 (Gillespie 1986).

Economic conditions worsened during the military's first year in power (table 2.6 at the end of this chapter provides Uruguay's basic economic indicators). Because of the oil shock in 1973 and the closing off of its beef exports to European Economic Community markets, Uruguay suffered severe balance of payments problems. Uruguay's fiscal deficit rose to 4.4 percent, and inflation accelerated to 77 percent (Larraín 1986).

Stabilization, 1974–81

In July 1974, Juan María Bordaberry, a democratically elected president in 1971 who retained his position for some time under military rule, appointed the internationally respected economist Alejandro Végh Villegas to serve as minister of economy and finance. Prior to Végh's appointment, members of the planning office (Oficina de Planamiento y Presupuesto) devised the National Development Plan for 1973–77. This plan argued for Uruguay to open its economy to the exterior, promote private sector investment, and stabilize and liberalize the economy (Macadar 1982, 26).

Végh focused on many of the same goals, including financial liberalization, fiscal reform, and gradual stabilization measures to improve the balance of payments situation and stabilize the economy. In one of his first actions, Végh liberalized capital inflows and outflows, freed domestic interest rates, and permitted deposits in foreign currency. He also changed the investment law in order to attract foreign investment. The new investment law guaranteed investors the right to repatriate all earnings and officially committed the central bank to supply foreign exchange funds (R. Kaufman 1979, 183). These policies brought badly needed foreign exchange reserves, which helped to address the country's capital account deficit.

Végh also instituted a stabilization program that eliminated the multiplicity of exchange rates and implemented a massive devaluation in the exchange rate to reduce trade imbalances. Following the devaluation, Végh introduced a passive crawling peg to maintain the devalued exchange rate (Ramos 1986, 28).[22] The increase in exports, as a result of exchange rate policy, improved the balance of payments deficit. The stabilization program also included a price and wage freeze to address inflationary pressures and an important tax reform to deal with fiscal deficits (R. Kaufman 1979, 183).[23]

Despite these open-market policies, Végh's overall program stressed gradualism.[24] His inability to privatize state-owned enterprises or reduce the expansion in public investment, both of which enlarged the fiscal deficit, suggest that Végh did not engineer an orthodox program.[25] In fact, public investment rose by 400 percent between 1974 and 1978 (Hanson and De Melo 1985, 920). Végh also initiated gradual changes in trade reforms, price controls, and industrial promotion programs. Although Végh removed quantitative restrictions on imports and eliminated import licenses, high tariff barriers remained (Favaro and Spiller 1991, 354).

The elimination of price controls also followed a gradualist course. Prior to 1974, the government set prices for most goods and services. Government authorities fixed the prices for 94 percent of the goods in the consumer price index (CPI) (Ramos 1986, 29). The government reduced its control over prices and deregulated 13 percent of goods in the CPI in 1975 (Larraín 1986, 11). A year later, the government freed prices on all competitively produced goods not in the CPI. By 1978, however, the government still controlled prices on 40 percent of the goods in the popular consumption basket (Ramos 1986, 28).

The government also continued to back industrial promotion programs. Through its use of preferential and subsidized credits, tax exemptions, and provision of foreign exchange, private companies could freely import machinery and equipment (De Melo, et al. 1985, 997). The government also progressively lowered export taxes, and nontraditional exports received financial subsidies and exemptions from the value-added tax (Hanson and De Melo 1985, 919). Though many of these programs helped to promote export growth, they also enabled inefficient companies and industries to survive.[26]

By 1978, many of Uruguay's leading economic indicators appeared positive, with strong output growth, a booming financial sector, accelerating exports, and new investment emerging (De Melo, et al. 1985, 995). But inflation persisted. Like Chile and Argentina, Uruguay introduced the *tablita*—the preannounced devaluation of the exchange rate—to reduce future inflationary expectations. The country also extended its trade reforms. Policy makers announced a five-year schedule for tariff reductions in 1978 with a uniform rate of 35 percent scheduled to arrive by 1985. Uruguay also began to dismantle its export promotion program and reduced price controls (Ramos 1986, 30–31).

Economic Collapse, 1982–84

Much like Argentina and Chile, however, the *tablita* led to the appreciation of the real exchange rate. This appreciation contributed to imbalances in its external accounts and significant balance of payments and current accounts deficits. The overvalued peso slowed export growth from 15 percent per year between 1974 and 1978 to less than 4 percent between 1978 and 1979. The volume of imports increased by 50 percent (Ramos 1986, 31).

The situation in Argentina also exacerbated Uruguay's external accounts deficit. As Argentina strictly adhered to its *tablita* with a lag, this resulted in an appreciation of the Argentine peso even greater than that of Uruguay's peso. The overvalued exchange rate offered travel opportunities for Argentines to Uruguay. Argentina also purchased much of Uruguay's exports. Once Argentina instituted its massive devaluations in March 1981 through 1982, exports to Argentina declined sharply and fewer Argentines visited Uruguay. This created a crisis in investor confidence about Uruguay's future exchange rate policy. Investors expected a devaluation. Given the openness of financial markets, this prompted a two-billion-dollar capital flight between January and November 1982 (Larraín 1986, 16). Uruguay also experienced a sharp cut in the inflow of foreign capital, as foreign investors doubted that the policies would continue. Uruguay concomitantly had a large increase in transfers to the social security system between 1981 and 1982, with transfers rising from 5.5 to 9.4 percent of GDP (López, et al. 1988, 11).

Faced with widespread bankruptcies, high levels of inflation, unemployment, fiscal deficits, and a burgeoning external debt, Uruguay abandoned its gradualist neoliberal program in November 1982. Trade protection increased with price floors placed on imported products, no privatizations occurred, and the financial market began to close. The government also suspended the tariff reduction program and freely floated the exchange rate following the collapse of the *tablita*. Over the next two years, policies typical of a transition went into effect, with no radical adjustments. According to Végh (1992b, 7), who returned to the finance ministry in late 1983 and stayed until the transition to democracy occurred, "Economic policy in a period of political transition is, essentially, a holding operation. The normal pressures for higher expenditure and lower taxes as well as for protectionist measures and regulations in favor of special-interest groups are stronger than ever."

Table 2.7 summarizes Uruguay's economic policies during the military period. From 1974 to 1982, the government initiated gradualist neoliberal policies. Policy makers liberalized capital markets and implemented a deep stabilization program. However, tariffs remained at high levels, as did number of prices controlled by government authorities. Industrial promotion programs also received support, and almost no firms were privatized. In late 1982, the government abandoned the gradualist neoliberal program. New forms of trade protection emerged, capital markets became less liberal, and the large role of the state continued, with its funding of industrial promotion programs and ownership of important sectors of the economy.

Table 2.7   Economic Policies in Uruguay, 1973–1984

Policy	1973	1974–1981	1982–1984
Stabilization	Yes (2)	Yes (2)	No (1)
Capital Reform	None (0)	Extensive (2)	Minimal (1)
Tariffs	High (0)	Reduced Slightly (1)	No Change (1)
Privatization	None (0)	None (0)	None (0)
Price Controls	Extensive (0)	Some (1)	Extensive (0)
Industrial Promotion	Minimal (1)	Extensive (0)	Extensive (0)
Total	3	6	3

2 = Strong Neoliberal Policies; 1 = Gradual Neoliberal Policies; 0 = Nonliberal Policies

Conclusion

The political-economic histories of Argentina, Chile, and Uruguay are remarkably similar. From the 1850s through the early 1930s, the Southern Cone countries adopted market-oriented economic policies that followed their comparative advantage in rural exports. The traumatic events of the Great Depression and World Wars I and II contributed to these countries moving away from an economic model based on primary-product exports toward inward-oriented industrial production in the 1930s and 1940s. In 1950, urban sectors that included activated unions succeeded rural groups on the political landscape. These urban interests insisted on subsidization of import-competing producers and trade barriers to protect against international competition, part and parcel of their backing of ISI policies through the 1970s. Economic problems caused, in part, by the inability of democratic leaders to break away from interest groups tied to uncompetitive industries, helped lead to military intervention in Argentina, Chile, and Uruguay in the 1960s through the 1980s.

Military regimes, free of political pressures, were supposed to overcome the economic problems faced by democratic governments and initiate and sustain the same market-oriented policies to produce high economic growth rates. As this chapter showed, however, policy choice differed among the countries. Chile initiated and sustained the most intense neoliberal experiment. Argentina and Uruguay, by contrast, initiated gradualist programs that they gave up. Why did Chile choose an orthodox neoliberal program, which it sustained, while the others favored more gradualist programs, which they abandoned? The next chapter addresses this question by examining the role of economic policy makers in policy choices.

Appendix

Table 2.2   Basic Economic Indicators in Chile, 1970–1989

Year	GDP Growth Rate	Inflation	Unemployment	Real Exchange Rate	Real Wages	Terms of Trade
1970	2.1	34.9	5.7	93.4	100.0	131.1
1971	9.0	34.5	3.9	85.6	129.0	98.3
1972	−1.2	216.7	3.3	64.7	115.0	69.0
1973	−5.6	605.9	5.0	74.4	64.0	100.0
1974	1.0	369.2	9.5	122.7	60.0	105.7
1975	−12.9	343.2	14.8	147.1	64.0	70.3
1976	3.5	197.9	12.7	124.1	77.0	75.7
1977	9.9	84.2	11.8	100.0	81.0	67.8
1978	8.2	37.2	14.2	111.4	83.0	67.7
1979	8.3	38.0	13.6	112.2	84.0	72.2
1980	7.8	31.2	10.4	97.2	96.0	69.2
1981	5.5	9.9	11.3	84.5	110.0	55.9
1982	−14.1	20.7	19.6	94.2	108.6	50.4
1983	−0.7	23.1	14.6	113.1	97.1	53.1
1984	6.3	23.0	14.0	118.2	97.2	114.6
1985	2.5	26.4	12.0	145.2	93.0	139.4
1986	5.6	17.4	8.8	159.7	94.9	144.9
1987	5.8	21.5	7.9	166.6	94.6	134.2
1988	7.4	12.7	6.3	177.6	99.2	148.9
1989	10.0	21.4	5.3	173.5	n.a.	126.1

Sources: For growth of GDP, inflation, real wages (1982–88), and terms of trade (1973–83), see Edwards and Edwards (1991, 12, 28, 117, 137, 213); for unemployment and the real exchange rate, see Corbo and Fischer (1994, 32–33); for real wages (1970–81), see Frieden (1991, 154); for terms of trade (1970–73, 1984–89), see International Monetary Fund (1978, 1991). Terms of trade is defined as the ratio of export to import prices. n.a. = not available.

Table 2.4   Basic Economic Indicators in Argentina, 1966–1983

Year	GDP Growth Rate	Inflation	Unemployment	Real Exchange Rate	Real Wages	Terms of Trade
1966	0.6	31.9	6.1	103.7	98.9	111.8
1967	2.7	29.2	6.5	105.9	96.7	107.4
1968	4.3	16.2	5.1	100.9	91.7	106.1
1969	8.6	7.6	4.5	103.3	96.4	100.5
1970	5.4	13.6	5.0	95.3	100.0	100.0
1971	3.6	34.7	5.9	103.9	105.2	113.4
1972	1.6	58.5	6.6	117.4	99.0	125.3
1973	3.4	60.3	5.5	139.8	107.2	142.0
1974	6.5	24.2	3.9	121.7	126.4	113.4
1975	−0.9	182.8	3.3	97.6	123.7	95.2
1976	−0.2	444.0	4.7	90.9	79.2	89.4
1977	6.0	176.1	3.3	89.6	75.6	93.6
1978	−3.9	175.6	3.0	80.6	77.2	91.9
1979	6.8	159.9	2.1	83.9	86.1	100.2
1980	0.7	100.8	2.4	94.2	100.0	117.8
1981	−6.2	104.5	4.8	98.6	91.2	124.6
1982	−5.2	164.8	5.3	86.2	79.3	105.2
1983	3.1	343.2	4.7	n.a.	102.6	101.8

Source: Di Tella and Rodríguez Braun (1990, 205–12). n.a. = not available.

Table 2.6   Basic Economic Indicators in Uruguay, 1971–1984

Year	GDP Growth Rate	Inflation	Unemployment	Real Exchange Rate	Real Wages	Terms of Trade
1971	−0.2	24	7.6	92.0	105.2	102.2
1972	−1.6	76.4	7.7	113.7	87.2	109.9
1973	−2.1	77.5	8.9	134.1	100.8	n.a.
1974	3.1	107.2	8.1	114.3	100.0	144.9
1975	5.9	66.8	8.1	134.5	88.9	106.5
1976	4.0	39.9	12.7	144.3	85.8	108.1
1977	1.2	57.2	11.8	142.1	75.6	97.8
1978	5.3	46.0	10.1	139.4	72.9	101.9
1979	6.2	83.1	8.3	121.9	66.9	103.6
1980	6.0	42.8	7.4	100.0	66.7	100.0
1981	1.9	29.4	6.6	101.3	71.6	103.2
1982	−9.7	20.5	11.9	122.9	59.2	103.3
1983	−4.7	51.5	15.5	230.2	46.8	93.3
1984	−1.8	66.1	14.0	n.a.	32.5	84.7

Sources: For GDP growth, inflation, the real exchange rate, and terms of trade, see Larraín (1986); for unemployment, see Ramos (1986, 26–27) and López Murphy et al. (1988); for real wages, see Hanson and De Melo (1985, 921), Ramos (1986, 26–27), and Banco Central del Uruguay (1986, 70). n.a. = not available.

THREE

The Effects of Institutions on Policy-Making Appointments

I know that every one will admit that it would be highly praiseworthy in a prince to possess all the above-named qualities that are reputed good, but as they cannot all be possessed or observed, human conditions not permitting of it, it is necessary that he should be prudent enough to avoid the scandal of those vices which would lose him the state, and guard himself if possible against those which will not lose it him, but if not able to, he can indulge them with less scruple.

—Niccolò Machiavelli, *The Prince*

The previous chapter revealed differences in the initiation and maintenance of economic policies by Southern Cone military regimes. Given that many Southern Cone policy makers openly pledged their support for orthodox policies, these different policy choices are fairly remarkable. The inconsistency between the pledges of policy makers and their actual policy choices leads us to ask why some military regimes implemented their policy preferences while others did not.

This chapter begins with a discussion of the prevailing wisdom on economic policy choice. The first section applies empirical evidence from the Southern Cone cases to assess the merits of alternative political economy explanations. This section demonstrates that though each theory explains part of the process of economic policy choice under military rule, none fully accounts for policies chosen in the Southern Cone. The next section elaborates on a theory introduced in chapter 1, which I call the by-product theory, to explain the apparent inconsistency. This theory identifies the importance of historical characteristics of the military and governing institutions installed by military leaders to explain economic policy-making appointments. Differences in the long-standing characteristics of the military, such as factionalism, and in the kinds of governing institutions established by military leaders, I contend, influence the appointment decisions of military leaders.[1] An empirical section follows, which confirms that the by-product theory provides the most complete explanation for policy choice in the Southern Cone cases as well as in Brazil and Peru.

Theoretical Perspectives on Policy Choice under Military Rule

Do long-held characteristics of the military and the kinds of governing institutions installed under military rule matter, or is it possible to explain policy outcomes in the Southern Cone on the basis of other factors? To explore these issues, this section considers alternative theories to explain the process of economic policy making: (1) international factors, (2) economic interest groups or class-based theories, (3) left threat arguments, and (4) ideology and institutions.

In an ideal world, this section would include quantitative data to test more rigorously the alternative theories. However, as Latin American data under the best circumstances are scarce and frequently unreliable (Frieden 1991, 10), finding reliable data for insular military regimes is even more challenging. Indeed, an important reason analysts probably choose not to study military regimes reflects data collection difficulties. The secretive nature of policy making under military rule makes attempts to collect useful information for quantitative measures almost impossible. Despite these limitations, the following section shows the evidence theorists generally use to support their claims and their effectiveness in explaining economic policy choice in the Southern Cone.

International Factors

In the internationalist literature, some (Haggard 1990; Lancaster 1988; Stallings 1990, 1992) argue that policy choice depends on external constraints, such as debt crises and changes in external lending practices by international organizations including the International Monetary Fund (IMF) and the World Bank, and commercial banks. The availability of funding from external sources affects policy choices and limits the range of feasible policy options. In the case of military regimes, the availability of funding from international organizations and commercial banks constrains decision making for various public projects or for renegotiating debt. This approach predicts that countries experiencing intense pressure to reform from multilateral organizations are most likely to initiate and sustain reform measures. Countries less reliant on loans from these organizations and commercial banks are less likely to initiate measures advocated by them.

The Southern Cone cases show the merits and limitations of internationalist arguments. Internationalists emphasize international factors to explain policy choices in the Southern Cone in the mid-1970s and early 1980s. In the mid-1970s, oil prices skyrocketed and revenue from oil sales flowed into commercial banks throughout the world, but especially into banks in the United States and Europe. The strong inflow of reserves encouraged banks to lend aggressively to many countries, including some military regimes. While military regimes posed some risk to investors because of their instability and potential to default on loans, bankers still lent liberally.

The enormous cash flow into the Southern Cone countries set few limits on their range of policy choices. This enabled Argentina, Chile, and Uruguay to accumulate massive amounts of capital in the 1970s. This capital could be used in a variety of ways, depending on the interests that linked domestic and international actors. In the early 1980s, however, the crisis in the more developed countries created a cash crunch for the Southern Cone countries. Developments in international financial markets increased interest rates on most loans, which led to a sharp rise in debt-service ratios. At the same time, foreign lenders began to withdraw from these countries. This left Argentina, Chile, and Uruguay with both huge imbalances in their foreign exchange reserves and enormous debts. The crisis situation forced these countries to adopt more fiscally restrictive policies to put their accounts in order.

International factors offer general insights into the policies chosen in the Southern Cone, but they do not adequately explain variations among the cases. As detailed in chapter 2, Chile, Argentina, and Uruguay adopted different economic policies from the 1960s through the 1980s. International factors also do not account for differences in their ability to sustain the policies. Based on GDP growth rates and unemployment, Chile suffered the most from the external shock in 1982. But it maintained its program, while Argentina and Uruguay abandoned theirs. In fact, Argentina deserted its first economic program in 1969, at the height of its economic success and with little influence from international financial sources.

In addition, internationalist theorists would argue that in the 1970s, countries had more freedom in their policy choices. These countries had greater access to international funding that enabled them to pursue less fiscally prudent policies. In the 1980s, cutbacks in international funding forced countries to reduce government expenditures, control the money supply, and increase revenues. Ironically, Argentina, Chile, and Uruguay attempted to initiate policies that did just the opposite. In the 1970s, these countries imposed more fiscal restraint in their economies and opened their domestic markets to international competition. In the early 1980s, at the height of the economic crisis, Argentina and Uruguay abandoned many of these policies and increased protection while proposing more inward-looking policies. In late 1983, Chile also reduced the severity of its orthodox program by increasing tariff rates, imposing price controls, and adopting nonuniform tariff rates. The Southern Cone cases suggest the importance of domestic factors in order to explain more fully economic policy choices.

Economic Interest Groups or Classes

Economic interest groups or class-based arguments provide an alternative explanation for economic policy choice. Some (Cardoso and Faletto 1979; Evans 1979) argue that international and domestic class alliances contribute to policy choices, while others (O'Donnell 1988; Frieden 1991; Silva 1991, 1993) contend that domestic economic interests alone determine policy choices. Interest-group and class arguments emphasize the role of powerful domestic interests who lobby politicians to get what they want. Under military rule, economic interests lobby officers and appointed officials who have taken roles normally occupied by politicians in democracies.

In an example of a class-based argument, Guillermo O'Donnell (1973) claims that late industrialized societies, such as in Argentina, Chile, and Uruguay, go through two developmental stages. In the first stage, late-developing countries need a small amount of capital to produce simple consumption goods in an easy phase of import substitution. Domestic enterprises, often receiving tariff protection and state subsidies, produce goods for the local market. As the easy stage of development exhausts itself, a deepening phase begins that requires much larger supplies of capital. Domestic capitalists see vertical integration of industrialization through domestic manufacturing of intermediate and capital goods as necessary for development. One way for domestic capitalists to obtain the needed infusions of capital comes from squeezing wages and repressing demands of workers. As democratic regimes tend to favor working-class interests, domestic capitalists support military takeovers. Once installed, military regimes in the Southern Cone make policy decisions that suppress wages in order to accumulate capital necessary for larger-scale import substitution industrialization. Large capital requirements also force governments to attract foreign investment. Orthodox economic policies presumably address issues of economic crisis and long-term economic stability, which international investors desire.

O'Donnell's argument provides a broad and interesting historical account of the policies pursued in the Southern Cone over the past forty years. As discussed in chapter 2, these countries pursued similar policies from the 1940s through the 1960s. It does not, however, explain why these countries chose different neoliberal policies under military rule. O'Donnell's theory leaves unexplained why Chile initiated and maintained orthodox policies while the others selected gradualist policies, which they abandoned. More important, O'Donnell argues that the deepening of ISI requires economic liberalization. To the contrary, liberalization attempts to eliminate or limit tariff protection and subsidies for domestic producers and open markets to international competitors. The harm to inefficient import-competing producers caused by liberalization explains why such producers rallied to block neoliberal reforms.

In an important example of an interest-group argument, Jeff Frieden (1991) argues that economic policies are the result of group pressures on policy makers. According to Frieden, interest-group pressures increase with the specificity of the assets held by members of the group, rise with the concentration of the group, and decrease with the level of class struggle. Higher asset specificity more closely weds the owner to its current activity and minimizes the availability of other uses to which the asset might be put. Higher concentration also facilitates the mobilization of personnel to lobby policy makers.

Interest-group arguments, like Frieden's, provide well-reasoned and useful explanations for economic policy choices under military rule in Argentina and Uruguay. Frieden's theory captures important insights for the Southern Cone and has received significant attention by scholars beyond Latin America. In both of Argentina's military regimes and in Uruguay, powerful interest groups, including the military, lobbied military officers and military leaders to block or suspend neoliberal reforms. In Argentina, Fabricaciones Militares, the military's industrial complex, and domestic manufacturers lobbied to maintain protection for their products, prevented privatization of state-owned enterprises, and created schemes to receive new forms of protection. In Uruguay, textile merchants, automobile manufacturers, and others blocked reforms, as did the military itself.

Interest-group arguments, however, are less convincing for explaining Chile's economic policy change from the inception of military rule in 1973 to radicalism in 1975.[2] In Chile, most officers and powerful domestic groups, including manufacturers, opposed privatization and liberalization policies (Edwards and Edwards 1991, ch. 4). In fact, from 1975 through 1982 almost 2,500 manufacturing firms filed for bankruptcy (Stenzel 1988, 329–31).[3] Small and medium-sized enterprises and entrepreneurial sectors, and domestic market producers in agriculture and industry especially lobbied against these policies, but they could not stop economic reform (Campero 1991, 132).[4] Former heads of the National Association of Manufacturers (NAM) and its members also vigorously opposed policies introduced in 1975, but policy makers ignored their pleas (Agüero 1992; Arteaga 1992). As Frieden (1991, 157) concedes, "Economic policy was made by economists who ignored sectoral demands and concentrated on restoring an investment climate favorable to the private sector." Frieden (1991, 158) further states that "there is little evidence that policy was made with sector-specific targets in mind." Moreover, while the world economic recession affected firms in Chile, including its conglomerates known as *grupos,* in 1981–83, Pinochet did not moderate Chile's policy course until late 1983, with the crisis brewing for more than two years. If powerful domestic groups held so much power, changes should have occurred in 1981, not in 1983, when complaints redounded not only from powerful interest groups but also from nearly all societal forces in Chile. In addition, orthodox policies returned in 1985 despite entrepreneurs disagreeing over policy choices.

Interest-group or class-based arguments reveal important parts of the policy-making process. These arguments help to understand the demand side of policy making. But to gain a greater sense of the internal workings of policy making under military rule, the policy-making process also needs to include the supply side. An analysis that focuses on military leaders and their policy-making appointments helps to explain when interest groups will affect policy choice.

Left Threats

In 1988, Guillermo O'Donnell revised his earlier theory to include the importance of left threats to policy choice. O'Donnell's (1973) previous work suggested why military regimes imposed economic policies supported by capitalists, but it provided less theoretical insight for explaining variations in policies among military regimes. In an attempt to explain variations among Southern Cone regimes, O'Donnell (1988) along with Stepan (1988) and Frieden (1991) contend that the level of threat from the left within each society prior to the military taking over affects policy choice. O'Donnell argues that the higher the left threat preceding military coups, the more orthodox the policy choices are and the greater the chance that the policies are sustained. Intense left threats produce strong cohesion among dominant classes against the popular sector and increase the willingness of rightist military leaders to adopt orthodox economic policies that harm or deactivate leftist organizations.

O'Donnell claims that differences in the left threat experienced by the Southern Cone countries prior to the military's interventions help to explain Chile's initiating and sustaining of more orthodox policies and Argentina and Uruguay's adoption of more gradualist policies. Salvador Allende's electoral victory in 1970 and introduction of Marxist policies created a more intense threat and more polarized society in Chile than guerrilla groups in Argentina and Uruguay. The higher threat in Chile stimulated the initiation of more orthodox policies. As orthodox policies have negative effects for leftist groups, Chile introduced these policies in order to reduce the left threat and to resurrect the economy.

While O'Donnell's argument provides a useful explanation for variations in the Southern Cone, methodological difficulties with defining the degree of left threat make it incapable of falsification (Remmer 1991). For example, did Chile's democratically elected Marxist government pose a greater threat than large terrorist groups in Argentina and Uruguay? Fernández (1976, 73–76) estimates that an alliance between the People's Revolutionary Party (ERP) and Montoneros in Argentina had a combined strength of 200,000. Chile's initiation of orthodox policies two years after the fall of democracy, not immediately following the coup, also raises doubts about the relevance of the left threat for policy choice. If the left threat played such a critical role in policy choice, policy makers should have implemented orthodox reforms immediately following the coup, not two years later, when the threat virtually no longer existed. Argentina's second military regime also experienced a more severe left threat than its first regime, but neither case sustained its reforms. Moreover, if military governments want to reduce left threats, they can initiate populist policies advocated by the left—as in the case of Peru—that attract left supporters and undermine the popularity and support base of leftist parties (or organizations).

Ideology and Institutions

Katherine Sikkink (1991) and others (Hall 1989; Goldstein and Keohane 1993) examine the effect of ideas and institutions to explain the adoption, implementation, and consolidation of policy choices. Sikkink argues that the ideas and ideology of policy makers and the president—who are aware of international and domestic constraints and opportunities—influence the adoption of economic policies. For successful implementation, these ideas must be embedded in institutions. For ideas to become consolidated, they must fit with existing ideologies of important economic and social groups and the state must have the organizational capacity to carry out the policies.

In the Southern Cone, the ideas and ideology of policy makers influenced policy choices. The strong commitment of Chilean economic policy makers to orthodox policies affected their policy choices. Institutions in Chile also entrenched these ideas. The existence of an insulated bureaucracy in Chile enabled policy makers to implement an orthodox program.[5] Policy makers in Uruguay and Argentina, by contrast, held different ideas on policy choice that led to less orthodox policies. The inability of policy makers to embed neoliberal ideas in their institutions impeded successful implementation of the policies. In addition, neoliberal ideas never fit with existing ideologies of important economic and social groups. Powerful import-competing producers and military interests tied to production of steel and other materials in Fabricaciones Militares in Argentina opposed neoliberal ideology. The historic influence of José Batlle y Ordóñez in Uruguay and his concern for state-led development also worked against neoliberalism.

The ideas and ideology held by policy makers are important for policy choice. Ideology alone, however, does not fully explain policy choice. These theories also need to explain the factors that contribute to the appointment of policy makers. While some may argue that the economic interests of leaders determine policy-making appointments, General Jorge Videla of Argentina and President Juan María Bordaberry of Uruguay advocated orthodox policies, but not all of their policy makers did. In contrast, Pinochet did not espouse orthodox policies in 1973. But in 1975, he appointed a team of similarly trained and doctrinaire economists. In addition, most important economic and social groups in Chile opposed the ideas of Chicago Boys, University of Chicago–trained economists, in the 1970s through the mid-1980s. The ideas of Chicago Boys did not fit with existing ideologies of important economic and social groups (De Castro 1992). Yet, Chile consolidated market-oriented policies to the point that its democracies continue to pursue many of the policies first enacted under military rule.

Each of these alternative theories offers possible explanations and powerful insights about policy choices under military rule in the Southern Cone. International factors constrain the choice of feasible policies. Powerful economic interests who lobby military governments have greater success in getting what they want. An intense left threat fosters policies that attempt to redefine and restructure society. Ideology affects policy choice. By themselves, however, these theories do not adequately explain variation in policy choice under military rule or the politics within military governments. In the next section, the by-product theory is offered as a detailed and generalizable explanation for why military regimes vary in their policy choices and to help us to understand the politics inside the military.

By-Product Theory

Policy-Making Appointments and Political Survival

Since the late 1960s, domestic economic policy choice and its effect on economic development have received much attention. Despite the increasing interest in economic policy issues, most of the policy choice literature has focused on democratic governments and the goals of democratic leaders. Military leaders who direct military governments have received minimal interest.

In one of the few works to discuss the role of military leaders on policy choice, Ames (1987) argues that military leaders in political offices hold much the same goals as democratic leaders. Like democratic leaders, at times military leaders want to survive in political office and increase their own power. Although most officers don't care about political office, those who achieve the presidency or its equivalent under military rule usually do since it takes a lot of effort. There are exceptions, such as when officers take over the presidency to oversee transitions. These officers realize that their rule is transitory, and are often chosen by their peers for just that reason. In addition, the fact that the main interest of leaders is the maintenance of office does not preclude them from having substantive preferences that go beyond staying in power. However, the need for short-term survival imposes a constraint on military leaders' efforts to achieve those preferences. Thus, if we accept that most military leaders identify political survival as an instrumental goal that prevails over immanent goals, the next question is what are the survival strategies available to military leaders and what factors influence the survival strategies they choose?

Before discussing the survival strategies, it is important to recognize differences between democratic and military governments. Although military rulers hold many of the same goals as democratic leaders, military rulers face different circumstances that affect the attainment of these ends. Unlike democracies, military regimes seize power illegally. Despite the initial popular support to mount a coup, military governments do not acquire the legitimacy democratic governments earn with electoral victories. Early support for a military regime usually evaporates quickly once tough decisions are made (Stepan 1971, 265). Military leaders also have no officially recognized support base, which makes their rule more tenuous.[6] In addition, as military governments usually redesign their constitutions or limit the powers of their supreme courts, the legitimacy of their judicial bodies are subject to question. Legal issues are problematic since military governments have no credible means to enforce agreements among junta members, and often rely on coercive threats to resolve matters. Because many of their commitments are not credible, they can lose the support of investors, who rely on long-term predictability. The potential for struggles within the armed forces escalating into civil war makes the lack of enforcement of agreements even more critical.

These circumstances, common to military regimes, limit the choice of survival strategies available to military leaders. One of the most common but least studied survival strategies involves appointments to policy-making positions. Military leaders can use the appointment of personnel to bureaucratic agencies, and especially in areas concerned with the economy, to extend their political careers. Appointments to economic policy-making positions are critical, as their decisions influence economic performance, which affects the military leader's survival.

We can conceive of various scenarios wherein military leaders use economic policy-making appointments to advance their political careers.[7] The three most common appointment strategies are patronage, co-optation, or technical merit. In one scenario, military leaders use appointments as forms of patronage to reward supporters or persons loyal to them. As in democratic governments, where political leaders provide party workers and loyalists with work opportunities and high-level positions in government (Geddes 1994; Schneider 1991), military leaders provide jobs and political openings for officers and other supporters. In providing employment for their friends and supporters, however, military leaders forgo potential economic benefits that they would have earned if they had hired the most qualified personnel.

Alternatively, military leaders adopt appointment strategies that promote consensus among rival leaders. Fear of a counter-coup by military rivals weighs into appointment strategies chosen by leaders. As mentioned earlier, because military governments have no official unbiased body or document to enforce agreements among junta members, this makes consensus among leaders on the choice of policy makers even more critical. Like the patronage option, the need for consensus works against the appointment of most qualified personnel. Moreover, most officers advocate protectionist and statist economic policies. These policies provide employment for officers in state-owned enterprises and protection and subsidies for military enterprises. Thus, most in the military, for self-interested or ideological reasons, prefer not to appoint technocrats.

Alternatively, leaders make appointments that appear to be based more on technical merit than on issues of political patronage or coalition building. In the case of economic policy-making appointments, leaders appoint economists who, on the basis of their training, are best qualified to manage the economy. If these policy makers implement policies that produce strong economic growth and promote economic development, they serve the career goals of their leaders in office.

This means in effect that economic policy making under military regimes is essentially an unintended by-product of the military ruler's strategy to retain power. Rulers need both good economic performance and political support to remain in office. Sometimes, as these appointment scenarios suggest, the need for short-term political support may hinder good economic results.

Military Factionalism and Economic Appointments

Military leaders, who supposedly favor the same types of policies and policy makers, often differ in their policy-making appointments. To explain appointment strategies chosen by military leaders, it is important to examine the political conditions and constraints that shape their decisions. Differences in long-standing characteristics of the military and in the kinds of governing institutions established by military rulers help to explain why leaders appoint different policy makers. These differences affect the political survival strategies chosen by military leaders, which in turn shape the appointment of economic policy makers.

According to *Webster's Third New International Dictionary* (1986), a faction is "a party, combination, or clique (as within a state, government, or other association) often contentious, self-seeking, or reckless of the common good." For our purposes, this definition suggests that the greater the level of contention among military services across time, the higher the degree of factional pressures in the military. To measure the degree of contention in the military, we need to examine the historical circumstances that give rise to these disagreements. As discussed in chapter 1, three factors clearly can contribute to factionalization and are, at minimum, good indicators of the presence of factionalization within the military: (1) the frequency of political interventions by the military, (2) the experience of the military with politicized promotions, and (3) the history of competition among the armed services for scarce resources.[8]

Frequent military interventions often promote divisions in the armed forces. After repeated political interventions, officers no longer focus solely on security issues, areas where they possess a high level of expertise and where a consensus among officers can be found. Instead, officers directly involve themselves in political and distributive decisions, which increases ideological dissension and creates proto-parties within the officer corps. Cliques form around charismatic officers who can articulate different visions of the military's proper role in politics. In addition, the more often the military intervenes, the greater the infighting and competition among officers to manage the government. In their competition to serve as leaders following military interventions, officers jockey with each other for high-level positions in the government. This struggle for power inflames factionalism. Through their frequent interventions, officers also learn about the potential economic benefits and perquisites that can be garnered from positions in the government. Competition for these benefits exacerbates military divisiveness.

Politicized military promotions also contribute to military factionalism. When democratic or military leaders make military promotions on the basis of officer loyalty, rather than merit or seniority criteria, this tends to politicize military officers. The lack of fairness in promotions divides the military and undermines discipline (Stepan 1971, 155). In addition, as each presidential succession brings with it the opportunity for democratic leaders to promote their own military supporters, this further politicizes the military force.

Military factionalism is also fostered when no service dominates the others in terms of manpower, equipment, and supplies. This lack of dominance encourages fierce competition and intense inter-service rivalries for scarce state resources.[9] It also forces the services to act more politically than they might otherwise. Officers lobby politicians for as much or more resources than the other branch receives.

An absence of these factors, by contrast, contributes to a relatively united and apolitical military. Armed forces that have not frequently intervened democratic governments, have no history of politically manipulated promotions, and have one service that dominates the others in terms of power and resources are usually apolitical and focused on military and security issues. Their professionalism promotes an esprit de corps among the services.

Whether the military is factionalized or not has important implications for appointment strategies chosen by military leaders. I contend that military leaders backed by factionalized militaries rely on consensus building among the branches in order to discourage counter-coups. As officers in factionalized militaries struggle among themselves to reach agreements that satisfy a broad range of interests within the leadership, they make economic appointments that serve their short-term interest in political survival but which come at the expense of their medium-term interest in economic performance. Political contenders from within their service branch or other branches induce rulers to offer cabinet appointments, jobs, and favors to military loyalists and competitors in return for short-term political support. Rulers appoint policy makers who help maintain cohesion in the military but who are usually not well-trained in economic policy decisions.

Interests within the military also work against the appointment of technocrats of a particular ideological coloration, namely neoliberal economists. In factionalized militaries, many officers served previously as directors of state-owned enterprises and in other bureaucratic capacities and are aware of the benefits that come from state employment, including high salaries, a car and driver, and the potential to loot enterprises or collect rents. Neoliberal economists, however, favor privatization policies that reduce opportunities for rent seeking (Krueger 1974; Bhagwati et al. 1984). Instead of revenues from state-owned enterprises and marketing boards flowing to officers, these revenues go directly to the private sector and its newly privatized firms, eliminating the military as middlemen. Since neoliberal economic policy makers threaten access to important state resources used by leaders to build their support, most officers are not expected to favor the appointment of neoliberal economists to economic policy-making positions.

Factions also attract interest-group pressures. Since the military serves as the most effective channel for exercising influence over military leaders, interest groups lobby officers. Protectionist interests, in particular, solicit officers to put up fierce resistance to the appointment of policy makers who support neoliberal policies. Contrary to many expectations, industry often is opposed to market reforms and will be key lobbyists. Fueled by the ISI model, import-competing producers, who rely on high tariffs, are among the most powerful industrial groups.

In less factionalized armed forces, military rulers face a less pressing threat of counter-coups. The long history of military unity and professionalism reduces the likelihood that officers will engage in political intrigue.[10] Fewer factions also limit the need for having many officers involved in the government. Most officers continue to focus on security issues. Those officers who do receive governmental appointments have been inculcated with strong traditions of discipline and hierarchy and are more likely to follow orders from their superiors. Consequently, interest groups have fewer opportunities to influence policy.

Governing Institutions and Economic Appointments

In addition to its direct effects on economic policy making, military factionalism may affect the kinds of institutions devised by military rulers. The governing institutions created by military regimes often reflect the underlying relations between the military services supporting that regime. For example, military factionalism may result in the creation of junta rule designed to distribute power and responsibilities equally among the services.

A consensus-oriented political structure is not as important in less factionalized military regimes in which less need exists to guarantee institutionally the distribution of power. The degree of factionalization in the military, however, does not determine with certainty which governing institutions the newly installed military regime will choose. Contextual factors specific to the particular country, and its history prior to and during the military intervention, also influence the kinds of governing institutions selected. Such factors might include the development of factions just prior to the military intervention and differing levels of support among service chiefs to stage a coup. The possible governing institutions installed by less factionalized militaries include collegial executives, strict succession systems under collegial or one-man rule, and one-man rule. These governing institutions affect policy-making appointments.

Under collegial rule, service chiefs from each military branch who make up the junta share decision making equally. This power sharing contributes to negotiation in appointments. While each military branch in a collegial government usually controls a specific area of the government, the appointment of top ministers requires consensual or unanimous support from the leaders. Given the likelihood for competition among the service chiefs to serve as junta leader, each adopts short-term survival strategies including appointing politically useful but not economic experts to policy-making positions. No junta member willingly sacrifices the political advantage of having one of his allies in important policy-making positions. Each service chief attempts to buy off support groups from within the military and its civilian allies to improve his position in the junta.

Gaining political support from military and civilian interests suggests that neoliberal economists, whose view conflicts with most civilians and officers, are unlikely to be selected. Indeed, as leaders struggle for prominence with each other in a collegial government, they try to mobilize civilian support for themselves by promoting policies advocated by powerful interest groups, especially in protectionist import-competing industries. The system of equality among service chiefs also may give each of them the authority to veto proposed appointments.[11]

Succession or rotational systems also work against the appointment of neoliberal economists. Succession or rotational systems, with either collegial or one-man rule, set specific timetables of three to five years or less for leaders to step down from office. When succession or rotation occurs every three to five years, contenders for governmental positions enter into political struggles prior to each succession or rotation. As in any political struggle, contenders make promises to attract supporters. Given the unpopularity of neoliberal policies with most interest groups, military officers gain civilian support by "campaigning" against these policies and its proponents. Once in office, these leaders repay their backers and attempt to attract supporters before the next succession or rotation, which works against neoliberal economists. The short time between successions or rotations also may not allow a team of experts enough time to implement their policy preferences. When new leaders enter office, they usually choose their own policy makers. As policy making requires time for considering, deciding on, and implementing policies, a succession or rotational system may not give policy makers enough time to enact their reforms.

Repaying debts to supporters and interest-group access are most intense when successions occur frequently. When successions or rotations occur annually, this system will be reminiscent of a collegial system, even with one-man rule. During their year in office, leaders will have almost no time to initiate new reforms. By the time leaders submit proposals for change, successors are making preparations to enter office. Leaders will thus seek policies that conform to the programs of former leaders and that their supporters back. Moreover, as policy makers have little time to evaluate problems in various industries, they may rely on advice and information from self-interested, pressure-group lobbyists, which further restricts policy-making autonomy.

A less factionalized armed force under one-man rule (from now on referred to as consolidated one-man rule), by contrast, is critical for rulers' medium-term interest in economic performance to supersede their short-term interest in political survival. As mentioned earlier, less factionalized militaries feel less pressure to appoint officers to governmental positions. Those officers who do receive governmental appointments are accustomed to promotions on the basis of merit and hierarchical discipline, that is, obeying orders of superiors. Interest groups thus need to lobby senior officers or service chiefs to influence policy. One-man rule also limits access points for interest groups. Under one-man rule, the leader has less need to consult with service chiefs prior to making important decisions. The leader faces fewer factions that force compromise with other military interests, and the leader does not share power, which requires consensual agreement. Of course, leaders cannot rule alone, as they can be replaced or overthrown. Consolidated one-man rule, however, confers greater autonomy on leaders in their policy-making appointments and policy choices. Moreover, military leaders have opportunities to retain the loyalty of military officers by manipulating promotions and retirements or by offering governmental positions, while pursuing their own policy goals. Through the control of military promotions, retirements, and political perquisites, the leader can make officers beholden to him. The long history of discipline and apolitical character of militaries under consolidated one-man rule provides an ambitious leader with freedom in policy choices, while doling out benefits to officers to insure their loyalty.

Greater autonomy in policy-making appointments does not insure that leaders will appoint neoliberal economists. But, in contrast to situations that compel leaders to expend political capital to satisfy immediate political considerations, leaders under consolidated one-man rule and efforts to achieve such rule can follow medium-term survival strategies. A strategy to promote survival and consolidate power may include the appointment of neoliberal economists. As neoliberal economists are considered knowledgeable in economic policy making, they may have a greater understanding of the policies necessary to obtain long-term economic growth.[12] In addition, policies endorsed by neoliberal economists, such as the reduction of state intervention in the economy and the elimination of protection, contribute to the decline and fragmentation of powerful interest groups that depend on the state for their survival. Their decline makes the leader less beholden to any group, which helps to consolidate the leader's power (Garretón 1986, 155).

Empirical Cases

The following sections document empirically the usefulness of the by-product theory through a review of the Southern Cone cases. Chile (1973–89) and Argentina (1966–69) exemplify cases of one-man rule, and Uruguay (1973–84) and Argentina (1970–73, 1976–83) illustrate cases of collegial and succession systems. Military forces in Chile and Uruguay are identified as less factionalized, while factionalism surfaced in both Argentine cases (see diagram 3.1).[13] These cases show that military characteristics and governing institutions installed under military rule shape survival strategies and influence the choice of economic policy makers. Military regimes in Brazil and Peru are also included to show the generalizability of the theory.[14]

Diagram 3.1   Characteristics of the Military and Its Governing Institutions

		Military Rule	
		One-Man	Junta
History of Military	Less Factionalized	Chile 1973–89	Uruguay 1973–84
	Factionalized	Argentina 1966–69 Brazil 1964–85	Argentina 1970–73 1976–83 Peru 1968–80

Chile

Effects of Less Factionalism in the Military

Chile's military supported the country's long-held democratic tradition. Except for a short period (1927–32), nearly 150 years of civilian rule marked Chile's apolitical, less factionalized military (Arriagada 1986).[15] The military received promotions based on professional criteria, and the army always dominated the other services in terms of manpower and resources (see table 3.1). This apolitical tradition delayed the decision to depose democratically elected President Salvador Allende (Valenzuela 1978). Fear of engaging the military in an internal war against constitutionalist military forces and irreparably damaging the prestige and reputation of the armed forces enabled Allende to retain power longer than he otherwise would have.

On September 11, 1973, the military branches and their service chiefs worked in concert to depose the democratic government and institute military rule. In an effort to limit factional pressures, the service chiefs proclaimed that the military would serve in the government "only as long as circumstances require" (Arriagada 1988, 5). The service chiefs also agreed to share power among themselves. They designated a junta gov-

Table 3.1   Military Personnel in the Southern Cone: 1972, 1977, and 1991

		Army	%	Navy	%	Air Force	%	Total
	1972	85,000	62	35,000	26	17,000	12	137,000
Argentina	1977	80,000	62	32,900	25	17,000	13	129,900
	1991	45,000	54	25,000	30	13,000	16	83,000
	1972	38,000	62	15,000	25	8,000	13	61,000
Chile	1977	50,000	59	24,000	28	11,000	13	85,000
	1991	54,000	58	25,500	28	12,800	14	92,300
	1972	12,000	78	1,800	12	1,600	10	15,400
Uruguay	1977	20,000	74	4,000	15	3,000	11	27,000
	1991	16,000	70	3,500	15	3,400	15	22,900

Sources: 1991, Wilkie et al. (1993, 373); 1977, The International Institute for Strategic Studies (1978, 67–72); 1972, Dupuy (1972, 42–66).

ernment with each service chief holding equal power and divided up control over cabinet ministries among the service branches. According to General Pinochet:

> I have no pretension to direct the Junta while it lasts. What we will do is rotate. Now it is me, tomorrow it will be Admiral Merino, then General Leigh and after, General Mendoza. I don't want to appear to be an irreplaceable person. I have no aspiration but to serve my country. As soon as the country recovers, the junta will turn over the government to whom the people desire (cf. Valenzuela 1991, 27).[16]

The junta also limited the potential for factional pressures by concentrating decision making in the four service chiefs. The junta continued the tradition of military subordination, though in this case, to the junta leaders and not civilians. By keeping the military out of politics, the junta leaders retained the military's apolitical positions and centralized power (Valenzuela 1991, 27–32). This concentration of power also minimized access points for interest groups. To lobby for policy changes, interests needed to pressure the four service chiefs rather than their underlings, who remained outside of politics and focused on security and national defense issues.

Toward One-Man Rule

Following the coup, the four service chiefs supported sharing power. A year later, however, General Pinochet adopted an ambitious political strategy that led to one-man rule. From the outset, military rule produced tensions within the junta, especially between Pinochet and the air force commander, General Gustavo Leigh. Having served as commander of the air force longer than Pinochet had as commander of the army, Leigh contended that he should hold the position of commander in chief of the armed forces.[17] Pinochet, by contrast, argued that since the army held the greatest proportion of military resources and personnel, he, as head of the army, should serve as commander in chief. A power struggle ensued between the two leaders.

In 1974, Pinochet took actions to preserve his political position and his position as leader of the armed forces. As a first step toward installing one-man rule, Pinochet created DINA, Dirección Nacional de Inteligencia, the centralized military intelligence agency. DINA's operation included an infrastructure of secret agents, unmarked vehicles, and clandestine detention centers (Arriagada 1988, 13).[18] Although the formation of DINA through Decree Law 521 (June 18, 1974) at first appeared as a way to coordinate and centralize the intelligence activities of the military services against opposition forces, DINA also served as a vital weapon in Pinochet's drive to install one-man rule (Valenzuela 1991, 47–50). An example of the advantages DINA conferred on Pinochet is the naming of an army officer as DINA's director, who in theory reported DINA's activities to the junta, but who in actuality reportedly directly to Pinochet. The army also represented the preeminent group within DINA, which drove General Leigh to withdraw his air force officers from DINA.[19] As Leigh stated:

> They [DINA] requested personnel from all branches, but it turned out that the officers who we sent to DINA were not given any executive work, only administrative jobs. In practice, the organization was directly subordinate to the President, although legally it was supposed

to be subordinate to the Governing Junta. So I pulled my people when I realized that I had no power over DINA (cf. Arriagada 1988, 18).

Given DINA's immense security activities in state agencies and in the military institution itself, DINA concentrated an all-powerful police apparatus in Pinochet's hands and dispelled any pretense of equality among the service chiefs.

A second method used by Pinochet to consolidate his unrivaled position within the junta came through Decree Law 527 (June 26, 1974), the Statute of the Government Junta. The Statute of the Junta "largely ratified the de facto structure of power among the members of the Junta" (Barros 1996, 26). Under D. L. 527, the junta declared Pinochet as both president of the junta and supreme chief of the nation. The junta leaders initially strongly resisted the statute, but they relented when they learned that the statute represented nothing more than a technical change necessary for the proper administration of the government (Valenzuela 1991, 37). The junta leaders, however, did not understand the full extent or the implications of the legislation. This statute not only did not recognize the junta's prerogative to designate the president, but it also conferred executive power on the president of the junta, who also served as supreme chief of the nation (Arriagada 1988, 15–16).[20] Pinochet held executive power without a fixed term and could not be dismissed by the other members of the junta.

As supreme chief of the nation, Pinochet also could appoint and dismiss cabinet ministers and other top officials with little consultation with the other junta members.[21] Pinochet used these appointments to assert the predominance of the army over the navy and air force and his preeminence over other army officers (Remmer 1991, 128). The new appointments gave Pinochet power over his rivals, including Leigh, as he could force resignations of competitor army officers and dole out promotions to officers who would feel beholden to Pinochet (Sigmund 1982, 107).[22] Pinochet could also change seniority and retirement rules for military officers, allowing some to stay beyond their commissioned terms, which further increased loyalty to Pinochet (Arriagada 1988, 132–39). Moreover, since their longevity depended on the supreme chief's wishes, these new appointees reported directly to Pinochet, fortifying his position relative to the other service chiefs.

In another change, Pinochet convinced the other junta members to approve Decree Law 806 in December 1974, which changed his title from supreme chief of the nation to that of president of the republic. Pinochet argued for changing his title, as most legislation referred to the office of the president of the republic when referring to the executive branch (Valenzuela 1991, 37).

Despite these changes, Pinochet felt constrained politically. Junta laws, for example, still required unanimous approval. In his quest for unlimited control, Pinochet used the power of appointments to consolidate one-man rule and diminish the standing of Leigh. From the beginning of the military takeover, Leigh had favored Keynesian ideas (Varas 1979). Leigh spearheaded the appointment of the first economic team, notable for its political and ideological heterogeneity (Arriagada 1988, 7). By 1975, however, "Chicago Boys," economists trained at the University of Chicago, dominated economic policy making.[23]

Pinochet, who previously repudiated market-oriented policies, appointed the Chicago Boys to neutralize the arguments and strength of Leigh (Fontaine Talavera 1992, 115; Valenzuela 1991, 40–42).[24] Prior to the appointments, Pinochet had witnessed the heated exchanges between "Chicago" economists who held subsecretarial positions within the government and Leigh. Pinochet appointed these economists (who held nearly identical views on economic policies) as opponents to the rival junta member in order to consolidate his rule. As Leigh proposed policies opposed by economists, this united team of economists could tear apart his arguments in front of military decision-making committees, making Leigh appear less competent among his colleagues. Chicago economists weakened Leigh's standing among military officers and within the junta.[25]

Economic factors also influenced Pinochet's appointments (Delano and Traslaviña 1989, 45). Because of the fall in copper prices and the rapidly rising cost of imported oil, Chile's balance of trade account worsened in 1974.[26] Human rights abuses also restrained most foreign interests from offering loans, which further exhausted foreign resources. The appointment of neoliberal economists addressed these issues. Based on their schooling, neoliberal economists held ties to officials from international organizations that increased credibility with lenders and attracted capital (Méndez 1992; Massad 1992). As Arriagada (1988, 42) writes:

> The economists in the government and the heads of the large financial conglomerates had succeeded in establishing themselves as the keys to the Chilean economy's gaining access to international finan-

cial circles. Clearly, this role was the civilians' most significant contribution to the military regime, and it was doubly important because of the sorry state of Chile's relations with major Western governments since 1973.[27]

The appointment of neoliberal economists also enabled Pinochet to consolidate his rule by weakening powerful interest groups. Most neoliberal economists opposed formal links between entrepreneurial organizations and the government (Campero 1991, 155).[28] Independent economists introduced market and labor policies that led to the collapse and fragmentation of many powerful interest groups (Drake 1998, 86). Groups such as entrepreneurs, who depended on the state to provide subsidies and protection from international firms, no longer could rely on state support. Their collapse made Pinochet less beholden to any group and helped to consolidate his power (Garretón 1986, 155).

By appointing these economists, Pinochet also finessed the usual trade-off between political loyalty and technocratic expertise. Pinochet consolidated his rule by weakening his competitors and doling out benefits to the military qua military through increased military budgets, military appointments to state-owned enterprises and cabinet positions other than economic policy making, and expanding the officer corps.[29] He hired neoliberal economists as his economic policy makers, securing the advantages of employing qualified personnel.

The apolitical nature of the military and the allotment of benefits to officers also helped Pinochet to insulate policy makers from interest groups. The military's apolitical traditions allowed Pinochet to separate the military as institution from the military as government, restricting the role and influence of the military in policy matters (Valenzuela 1991, 31–36). Apolitical traditions predisposed most officers to stay out of governmental functions and to devote themselves to security activities (Foxley 1992). Those officers who did receive government positions responded to the government line of authority and did not serve as representatives of the armed forces (Agüero 1989). Particularistic benefits to the armed forces also retained their loyalty to Pinochet.[30] Military loyalty to Pinochet enabled him to insulate economic policy makers from military interests, which obstructed interest-group access.

Consolidated one-man rule and efforts to achieve it enabled Pinochet to appoint neoliberal economists in economic policy-making positions and to insulate these policy makers from societal and military influence, as part of a strategy for achieving political ambitions. Pinochet implemented a political survival strategy necessary to thwart competitors, provide benefits to officers, and employ technocrats.

Argentina

Origins of Military Factionalism

The history of Argentina's military shares few parallels with Chile. Politicized military promotions, intense inter-service rivalries, and the frequency of political intervention by the armed forces fostered strong factions in Argentina's military. From 1930 through 1983, military forces overthrew civilian governments six times: in 1930, 1943, 1955, 1962, 1966, and 1976.[31]

The frequency of military coups contributed to the long history of factions in Argentina's military. Initial factions emerged in the early 1940s over the role of the military in politics and because of officer loyalty to previous or current military leaders (Potash 1969, 163).[32] Some officers supported military intervention, while others called for a return to professional military values. President Juan Perón aggravated these factions by politicizing military decisions. Perón undermined professional norms in the armed forces by providing benefits to loyal officers and by using political criteria in decisions affecting the officer corps, making them beholden to him. Perón also retained control over military promotions, integrating the military with his national movement (Potash 1980, 112, 214). Unlike Chile, where General Pinochet as commander in chief of the armed forces justified his military promotions on the basis of his position in the military, Perón, now a civilian, had little legitimate basis for control over promotions. Perón's influence over military policy fostered new factions (Snow 1979, 73).

Once the military deposed Perón in 1955, factions grew and inter-service rivalries intensified.[33] Although the army held and continues to hold the most manpower and resources (see table 3.1),[34] which tends to reduce rivalries among the services, Perón's politicized promotions stirred up opposition to him. It took the navy's solid opposition to help bring down Perón. The prestige earned by the navy for its ability to determine political outcomes escalated inter-service rivalries, as naval officers demanded more power (Carranza 1983, 131).

Intense conflicts among the armed service branches and within each service stimulated power struggles and repeated coup attempts between 1955 and 1962 (O'Donnell 1988, 51–52). By 1962, these factions merged into two camps: the colorados (reds) and the azules (blues). While the colorados demanded military rule for an indefinite period, the azules argued for restoring military professionalism. The azules opposed military involvement in partisan politics and defended constitutional government (Wynia 1986, 77).[35]

In September 1962, the colorados and azules engaged in armed confrontation, with the azules claiming victory (Rock 1987).[36] Heady from their conquest, the azules attempted to reinstitute professional values and to increase the cohesion of the armed forces by introducing national security doctrines and recasting vertical lines of command. These national security doctrines emphasized organizational accomplishment and superior capability within the armed forces, a high degree of corporate identification, and national security ideology as means for promoting greater unity and military professionalism (O'Donnell 1976, 212). The azules also tried to separate the armed forces from the rest of society by placing them above politics.

Military Factionalism under One-Man Rule (1966–70)

In 1966, societal pressures led the military to intervene again. In contrast to previous coups, the leader of the army, General Juan Carlos Onganía, declared that the military would serve for a long and indefinite period. Onganía, head of the azules, attempted to maintain recently introduced national security doctrines to promote military professionalism. Onganía instituted one-man rule, retiring from active duty and divorcing himself from the armed forces. Onganía created hierarchical governmental institutions and enforced specialization by the armed forces in security issues to separate the military from politics. He also appointed civilians to nearly all the highest positions of the government. By excluding the military from governmental affairs, Onganía hoped to reduce factionalism and foster an apolitical military (Ricci and Fitch 1990).

Onganía also favored economic policies to minimize military divisions. Due to the economic problems caused by his early policies, Onganía initiated a fairly austere economic program in late 1966. This policy change provoked officers to demand a greater voice in political decisions (Snow 1979, 140). Onganía responded by creating a national security council composed of himself, the five ministers of state, and the commanders in chief of the service branches, which institutionalized military input into policy choices.

Efforts to sustain an apolitical military, however, became more difficult as factions reemerged in response to Onganía's policies. One faction, the paternalists, supported authoritarian rule but with the military detached from politics. Others supported military involvement in politics, but they espoused different policies. Nationalists advocated a strong state and measures to co-opt union support by protecting the domestic market. Liberals, by contrast, wanted to open the domestic market to external competition (O'Donnell 1988, 55–57).

Onganía, head of the paternalists, responded to tensions within the armed forces by appointing civilian paternalists to work in the highest cabinet positions—but outside of the economic ministries—while appointing some civilian liberals in the economic cabinet.[37] By appointing members of different factions, Onganía hoped to reduce support for a counter-coup. Onganía also acceded to nationalist pressures by creating a secretariat as a veto over policies proposed by the economics ministry (O'Donnell 1988, 76).

The main reason many military officers opposed liberal economists and their policies, especially paternalists—devout, conservative Catholics—who pressured Onganía to favor populist and nationalist goals, was concern about the survival of Fabricaciones Militares (FM), the military-run enterprises (Lewis 1992, 283). Created in 1941, FM included both heavy industrial and light manufacturing sectors. Its heavy industry produced metals, chemical products, petrochemicals, and fertilizers. The light manufacturing sector made machinery and electrical goods. To survive, however, these enterprises depended on high subsidies and protection from external and internal competition. The training officers received about the need for a strong state for security and development also provoked military opposition to liberal economists.

These military factions became fertile ground for the expression of grievances of interest groups (O'Donnell 1988, 194). Since the military served as the most effective channel for exercising influence over the military president, interest groups lobbied military officers, which inflamed already heated factional disputes. Direct involvement in partisan issues destroyed vertical patterns of military authority and aggravated factions. As the military became more factionalized, this stimulated more demands being filtered through them (O'Donnell 1978, 157).

Over the next two years, Economic Minister Adalbert Krieger Vasena's team applied stabilization measures, reduced tariffs, and imposed price controls to confront inflation. By 1969, Argentina's economy began to recover, but nevertheless opposition persisted from military factions who opposed opening the economy (O'Donnell 1988, 103–14). Because he was retired, Onganía was not able to use control over promotions and retirements to insure officers' loyalty and reduce factional pressures (Remmer 1991). In addition, if Onganía attempted to change military promotional procedures, he would risk a counter-coup from competitor officers.

The *cordobazo* in 1969 showed the fragility of Onganía's rule and the politicized nature of the military. During an economic recovery, strike activity and student unrest erupted in Córdoba, with the complicity of some military factions, sharpening discontent among the armed forces (Roth 1980; Rock 1987). According to O'Donnell (1988, 156), the *cordobazo* happened precisely during an economic recovery because of attempts by paternalists and liberals to "king their pieces." During the economic recovery, paternalists argued for a greater distribution of resources while liberals wanted to open the economy more. Nationalists also supported populist positions, including a greater role for the state in policy making and an end to economic denationalization, further aggravating tensions within the regime.

The *cordobazo* left Onganía with a choice between acquiescence to military demands for policy changes or confronting a counter-coup and immediate dismissal from power. Onganía adopted a survival strategy to appease officers and strikers in Córdoba. Onganía forced his economic minister to resign and sacked other liberals from his cabinet. By responding to the demands of officers, Onganía hoped to remain in power. Within a year, however, the army forced Onganía to resign.

Military Factionalism under Collegial Rule (1970–73; 1976–83)

The military chose General Roberto Levingston as Onganía's successor, who would work in a collegial setting as one of four participants in making important decisions. Like Onganía, Levingston gave the impression that he would share cabinet appointments among different military factions. Levingston, however, soon showed his allegiance to nationalist economic ideas. Levingston offered concessions to workers and domestic firms in order to broaden his support base and prolong his presidency. These concessions, however, did not prevent banned political parties from banding together in November 1970 to demand an immediate return to democratic rule. Three months later, Córdoba erupted again.

Following the upheaval in Córdoba, the military replaced Levingston with General Alejandro Lanusse. Like Levingston, Lanusse used concessions in an attempt to attract support among many groups, including unions, while isolating extremist groups. Despite these concessions, the popularity of military rule declined, and public calls for a return to democracy increased. Aware of popular sentiment toward the military, Lanusse made the extreme concession of lifting the ban on Peronism. Lanusse believed that by negotiating with Peronists, he could increase his popularity (Wynia 1978, 192). Popularity played a critical role in Lanusse's decisions, because he wanted to prolong his presidency after democratic elections. Lanusse, however, miscalculated his support base.

Democratic elections led to Juan Perón's return as president and an end to Lanusse's political career in 1973. A year after taking office, Perón died, leaving Perón's vice president and wife, Isabel Perón, in office. Over the next two years, economic and political turmoil spread throughout the country, as inflation and violence mounted. While Perón attempted to address economic problems, guerrilla groups including the Montoneros and Ejército Revolucionario del Pueblo (ERP) kidnapped and assassinated businessmen, police personnel, and army officers. The ineffectiveness of the government in responding to economic problems and political violence induced another military intervention (Waisman 1989; Cavarozzi 1986).

The military that took power in 1976 showed even more concern for preserving the unity of the armed forces and opposed granting dictatorial powers to any branch of the military, let alone one person. The military installed a government with clearly defined rules of succession for both the office of the president and the members of the junta, and an institutional arrangement of direct and equal participation among the service branches (Fontana 1987, 3). The junta made decisions through majority rule, except in the case of designation or removal of the junta chief, which required unanimity. Power sharing in this government went to an extreme, with each branch acquiring one-third power in decision making.

Equality among the services influenced the appointment of cabinet ministers, including economic policy makers. As each service favored different personnel, their differences contributed to the appointment of a less coherent economic team. Collegial power among service chiefs and within each service branch implied arduous inter-branch negotiations, especially in the appointment of the economics minister (Fontana 1987, 44, 49). These negotiations led to the selection of José Alfredo Martínez de Hoz as the first economic minister following the military coup. A trained lawyer, who had served as economics minister in the early 1960s and president of a large business, Martínez de Hoz presented the military with an articulate spokesperson on economic policy matters. He appealed both to big business and to military circles because of his strong opposition to subversive activities and communism and his support for gradualist reform (Martínez de Hoz 1990). Martínez de Hoz also appealed to the military from an economic perspective because he sought an economic plan of financial and monetary reform without producing massive unemployment, a concern of officers who did not want to create a ready group of recruits for guerrilla organizations.

Following the appointment of members of the "economic team," conflicts arose between military officers and team members. Admiral Emilio Massera, chief of the navy, expressed his opposition to Martínez de Hoz's policies and support for populist ideas (Schvarzer 1983). General Díaz Bessone, head of a sector of the army, joined Massera in his opposition to Martínez de Hoz and to General Jorge Videla, the junta leader, who backed his economic minister (Videla 1992).[38] As a power struggle ensued among the service chiefs, none of these men would compromise on the direction of the economy. This lack of cohesion in Argentina's state apparatus further weakened the chance of choosing a coherent team of experts (Stepan 1985, 330). Moreover, even if the armed forces agreed to appoint many experts for policy making, the need for unanimous agreement of officers would make it difficult to insulate economic policy makers from service branch negotiations.

The lack of coherence among economic team members also weakened their ability to sustain neoliberal policies. While some members supported rapid tariff reductions and privatization of state enterprises, others wanted to maintain protection, which lessened the possibility of converting already reluctant military officials to support such policy changes.

The institutional structure of power sharing also affected policy choices. As part of this power sharing, the junta submitted all important economic proposals to the Legislative Advisory Committee (LAC). The LAC, composed of nine members—three active members from each service—provided advice to the junta on legislative matters and could delay, change, and veto presidential initiatives when the executive exercised legislative functions (Fontana 1987, 31). Thus, not only did the junta leader have to deal with other service chiefs who held veto power, but the LAC reviewed all important initiatives, increasing the opportunity for officers to derail orthodox plans (Epstein 1985). In addition, if the LAC and the junta disagreed on a policy issue, "teams of inter-service compatibilization" would attempt to unify the divergent opinions on the particular issue (Fontana 1987, 30). Efforts by these teams to broker compromises provided opportunities to marginalize orthodox policies.

Power sharing also affected interest-group lobbying. At first, big business supported Martínez de Hoz. In his first year, the minister had protected business from foreign competition through an overvalued exchange rate and high tariffs. Over time, however, Martínez de Hoz reduced tariff levels and other forms of protection for local producers. Businesses responded by lobbying sympathetic officers, who pressured the military government (Epstein 1985).[39] The influence of the military over policy, through the LAC and the rotation of service chiefs, guaranteed military input in policy decisions and provided opportunities for interests to influence policies.

In 1980, military interventions in policy choices contributed to tensions in the armed forces. Internal squabbles within Argentina's armed forces grew, as shown by the less than automatic selection of Videla's successor, General Roberto Viola, as the new junta leader (Pion-Berlin 1985). Prior to his selection, Viola had made promises to attract supporters. Aware of broad-based opposition to market-oriented policies, Viola proclaimed his support for policies advocated by many in the military and business groups. Supporters of Viola saw him as "open to dialogue with the traditional political parties and to negotiation with the organizations of the various sectors of production" (Fontana 1987, 120).

In 1981, in fulfillment of earlier promises, Viola deliberately selected policy makers who protested his predecessor's policies (Wynia 1982). The policy makers promptly abandoned the *tablita*, the preannounced devaluation of the exchange rate, increased the size and scope of industrial promotion programs, abandoned the tariff reduction program, and called for large devaluations. Investors responded by sending capital abroad, spiraling the economy into a deeper recession. Within a year, the army replaced Viola with General Leopoldo Galtieri. For the first time, the military confronted active opposition from all parts of society, which included unions, politicians, and business owners (Fontana 1987, 119). In April 1982, Galtieri invaded the Malvinas/Falkland Islands, hoping to stir up nationalistic support for his rule.[40] British forces put down the

Argentine offensive in short order, creating an even more divided army (Rock 1989). After Galtieri's fall, the transition to democratic rule began.

Uruguay

Less Factionalized Military under Collegial Succession

Like Chile, few factional problems existed in Uruguay's military (McDonald 1975; Rouquié 1987). The armed forces historically isolated themselves from civilian affairs and never intervened in the first 150 years of Uruguay's independence (Moore 1978; Myers 1988). The use of merit-based promotions and dominance of the army against the other services (see table 3.1) fostered a high degree of professionalism in Uruguay's military.

In the early 1970s, however, economic and political turmoil erupted in Uruguay. Depleted foreign exchange reserves, climbing foreign debt, and high inflation exhausted Uruguay's economy (Finch 1989). The Tupamaros (MLN), a Marxist-Leninist guerrilla group, escalated political violence by setting off bombs and committing other acts of protest and aggression. Responding to requests by civilians for action, military officers brutally put down these protests.

In February 1973, President Juan María Bordaberry, democratically elected two years earlier, replaced his defense minister, Armando Malet, an active proponent of military intervention, with retired General Antonio Francese, a strict constitutionalist. Military officers expressed outrage over Malet's dismissal. Fearing for his political life, Bordaberry negotiated with the military, especially with leftist officers, and agreed to support military communiqués four and seven, which promoted a nationalistic economic program. Bordaberry also incorporated officers into all levels of government through the creation of the national security council (COSENA), an agency under military control with wide-ranging executive powers. COSENA would oversee all important governmental activities (Gillespie and González 1989).

In June 1973, following the legislature's refusal to lift the immunity from prosecution of Senator Enrique Erro for his suspected subversive activities, Bordaberry dissolved the National Assembly and put an end to democracy (Johnson 1982). Prior to the coup, however, significant military factions formed for the first time in 150 years. Military factions developed around disagreements over the imposition of military rule and the choice of economic policies. In contrast to Chile's military forces, which almost universally backed the military coup, dissension surfaced in Uruguay's armed forces over the military takeover (Gillespie 1991). This dissension may have influenced the military's decision to take over in increments rather than commit a definite coup.

One faction supported a "Peruvian" course, arguing for the imposition of military rule in order to promote a large state role in development and implement populist policies (E. Kaufman 1979). Another faction rallied for a hard-line or "Brazilian" course that supported military rule to help fight "subversion" and to foster internal order and security. "Brazilianists" favored economic development "based on linkages with foreign investment and technocratic decision-making" (Handelman 1981a, 222). A third faction called legalists—mostly naval officers—remained loyal to the president and favored civilian rule.

Despite these initial factions, the differences did not coalesce into permanent divisions. An important reason is the long history of unity in Uruguay's military. Indeed, military forces had never intervened in democratic rule. The military also had no experience with politicized promotions, and one service dwarfed the others in terms of manpower and resources. Military purges brought a return to unity and substantially reduced factional pressures (Rial 1986).

The armed forces and the president made the June 1973 coup appear to hold some semblance of democratic rule. The president dissolved the National Assembly as part of the emergency powers reserved for him in the constitution. Moreover, the military retained the legally elected civilian President Bordaberry and replaced the National Assembly with a Council of State comprising far-right members of the main political parties.

As a complement to these "democratic" measures, the military constructed governing institutions that prevented a concentration of power. Like Argentina (1976–83), Uruguay's military adopted a consensus-oriented system that relied on a rigid collegial system with strict rotations. Military officers rotated assignments, preventing the accumulation of a personal following by any single officer (Moore 1978). The military also maintained automatic retirement rules that helped prevent the emergence of a military strongman (Rial 1989, 103). Uruguay's system rotated the president and military posts (including service chiefs) and elected the service chiefs through votes of high-ranking officers from the Junta de Oficiales Generales, ensuring a deconcentration of power. The Junta de Oficiales Generales, composed of twenty-one top-ranking generals from the three service branches, tried to assure participation of all three branches in decisions.[41] While service chiefs made most decisions, they consulted with the Junta de Oficiales Generales prior to making important decisions, which fostered consensus (Gillespie 1991).

The focus on consensus, however, "engendered significant internal veto power, opened up multiple lobbying points for civil society, and reduced the capacity of state planners to implement the sweeping policies they proposed" (Stepan 1985, 326). Based on their training, most officers rejected neoliberal policies, which affected policy-making appointments (*El Proceso Político* 1978). While President Bordaberry advocated orthodox policies and appointed Harvard-trained economist Alejandro Végh Villegas as his finance minister in 1974, the army chose officers or friends for economic positions (Handelman 1981a).[42] Consensus under collegial rule and input from over twenty military officers worked against the appointment of neoliberal economists.

Frequent rotations of service chiefs also reduced opportunities to appoint neoliberal economists. High-ranking contenders competed with others for service chief positions. As in any political struggle, contenders made promises to attract supporters. Given the opposition to neoliberal policies by most in the military and interest groups, prospective service chiefs rarely supported neoliberal economists. Indeed, once in office, service chiefs used governmental positions to repay supporters (Rial 1989, 106).

Collegial rule with strict rotations and the large contingent of officers also increased interest-group contact with the military. The concentration of power in the armed forces limited the value of seeking nonmilitary political allies (Moore 1978). In addition, military opposition to Végh's attempts to apply neoliberal policies contributed to a close relationship between protectionist industrialists and the military (Handelman 1981b).

To help gain the upper hand over interest groups and to maintain himself in office, President Bordaberry attempted a survival strategy similar to Pinochet's. Bordaberry, who corresponded with Pinochet on policy matters (Valenzuela 1991), claimed that he wanted the power that Pinochet had garnered in Chile (Bordaberry 1992). Bordaberry tried to abolish all political parties, cancel the 1976 elections, force the withdrawal of officers from the government, and create a corporatist state. As a civilian president, however, Bordaberry did not have the resources to create a docile military. While Pinochet controlled the promotional and retirement criteria of the Chilean armed forces, making officers beholden to him, Bordaberry held no control over these decisions. The Junta de Oficiales Generales oversaw military promotions (Rial 1989, 103). Moreover, Bordaberry's attempts to remove military officers from administrative positions antagonized hard-line officers, many of whom held governmental positions (Handelman 1981a). Bordaberry's antidemocratic declarations and quest for power led to his dismissal by the military in 1976.[43]

The military installed Alberto Demicheli as interim president and replaced him with Aparicio Méndez, the military's civilian puppet. In 1982, the military chose one of their own as president. By this time, however, two years after the failed plebiscite to change the constitution,[44] legitimacy and economic problems made it unlikely that a military official could concentrate power.[45] The collegial system and rotational structure also impeded one person from amassing significant power in the government. Over the next two years, the transition to democratic rule began.

Brazil

Military Factionalism under Presidential Succession

Brazil demonstrates the effect of a factionalized military and a presidential succession system on policy-making appointments. It shows that the process of presidential succession provides multiple access points for officers and interest groups to influence policy. It also documents how the military's factionalized history reinforces the need for consensual decision making from among the officers' corps.

Designating Brazil's military as factionalized may seem controversial. Alfred Stepan (1971, 1973, 1988), a foremost scholar of the Brazilian armed forces, has written about the maintenance of professional values in Brazil's military. On the other hand, Brazil's military has a long history of political intervention and politicized promotions, which is indicative of factions.

Military rule began in the late nineteenth century and persisted in much of the twentieth century. Military involvement in the affairs of the Old Republic endured during and after World War I. This involvement included revolts by junior officers in 1922 and 1924, military coups in 1930, 1945, 1954, and 1964, an attempted coup in 1961, and the beginnings of a coup in 1955 (Roett 1972, 92–98).[46] Brazil's military also has a history of politicized promotions. Although Stepan (1971, 55) contends that Brazil adhered to universalistic bureaucratic norms for promotion and assignment within the military, he also documents (1971, 68) many examples of presidents co-opting military support through appointment strategies from 1937 through 1964. Indeed, Stepan (1971, 165) argues that "promotions within the military in Brazil have always had a political content." The high frequency of military intervention and use of politicized military promotions may explain ideological differences among the Brazilian armed forces.

Although factions emerged in the military over several issues, most in the armed forces advocated the same kinds of economic policies. Except for those trained at the Escola Superior de Guerra (ESG)—Brazil's Superior War College—most officers backed self-sufficiency, heavy industrialization, import substitution, and Brazilian control over production and technology (Schneider 1991, 50). These economic ideas would affect cabinet appointments and policy choices once the military took power.

In 1964, officers deposed President João Goulart and took charge of the government.[47] Military rulers installed governing institutions that differed markedly from those found in the Southern Cone cases. Brazil initially chose to purge but not close the Congress and "adhered to the existing norms of presidential rotation with fixed terms" (Stepan 1985, 334). Following Brazil's presidential term limits under democracy, the military president would serve one term.

Presidential succession had important effects on the appointment of economic policy makers. As discussed earlier, succession struggles force contenders to make promises to officers whom they later repay with bureaucratic positions or their preferred policies. As most officers in Brazil favored statist policies, presidential candidates were unlikely to campaign in favor of the appointment of neoliberal economists. Policy makers working in a succession system also may not have enough time to initiate and sustain a neoliberal program. Incoming presidents usually choose their own policy makers. This shuffling of policy makers limits the time new appointees have for considering, initiating, and maintaining policy reforms (Schneider 1991, 31).

The succession system and military factions had little influence on the initial military government (1964–67) since no presidential succession had yet occurred. Moreover, officers are usually united immediately after mounting a coup. Over time, however, the succession system and reemergence of military factions would shape policy-making appointments.

In 1964, many of the coup conspirators who received their training at the ESG took over key positions in the government.[48] The military president, General Humberto Castello Branco, who had developed close ties to the ESG, came from an apolitical, military legalist tradition and opposed any extension of his rule (Baretta and Markoff 1987, 50). In his economic thinking, Castello Branco and others affiliated with the ESG connected the attainment of national security with national development. Unlike most officers, Castello Branco favored using private and foreign resources to develop Brazil. Indeed, the ESG espoused gradualist market-oriented policies.

The initial economic appointments reflected the interests of the ESG-dominated government. The original economic team included some neoliberal economists who influenced economic policy choices.[49] Facing a serious economic crisis, economists such as Planning Minister Roberto de Oliveira Campos and Finance Minister Octávio Gouvéia de Bulhões initiated gradualist neoliberal policies and renounced the nationalist rhetoric of the previous government (Skidmore 1988, 23, 55). Policy makers instituted a stabilization program that was relatively market-oriented by Brazilian standards. The program included policies to facilitate inflows of foreign capital, promote exports, reduce tariff protection, and revise or eliminate taxes on exports and overvalued exchange rates (Frieden 1991, 105). The policy makers also reduced the public sector deficit by slashing all nonessential expenditures, increasing tax revenues, and stabilizing wage rates.

Over time, these policies provoked hostility from military factions, societal interests, and structuralist technocrats (Skidmore 1973, 25). When Castello Branco stepped down in 1967, he had no control over the selection of his successor. Because the views of Castello Branco and the ESG represented a minority wing of the military and because the country was in a deep recession, officers rejected all of his choices for the next president (Stepan 1971, 248).[50] Hard-line and junior officers helped to select Castello Branco's successor, General Artur da Costa e Silva, and other officers and policy makers who joined the new government.[51]

The Serviço Nacional de Informações (SNI), the military intelligence agency, also affected presidential succession, and later, policy-making appointments. Created three months after the military intervened in 1964, SNI steadily increased its power and control over decisions made by the regime. Under the law, SNI maintained an office in every ministry and state enterprise. In these offices, SNI officers examined all important materials, explored the security implications of any policy, and screened personnel. SNI reputedly had veto power over nominees, though no cases have been reported of the SNI blocking nominations or firing officials.[52] Nonetheless, SNI "dissuaded some potential candidates, and thereby narrowed and homogenized the pool of elite bureaucrats" (Schneider 1987, 51).

In addition to presidential succession, many officers—especially in the office of the president—directly affected policy choice. According to Schneider (1987, 51), "The military staffed much of the office of the Presidency, giving them policy influence and giving other officers access through them to the President." Top generals also had policy preferences that the "President was obliged to consider" (Schneider 1987, 51). Moreover, some officers held positions in economic ministries that enabled the military to influence policy.

Following the first succession in 1967, the new cabinet included not a single carryover from the previous government. Like most military rulers, Costa e Silva rewarded the military and civilian factions that supported his candidacy with some top economic appointments. He also used cabinet appointments to incorporate "promising politicians into the government, and to nominate some representatives from the major civilian support groups" (Schneider 1991, 240). Economic policy making now rested in the hands of technocrats and economists who backed the nationalist stance of most officers (Skidmore 1988, 68). Led by Minister of Finance Antônio Delfim Neto, the government introduced a heterodox program that intended to loosen fiscal, monetary, and wage policies in order to spur aggregate demand. Delfim Neto and his "boys"—loyal former students who occupied many policy-making positions—stimulated demand by easing credit, funneling greater international loans to domestic interests. The government abandoned the restrictive austerity programs of the previous administration and employed a strategy to accelerate growth through ISI and an export-promoting investment program in the public and private sectors (Werneck 1991, 54). The government also introduced wage, price, and exchange rate controls.

Within two years, Costa e Silva suffered a stroke, which forced another presidential succession. Each service, and in particular its most senior officers, nominated its top three or four choices for president.[53] After much discussion, the services selected General Emílio Garrastazu Médici in October 1969. Médici appointed a new cabinet with Delfim Neto and Planning Minister João Paulo dos Reis Veloso being the only carryovers. Médici depended on the active support of an officer corps dominated by the hard-liners (Skidmore 1973, 17). Even Delfim Neto, who possessed tremendous influence in policy decisions, understood that he needed military support if he wanted to remain in office (Schneider 1987, 242).[54]

Participatory and consensual decision making from senior and junior officers described policy choice in Brazil after 1967 (Skidmore 1973, 17).

Frequent presidential successions and consensual decision making also facilitated interest-group influence. Modern industries, capital goods and consumer durable producers, large agribusiness outfits, and financial interests lobbied policy makers and officers to achieve their economic goals (Frieden 1991, 136). Because of its access to foreign loans, the regime obtained resources to satisfy these politically important economic interest groups.[55]

The Banco Nacional de Desenvolvimento Econômico e Social (BNDES), in particular, became an important focus for interest-group lobbying. According to some estimates, BNDES accounted for four-fifths of the lending to Brazilian industry (Frieden 1991, 112). BNDES had a nationalist reputation, which it brought to its policy battles, making it an easy access point for import-competing producers. Officials from BNDES also influenced bureaucrats in other sectors to support a nationalist development strategy (Schneider 1991, 222).

Delfim Neto and his team maintained heterodox policies that expanded the size and influence of the state sector until the next scheduled succession in 1974. For example, of the thirty largest nonfinancial firms by net assets, the state owned thirteen in 1967, seventeen in 1971, and twenty-three in 1974 (Stepan 1985, 331–32). The government also provided generous subsidies to private interests. These policies produced the economic "miracle" whereby annual industrial output rose 10.9 percent, GDP growth increased by 11.3 percent, and per capita GDP climbed 8.4 percent (Frieden 1991, 117).

Despite these spectacular growth rates, the presidential succession under a factionalized military proved troublesome (Skidmore 1988, 149). As in any presidential succession, the period prior to it contained much uncertainty. In May 1973, with the support of the SNI, General Ernesto Geisel won a consensus within the military.[56] Geisel's selection marked the reascension of the Castellistas (Ames 1987, 144). The fact that his brother served as minister of defense may explain how Geisel outmaneuvered Médici and his hard-liner allies in the succession process (Skidmore 1988, 149).

In March 1974, Geisel attempted to continue the economic "miracle." However, pressures mounted from former protagonists of the regime (e.g., the church and professional associations), who strongly opposed the repressive character of the government (Martins 1986, 82). Geisel responded to these pressures by having a political opening, known as an *abertura,* that resulted in reasonably free elections in November 1974, with the opposition party scoring some impressive victories. Efforts by the military to attract greater popularity gave officers and a small group of civilians more access to policy makers. Prospective presidential candidates and legislators also provided interest groups with widespread influence on policy choice.

As a result of this influence, Geisel installed a new cabinet with Mário Henrique Simonsen replacing Delfim Neto. Simonsen had established close relations with the leaders of the São Paulo business community, which eased the way for his selection. Like Delfim, Simonsen believed in government intervention and developmentalist policies (Frieden 1991, 118). Simonsen expanded state involvement in the economy at the same time that he designed policies to benefit the business community. Simonsen increased investment in state enterprises and huge state-sponsored projects from 1975 through 1979, which supplied basic inputs to modern industry.[57] The state also benefitted local producers by providing them with subsidies and protection from international competitors and by serving them as an important customer.

The expansion of state enterprises and protection for local industries, however, created economic difficulties. Government deficits and inflation soared at the same time that growth diminished (Rabello de Castro and Ronci 1991, 163). OPEC's tripling of the price of oil compounded problems, as Brazil depended on imports for 80 percent of its oil consumption (Skidmore 1988, 178). By 1977, inflationary pressures and balance of payments crises persuaded Simonsen to shift toward austerity and monetary restraint (Ames 1987, 189–92).

In 1978, Geisel supported General João Baptista Figueiredo in the succession struggle. Figueiredo, inaugurated in March 1979, attempted to follow the same economic course by maintaining Simonsen in the cabinet, although this time as planning minister. He also appointed Delfim Neto as minister of agriculture. In August 1979, Figueiredo replaced Simonsen with Delfim as planning minister. Figueiredo hoped to rekindle Delfim's earlier magic and please his business-community constituents (Frieden 1991, 127).

Economic circumstances, though, forced Delfim to reverse course and accept policy prescriptions of the IMF. In 1981, Brazil recorded a negative GDP growth rate (-3.4 percent) for the first time in at least forty years and inflation swelled to 100 percent (Werneck 1991, 57). Even as Delfim attempted to create a wage policy to address inflationary pressures and squeeze worker salaries, opposition from politicians and others galvanized to forestall enactment of some wage policies (Ames 1987, 201). Indeed, most wage reductions put in place during the 1980s would be "wholly compensated for by a rise in 1985" (Werneck 1991, 75). Moreover, the government often missed targets for public deficits and monetary expansion. Access to policy making by interest groups and officers opposed to market-oriented policies interfered with their implementation. In the end, economic crisis mobilized many of the regime's original supporters, including the industrial sector, to speed up democratic liberalization.

Peru

Military Factionalism under Collegial Rule

Peru (1968–80) demonstrates how military factionalization and junta rule promoted the need for broad consensus among the military establishment. This broad consensus along with General Juan Velasco Alvarado's own economic views discouraged the appointment of neoliberal economists. The Peruvian case also suggests that even when a ruler favors economic adjustment, as in the case of General Francisco Morales Bermúdez in 1975, factional pressures offer access to interest groups and officers— most of whom favor protectionism—to influence policy making.

Military rule in Peru shares similarities with Argentina's second military government. Like Argentina, the Peruvian armed forces had frequently intervened in political affairs. With the exception of two democratic interregnums (1939–48 and 1956–62), the military had dominated the political scene since 1930 with the support of agricultural exporters, large landowners, and bankers (Cotler 1978, 192).[58] These interventions helped to create military factions. One faction, known as progressives, supported reforms to eliminate mass poverty through income redistribution and socialist policies. The Movimiento Laboral Revolucionario, a proto-fascist faction on the extreme right, backed greater private investment and initiative. A third faction, centered politically between the other factions, advocated ISI on a national and regional level (North 1983, 251–64).[59] In general, the army leaned to the left, while the air force and navy upheld a more rightist stance.

In October 1968, General Juan Velasco Alvarado and several colonels from the progressive faction deposed the democratic government on the eve of presidential elections. The Gobierno Revolucionario de las Fuerzas

Armadas (GRFA) took steps to maintain military unity. Unlike previous interventions, where the military acted in the interest of the oligarchy, this time the military acted on its own (McClintock 1989, 348). The leaders of the GRFA created governing institutions that solicited input from many military circles before making policy choices. The governing institutions consisted of the military president, the revolutionary junta made up of service chiefs from each branch of the armed forces, and the heads of the ministries. As officers occupied most of these positions, this fostered a broad consensus among the military establishment on policy decisions (Cleaves and Pease García 1983, 222). The commanding generals of the army, navy, and air force also selected the president of the government and countersigned all his acts through unanimous agreement, which reinforced Peru's consensus.

The military also set up the Presidential Advisory Commission (COAP). Made up of thirteen colonels under the direction of an army general, COAP acted as the president's staff, coordinating laws before presenting them for a final vote in the cabinet. COAP guaranteed that many officers participated in policy choices.

Appointments of officers who dominated policy-making positions also assured military influence in policy decisions (Einaudi and Stepan 1971, 24). In fact, the minister of the economy was an officer who later served as president of the junta. Each ministry was designated to one of the services, which may explain why "all ministers were either generals (including the air force) or admirals in active service appointed by the president from a list of three names provided by the commander of the respective service branch" (Cleaves and Pease García 1983, 222). Officers also secured the subminister positions in nearly all the ministries, held top positions in major government agencies, and comprised the entire body of COAP (Palmer 1980, 100). Like Argentina, Peru's GRFA installed governing institutions that ensured broad consensual agreement from each service and from different factions, which limited the appointment of neoliberal economists to policy-making positions (Paredes and Pasco-Font 1991, 229–30).

The views of General Velasco also prevented the appointment of neoliberal economists. Like most GRFA members, Velasco and other officers supported populism largely because of their military education. In their training, many officers and instructors at the Centro de Altos Estudios Militares—the national war college—had taken economics courses in Santiago, Chile, in the 1950s and 1960s through the auspices of the Economic Commission for Latin America (ECLA) and the Institute for Social and Economic Planning. Officers learned that underdevelopment "stemmed from disproportionate economic and political power in the hands of an anachronistic upper class, lack of national integration, a weak state, and inordinate dependence on the international market" (Cleaves and Pease García 1983, 216). These officers returned to Peru to train others in dependency theory (Stepan 1973).

Actions taken by the United States in the 1960s dovetailed with dependency arguments. U. S. support for the International Petroleum Company (IPC), its refusal to sell Peru supersonic jets (while providing them to other Latin American countries), and its rejection of economic aid to ailing Peru in the mid-1960s (while continuing to aid President Frei in Chile) convinced officers that the government needed to address inequities in the world economic order.

The initial policies demonstrated the nationalist influence of officers. The military nationalized IPC's oil wells, installations, and refineries, and expropriated large land estates including sugar-exporting plantations. Over time, the military radicalized its program by nationalizing many Peruvian and foreign firms involved in banking and commercial sectors, natural resource extraction, basic industry, and the provision of services (Paredes and Pasco-Font 1991, 232–35). The government took over such prominent foreign-owned firms as ITT (1969), Chase Manhattan Bank (1970), Cerro de Pasco Copper Corporation (1974), and Marcona Mining (1975). The share of Peru's GDP owned by the state skyrocketed from 13 percent to 23 percent between 1968 and 1975 (McClintock 1989, 355).

Populism also pervaded the government's views on foreign capital and industrialization policies. To curtail the role of foreign capital, the government created a regulation board to prohibit foreign purchases of "viable, locally owned firms, and to exclude foreign participation from sensitive areas" (Skidmore and Smith 1989, 212). The government also initiated a strict ISI strategy to reduce foreign dependence and to promote domestic industrialization through fixed exchange rates, price controls, and unlimited trade restrictions (Schydlowsky and Wicht 1983, 98). The GRFA subsidized foodstuffs and energy for the household sector and administered wage increases.

In late 1973, unity in the military government began to crumble and factions reemerged. Five years of radical populist policies helped produce economic crisis, which fostered deep military divisions (Abugattas 1987, 126). Between 1970 and 1975, Peru's foreign debt more than tripled, petroleum, food, and arms imports soared, while exports stagnated (McClintock 1989, 350). A balance of payments crisis loomed and inflation accelerated. Yet, with growing factionalization and extreme economic chaos, Velasco maintained the policies. Indeed, he even reduced the price of gasoline and expropriated a mining enterprise to co-opt popular support.

The growing factionalization of the GRFA opened up multiple lobbying points for interest groups, which further inflamed military divisions. Industrial and commercial interests exploited the internal strife in an effort to reduce the state sector. These interests eroded the regime's main base of support. The presence of officers in government also provided access points for officers outside government. In addition, military factions sought alliances to strengthen their positions within the GRFA, which opened up access points to interest groups (Abugattas 1987, 126). Many military ministers became spokespersons for narrow economic interests (Cleaves and Pease García 1983, 229). Growing military factionalization and economic crisis contributed to Velasco's fall from power in 1975.

The second phase of military rule, headed by General Francisco Morales Bermúdez from the centrist military faction, made even greater efforts to satisfy the officer corps. President Morales Bermúdez attempted to keep "senior officers informed and consulted them on the problems facing their government" (Cotler 1986, 157). Factionalization in the military, however, continued to escalate. Rightists staged an uprising in July 1976, followed a month later by a leftist putsch attempt led by junior officers (Abugattas 1987, 128).

The precariousness of the economic situation made Morales Bermúdez and others realize the need for economic adjustment (Wise 1990, 185). Yet, as Cleaves and Pease García (1983, 234) point out, "The government confronted the economic crisis of 1975 to 1978 with successive attempts at stabilizing policies, reaching agreements first with the United States banks and later with the International Monetary Fund, but found itself incapable of sufficient discipline to apply their provisions." Intense pressures within the military forced Morales Bermúdez to include high-ranking officers in decision making, who maintained their opposition to "shock treatment" policies recommended by the IMF (Cotler 1986, 162).[60]

Due in part to the interests of these officers, public sector expenditures fell little, and tariff and nontariff barriers increased (Paredes and Pasco-Font 1991, 212). The government deficit remained at 10 percent of GDP through 1977, and social subsidies expanded to more than 5 percent of GDP (Wise 1990, 186). The failing economy provoked intense strikes and popular protest, which led to the announcement of a transition to democracy on July 28, 1977 (McClintock 1989, 351).

Summary

This chapter showed the effect of differences in long-standing character-istics of the military and in the types of governing institutions installed by military leaders on political strategies of military leaders. These sur-vival strategies affect the appointment of economic policy makers and, more generally, economic development. Consolidated one-man rule grants greater freedom in the appointment of economic policy makers than factionalized armed forces, or less factionalized militaries under collegial rule, or systems of succession. Although consolidated one-man rule does not guarantee the appointment of neoliberal economists, it provides leaders with an opportunity to appoint neoliberal economists as part of a strategy to promote their survival and consolidate power that may not be available in other institutional settings.

This chapter also demonstrated how the selection of cabinet minis-ters can, in unusual circumstances, satisfy both political and economic goals. Instead of survival strategies always hampering economic perform-ance through the appointment of less-qualified but more politically ex-pedient officials, survival strategies can lead to both the appointment of technocratic expertise and the survival of military leaders. Chile (1973–89) contrasted with Argentina (1966–73; 1976–83), Brazil (1964–85), Peru (1968–80), and Uruguay (1973–84) by appointing many neoliberal econo-mists to economic policy-making positions. These cases showed how dif-ferences in military characteristics and in the kinds of governing insti-tutions shaped appointment prospects and reduced the opportunity to choose economists in Argentina, Brazil, Peru, and Uruguay. In Argentina, Brazil, Peru, and Uruguay, the need for consensual agreement reduced the likelihood that military officers could agree to support the appointment of neoliberal economists.

Differences in cabinet appointments under military rule lead to the question of what role policy makers and their ideas play in the selection and sustaining of policies. The next chapter addresses the importance of neoliberal economists as economic policy makers for explaining policy choices and the maintenance of policies.

FOUR

The Effects of Neoliberal Economists in Economic Policy Making

The power of vested interests is vastly exaggerated compared with the gradual encroachment of ideas. . . . The ideas of economists and political philosophers, both when they are right and when they are wrong, are more powerful than is commonly understood. Indeed the world is ruled by little else.
—John Maynard Keynes, *The General Theory of Employment*

Chapter 3 discussed the political survival strategies available to military rulers and the constraints that affect their economic policy-making appointments. This chapter stresses the importance of policy makers for explaining different policy choices. Specifically, it examines the relationship between neoliberal economists in policy-making positions and policy outcomes for the Southern Cone cases. I argue that policy makers with shared ideas can have a direct effect on policy choices when they control most economic policy-making positions. Moreover, when these decision makers are considered experts in economic decision making, and share much the same economic ideas, this increases their policy-making autonomy from interest groups and political leaders. This chapter also analyzes how economists serving as economic policy makers attempt to lobby military leaders and officers, and society in general, to generate support for their policies.

Neoliberal Economists and Policy Outcomes

Over the past decade, many studies have shown the influence of ideas on economic policy choices (cf. Jacobsen 1995). Researchers in the rapidly growing ideational literature see the spread of ideas and innovations as responsible for changing policy discourse and affecting policy decisions. While many theorists, including those who support interest-group-driven approaches, agree that ideas influence decision making, if only as a mediating variable, there are often questions about where ideas come from and how they get translated into policy decisions. Why, out of all the ideas floating around, certain ones are selected is a common concern. Some recognize the difficulties in describing the role of ideas.[1] Hall (1989, 4), for example, acknowledges that failure to specify the conditions under which ideas acquire political influence "leaves a large lacuna at the center of our understanding of public policy." Nonetheless, much of the ideational literature asserts that ideas matter without explaining where ideas originate and how they affect policy choices.

In addition, although the literature is relatively successful at explaining major shifts in policy, it bogs downs in its understanding of more routinized and normal policy making. For instance, effective arguments are offered to explain the diffusion of Keynesian ideas to policy makers in the postwar years. But attempts to account for incremental policy changes are incomplete.

To address these concerns, work on epistemic communities—a subfield in the ideational literature—shows how networks of knowledge-based experts influence policy decisions. Epistemic community analysts argue that experts help to frame, develop, and clarify ideas and information and thereby either limit the range of policy options or create a middle ground among choices.[2] Despite these analysts' efforts, epistemic studies leave a gap in our understanding of how experts determine or facilitate the implementation of policy choices. Indeed, it is unclear how scientists, who publish articles and present papers at professional meetings, are able to influence directly the policies debated and eventually implemented by government officials.

The role of similarly trained economists in economic policy-making positions, however, may help to explain where ideas come from and how policy choices are implemented. It may also help extend and revise the ideas literature. When a large number of neoliberal economists work in the economic policy-making process and serve as the actual policy makers, they form an "epistemic community of knowledge" (Ikenberry 1992).[3] In contrast to works on epistemic communities, I examine the black box through which the ideas of experts translate into routinized or revolutionary policy decisions. When similarly trained experts work in the policy-making arena and dominate positions of decision making, the mechanism by which ideas shape policy and perhaps even public opinion becomes clearer. The training and economic ideology of the policy makers makes them a cohesive team with a commitment to the same ideas and policy choices (Kaufman 1990).

Earlier studies showed the role of similarly trained economists for the application of Keynesian policies. In the 1930s, Franklin Roosevelt appointed a team of policy makers chiefly from Harvard University, who implemented Keynesian policies (Ikenberry 1993; Salant 1989). Keynesian economists also developed close contacts with economic policy makers in Norway and Sweden (Pekkarinen 1989). Economists opposed to Keynes's ideas impacted economic policies in Italy (De Cecco 1989), Germany (James 1989), and France (Rosanvallon 1989).

Britain's experience perhaps best illustrates the importance of economists for Keynesian policies. In the 1930s, when John Maynard Keynes wrote prolifically on the need for government intervention in the economy, Britain had difficulties in applying his ideas. Britain's public commissions employed a motley group of extra-governmental figures including industrialists, trade unionists, and professional economists, which led to less than coherent advice. This prompted the subsequent appointment of a smaller committee of economists, who then promoted and installed Keynesian policies.[4]

Like their Keynesian predecessors, neoliberal economists also share many similarities that evolve through their earlier educational experiences. As chapter 6 will detail, many of these economists earned advanced degrees at universities in the United States over the last forty years, where faculty members stressed the advantages of free-market policies.[5] Whereas economics departments at many European and Latin American universities—especially those with ties to the Economic Commission for Latin America (ECLA)—trained students to believe that structuralist and developmentalist theories that granted the state a prominent role provided the best path for achieving economic development, most U.S. universities tended to emphasize just the opposite. Many of these economists returned to their home countries to work in universities and institutes that allowed them to inspire another generation of students who strongly favored the free market.[6]

Once neoliberal economists are appointed to policy-making positions, they are better able to resist pressures emanating inside and outside of the government than policy makers without such backgrounds are. Given their expertise in economic policy making, economists do not solicit or believe that they need advice from individuals outside their community, enhancing their autonomy (Hirschman 1989). As economic policy makers stonewall interest groups, these groups will attempt to lobby military officers to intervene on their behalf. Military officers, however, are unlikely to have much success in changing economic policies, as the united economic team (based on its ideas, which has helped to create a professional subculture) becomes nearly impenetrable.[7] The only way for military factions to cause policy change is to replace members of the economic team.

As argued in chapter 3, however, leaders select policy makers on the basis of their contribution to the leader's political survival. As long as policy makers continue to contribute to the leader's survival, the leader has few incentives to replace them. This does not imply that military leaders will only maintain economically successful teams. Leaders may retain teams that produce poor economic results for longer than is expected in order to satisfy factions or interest groups whose support they need to survive. In the end, neoliberal economists in policy-making positions increase the chance that neoliberal policies are initiated and sustained.

Background of Ministers

Economic policy making in military governments, as in democracies, usually occurs at the highest levels of the executive branch. Besides directives from the military junta, economic policy makers from the ministry of economics, the ministry of finance, the ministry of commerce, the central bank, and the office of planning and budgeting generally make economic policy decisions. The following sections examine the background of the ministers and subministers within these respective departments in the Southern Cone to determine the proportion of neoliberal economists in these ministries and to understand how policy makers influence policy choices.

Chile

Initiation of Economic Policies

The military regime (1973–89) that overthrew Salvador Allende's government in 1973 had little idea of what to do with the collapsing Chilean economy. Following the coup, military officials assembled a group of respected businessmen, lawyers, and economists to obtain their advice on the economy. Based on these discussions, officials decided that they wanted Raúl Sáez, an economist and former finance minister known for his support of gradualist policies, to direct the finance ministry. While Sáez declined the offer and instead worked as advisor to the finance ministry, the military installed their own man, Admiral Lorenzo Gotuzzo, and other personnel with little formal economic training in economic policy-making positions (Montecinos 1988). These policy makers were not prepared to adopt orthodox neoliberal policies or to manage an economy (Léniz 1992; Medina 1992). Indeed, the military generals, including General Pinochet, wanted to continue protecting the economy (De Castro 1992; Matthei 1992; Frez 1992). According to retired naval officer Roberto Kelly (1992), more officers preferred socialist policies to the free market in the early 1970s.

A year later in 1974, economic and political turmoil came to a head. The fall in copper prices and the surge in the cost of imported oil exacerbated Chile's balance of trade problems. Widespread human rights abuses also erupted that prompted the former president and leader of the Christian Democrats, Eduardo Frei, to express his opposition to the military government (Spooner 1999, 101). These abuses also convinced many economists either not to associate with the military regime (Meller 1992) or to disassociate themselves from the regime (Massad 1992).

Serious economic problems and human rights abuses contributed to personnel changes, as did General Pinochet's political survival tactics and personal ambition.[8] The most important changes came with the promotions of Jorge Cauas, an economist trained at Columbia University as the superminister (minister of finance), Sergio de Castro, a University of Chicago–trained economist as the minister of the economy, and the inflow of many other University of Chicago–trained economists. Over the next few years, "Chicago Boys"—economists trained in neoliberal doctrine at the University of Chicago—invited more economists into all levels of economic policy making. The proportion of neoliberal

Chart 4.1   Percent of Neoliberal Economists in Economic Policy
Making in Chile, 1973–1989

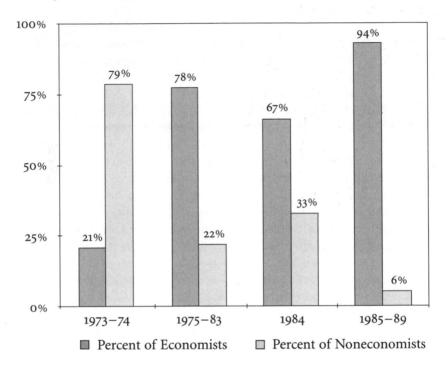

Sources: Montecinos (1988); Chilean central bank; Chilean planning office.
Note: Entries represent the number of policy positions held by economists per
year summed for the total number of years covered. Economic policy-making
positions in Chile are: finance minister and subsecretary of finance, secretary
and subsecretary of the economy, director and assistant director of ODEPLAN
(the planning office), budget director, and president and vice president of the
central bank.

economists in economic policy-making positions (see chart 4.1) jumped
from 21.4 percent in 1973–74 to 77.8 percent in 1975–83, with most having
earned advanced degrees in the United States.[9] These appointments contributed to a strong technocratic character and high level of expertise in
economic policy making.[10]

Following the appointments, neoliberal policy makers replaced gradualist policies with an orthodox program. Policy makers reformed the fi-

nancial and labor markets, dropped tariffs to 10 percent on all products with the exception of automobiles by 1979, privatized many state-owned enterprises and the social security system, and reduced virtually all forms of protection. In 1984, when the proportion of economists decreased by 11.1 percent, the intensity of neoliberal policies declined, as indicated by rising and nonuniform tariffs, the imposition of price controls, and greater state intervention in the economy.[11] By 1985, however, more neoliberal economists (93.5 percent) entered the economic team and orthodox policies returned with some changes. Economists spearheaded new reforms including privatization of traditionally state-owned enterprises and reduced levels of protection. Thus, when the highest proportion of neoliberal economists worked in economic policy making (1975–83, 1985–89), the intensity of neoliberal policies increased.

Coherence among Policy Makers

The relationship between neoliberal economists and orthodox policies leads us to examine the ability of economists to insulate themselves from interest groups. Contrary to conventional wisdom, pressure from interest groups is perhaps more intense in military regimes than in democratic governments. Unlike democracies that are flush with legitimacy following elections, because military regimes overthrow governments frequently without the clear backing of the populace, these regimes confront legitimacy questions almost from the start of military rule. And these questions linger and persist. In addition, the appointment of officers to bureaucratic positions may foster pressure among military factions, further restricting policy-making autonomy. Faced with these apparent obstacles, how did economists acquire policy-making autonomy and develop coherent ideas amongst themselves in order to block interest-group lobbying?

Partly as a result of institutional constraints associated with a consolidated one-man rule, General Pinochet gave economic policy makers a lot of leeway in economic policy making. The backgrounds of policy makers, many of whom had studied economics at similar schools in the United States and Chile, also contributed to their independence from traditional influence on policy. An agreement reached between the University of Chicago and Universidad Católica in Santiago in the 1950s provided many Chilean graduate students with the opportunity to study economics in the United States. As part of the agreement, students earned advanced degrees at the University of Chicago, in a school whose economics faculty fiercely defended the free market. Upon completion of their studies, most of these students returned to Chile as professors, principally to the Universidad Católica, though some worked at the Universidad de Chile, to train a new generation of economists.[12] Many of these individuals later formed a "critical mass" of economic policy makers in the military government (Donoso 1992; Costabal 1992). Members of the policy-making team became the equivalent of a highly cohesive political party (Valenzuela 1991). The classmate or professor/student relationships developed during this period contributed to both personal loyalties and to the coherence of their ideas (De Castro 1992; Bardon 1992).[13] The coherence of their program and their ideas also helped to convince the military to select these new economic policy makers (De la Cuadra 1992).

An amusing example of the economic team's coherence comes from the experience of a Japanese conglomerate. Sergio de Castro (1992), Chile's finance minister from 1976 through 1982, recounted a story about a Japanese conglomerate that arrived in Santiago in the late 1970s to consider investment opportunities in Chile. After one week, the leader of the conglomerate returned to de Castro and told him how impressed he was with their communication system. The leader had visited several departments within the government and had received the same answers to his questions from government operatives. The Japanese businessman assumed that these similar responses resulted from special internal communication engineered by the finance minister, when in actuality the responses were uncoordinated. The fact that at least forty to sixty persons within the different departments had studied at similar schools and spoke the same orthodox language led them to give similar responses without consulting with each other.[14] As José Piñera (1991a, 6), the chief architect of the labor, social security, and mining reforms stated,

> [The economists] constituted a team that could work together to get things done without becoming mired in endless debates and infighting. The fact that this team of like-minded and similarly trained economists was available to take the reins of policy during this crucial period in Chile's history is, I believe, the principal reason why Chile was able to launch and sustain its ultimately successful economic reforms.

Personal attachments among economic policy makers also fostered a closed-camp atmosphere that made it difficult for interest groups to lobby successfully for change (Arteaga 1992; Pérez de Arce 1992). This is important because "without the cohesiveness and single-mindedness that only a team can provide, any attempt at comprehensive reform, if it does not fail through simple lack of coordination, is sure to fall prey to factionalism and special interest politics" (Piñera 1991a, 7).

Events in the mid-1970s illustrate the difficulties interest groups had in influencing policy makers. In one event, appliance manufacturers invited the minister of finance to a meeting in order to discuss the impact of tariff reforms. These producers contended that lowering tariffs on their appliance lines would force the closure of plants and the layoff of nearly one thousand workers. Finance Minister de Castro examined their books and agreed that tariff reforms would have negative consequences for the industry. Shortly after the meeting, de Castro introduced tariff reductions, forcing producers of white line products to close their plants (Agüero 1992).

Neoliberal polices severely damaged the interests of important parts of business and the middle class, crucial elements of support for the military coup. From March through May 1975, for example, the Chilean government laid off more than one hundred thousand white-collar employees in public administration, in a country of barely over nine million inhabitants (Stenzel 1988, 329–31). As Fernando Agüero (1992), the vice chairman of the National Association of Manufacturers (NAM) from 1982 through 1986 and its chairman from 1987 through 1990 said, "If the business community had the power to avoid the revolution [by the economists], they would have done whatever was necessary to stop it." The former chairman of NAM in the 1970s concurred, stating that while business strongly resisted opening the economy, the economists nonetheless "took away the roof from the green house" (Arteaga 1992).

Others have also documented the inability of interest groups to affect policy-maker decisions. Eduardo Silva (1991, 100), for example, claims that the authoritarian policy process isolated the Chicago Boys "from virtually all groups, except the top directors of a handful of powerful Chilean conglomerates who agreed with them." Silva (1991, 123) further adds that "domestic market producers in agriculture and industry protested tariff reforms, but to no avail." Indeed, business owners had almost no influence over the economic team between 1975 and 1982 (Campero 1991, 131–33). As a former central bank president stated in the mid-1970s, "The fact that more than 90 percent of the people are against our policies is proof that the model is working, that it has affected everybody and that it has privileged nobody" (cf. Frieden 1991, 157). Policy makers initiated policies that nearly everyone opposed, including entrepreneurs (De la Cuadra 1992).

Although the economic team's cohesiveness helped them to initiate orthodox policies, to maintain themselves in governmental positions the team also required the backing of General Pinochet. As the leader in charge of most appointments, Pinochet controlled the team's ability to remain intact. In 1983, for example, violent street protests and economic chaos[15] forced Pinochet to change personnel in an attempt to reduce pressure (Larroulet 1992a; Cáceres 1992). From all segments of society, more open criticism and frustration set in with respect to Pinochet's handling of the economy, and with his support for the Chicago Boys.

In an effort to defuse tensions, Pinochet appointed Sergio Onofre Jarpa, a well-known National Party leader, as minister of interior (Spooner 1999, 191). Jarpa, a staunch opponent of neoliberal policies, tried to eliminate all Chicago Boys from economic policy making (Bardon 1992; Meller 1992). Following the appointment of Jarpa and Finance Minister Luis Escobar Cerda, the proportion of economists declined in 1984, as did the intensity of neoliberal policies. Jarpa and Escobar argued that Chile's economic problems resulted from policies associated with Chicago Boys, and they insisted on the appointment of "individuals linked to the traditional, prostatist business world" (Constable and Valenzuela 1991, 198). When pressure fell in 1985,[16] Pinochet replaced Jarpa and Escobar with economists,[17] some of whom had worked in the 1975 through 1983 period. Their return solidified the program (Larroulet 1992a; Pion-Berlin 1986, 329).

Maintenance of the Policies

The cohesion of the economic team had important implications not only for the initiation of orthodox neoliberal policies, but also for sustaining the policies. In interviews with economic policy makers, military officers and leaders, and academics, nearly all stressed the role of three people— Sergio de Castro, Miguel Kast, and José Piñera—in maintaining the coherence of the economic team in the 1970s through the early 1980s. These three men took actions to convert and persuade military officers and leaders, and society in general, to support neoliberal policies.[18]

The role of Sergio de Castro in solidifying the program is well documented. As one of the first students to embark in the program developed between the University of Chicago and Universidad Católica, de Castro returned to Chile with free-market ideas previously almost unheard of in the economics profession. De Castro later served as the dean of the economics department at the Universidad Católica, where he and his colleagues trained in Chicago developed a stronghold in the department. Once General Pinochet appointed him to the position of minister of finance in 1976, de Castro appointed many of his friends, colleagues, and students, who took over sixty positions within the public sector (De Castro 1992; Silva 1992). These persons believed devoutly in the religion of neoliberalism and saw de Castro as their leader and/or professor (Fontaine 1988; Meller 1984). In fact, opposition economist Oscar Muñoz (1992) argued that the ideological economists who worked under de Castro perceived their economic ideas as a religion—"as truth." De Castro's ability to outdebate and to educate his detractors impressed Pinochet and convinced him of the merits of orthodox policies (Harberger 1992). While Pinochet may not have advocated neoliberal policies at the beginning of the military government, by the late 1970s he had become a committed believer, thanks in large part to de Castro's economics lessons (De la Cuadra 1992). The fact that these policies promoted strong economic growth in the late 1970s further reinforced Pinochet's neoliberal convictions. Once de Castro appointed his team and convinced Pinochet of the virtues of neoliberal policies, interest groups found it very difficult to influence economic policy decisions.[19]

The importance of Miguel Kast comes from his recruitment activities. Kast, a charismatic and strong-willed right-wing Catholic, recruited students to earn advanced degrees in Chicago so that they could then return to work in the public sector or to teach a new generation of students at a Chilean university (Fontaine 1988).[20] As part of the recruitment and indoctrination process, Kast invited his undergraduate economics students to dinners that often lasted well into the evening in order that they might learn and absorb the orthodox ideas he espoused (Lavín 1988). By 1978, Kast held the position of head of ODEPLAN, the planning ministry, enabling him to fill many planning positions available not only in Santiago, but also in the outlying areas of Chile.[21] Kast helped to promote a third generation of Chilean economists to study at the University of Chicago and then to work in the government (Larroulet 1992a). As such, Kast played a key role in the consolidation of the Chicago team (Valenzuela 1991, 71).

In contrast to de Castro and Kast, José Piñera earned his reputation through his groundbreaking work in social security reforms, labor laws, and mining legislation. To accomplish these changes, however, Piñera (1991a) recognized the importance of the media for educating and convincing the public of the benefits of his policies. While military regimes often use repressive tactics in order to force public acquiescence, these regimes still need public support.[22] Piñera relied on legal measures to earn support for his proposals. Policies such as privatization of the social security system received vocal opposition. To counter opposition pressure, Piñera wrote newspaper articles and held weekly television presentations revealing the benefits of social security reforms, while elaborating on the disarray in the poorly managed, state-run social security system.[23] Once Piñera garnered enough support to implement reforms in social security, labor laws, and mining, the policies appeared almost irreversible. Not only had interest groups formed based on the new policies, but also the high cost of trying to reinstate a nearly bankrupt public social security system further sustained the reforms.

Argentina

Effect of Economists on Policy Coherence and Interest-Group Influence

The appointment of policy makers in Argentina differed markedly from Chile. Like Chile, Argentina had many trained economists available when the military took over in 1966.[24] Unlike Chile, however, the military chose few of them to work in economic policy making (Dagnino Pastore 1988). From 1966 through 1969, neoliberal economists made up only 31.2 percent (see chart 4.2) of the economic policy-making positions. In 1966, Juan Carlos Onganía selected Jorge Nestor Salimei as minister of economy and labor.[25] Salimei, an entrepreneur, "found himself directing a heterogeneous team that included other 'Catholic entrepreneurs,' some liberals, and some Christian Democratic técnicos" (O'Donnell 1988, 66). This heterogeneous team developed internal conflicts that created access points for interest groups connected to inefficient, import-competing industries, Peronist-created labor unions, and military enterprises. In his attempt to satisfy these various interests, Salimei initiated expansionary economic policies that aggravated Argentina's economic difficulties.

Following the economic debacle, Onganía replaced Salimei with Adalbert Krieger Vasena in January 1967. Krieger Vasena, a well-respected economist in international circles, assembled a team with a few prominent economists. Young *técnicos*—middle-ranking executives or consultants to large corporations (and not economists)—made up most of the team

Chart 4.2   Percent of Neoliberal Economists in Economic Policy Making in Argentina, 1966–1983

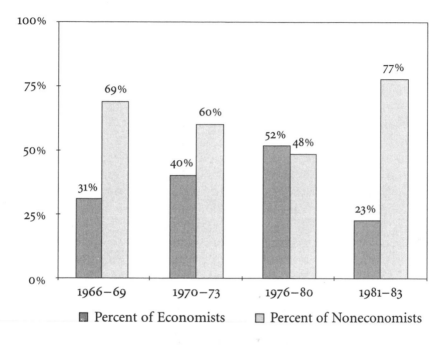

Sources: Argentine finance ministry, central bank, and planning office.
Note: Economic policy-making positions in Argentina are: secretary and subsecretary of finance, minister and subsecretary of the economy, secretary and subsecretary of SEPCE (the planning office), secretary and subsecretary of commerce, and president, first vice president, and second vice president of the central bank. The percent of economists increased from 1970 through 1973, but most of these economists received their training not in the U. S. but in schools that favored structuralism over neoliberal approaches to economic policy making.

(O'Donnell 1988, 73). Krieger chose gradualism over orthodox policies, which brought some economic order in the late 1960s (Simone 1992). In 1969, however, following the *cordobazo*—automobile workers' strikes and student unrest in Córdoba—Onganía forced Krieger to resign. The proportion of neoliberal economists in policy-making positions never grew significantly after this, and gradual neoliberal policies withered away.

In 1973, the military ceded power back to democratic forces. The return of Juan Perón to the presidency, nearly two decades after his ouster by military forces, prompted many of his followers to believe that change would occur almost immediately. A year after taking office, Perón died, leaving his vice president and wife, Isabel Perón, as the new president. Over the next two years, economic and political turmoil spread throughout the country.

By March 1976, the explosion of guerrilla activities spearheaded by the Montoneros and the Trotskyite ERP and economic chaos propelled another in Argentina's long tradition of military coups. In his first address to the country, the new economic minister, José Alfredo Martínez de Hoz, discussed the seriousness of the economic problems. His prescriptions, however, continued to favor gradualist policies (Memoria 1981; Simone 1992). Martínez de Hoz believed that the country's economic problems stemmed from a lack of confidence, and he proposed a gradualist program to reduce inflation (Folcini 1992).[26] As part of the program, industries continued to receive protection, privatization only occurred in peripheral areas, and fiscal restraint garnered minimal attention.

In 1978–80, Martínez de Hoz used stronger neoliberal language and, in fact, stepped up the program. A few economists supportive of orthodox policies replaced members of the economic team who had expressed reservations toward these policies. The lower proportion of neoliberal economists (51.9 percent) compared to Chile (77.8 percent), however, inhibited the adoption of an orthodox program. The Argentine team held heterogeneous economic beliefs compared to the Chileans, which made it difficult for the team to convince the military government to sustain neoliberal policies (Diz 1992; Estrada 1992; Solanet 1992). Even when Martínez de Hoz—with the backing of junta leader General Jorge Videla—attempted to put through more rigorous policies, the vulnerability to interest-group pressures seemed inalterable (Wynia 1986; Schvarzer 1983).[27] The original economic team included representatives of agriculture and industry, which gave automatic access to interests in these fields (Frieden 1991, 211).

The market for canned peaches exemplifies interest-group influence. Under military rule, the price of domestic canned peaches remained above the international market price. Given the high domestic price, international suppliers attempted to exploit Argentina's market, but virtually no foreign peaches entered. The reason was that in the world market, most canned peaches came in 500-gram containers. In Argentina, however, the government imposed a restriction on the importation of canned peaches.

Only peaches in 550-gram containers or larger could enter the country (Arriazu 1992). Specific legislative provisions enabled domestic peach producers to avoid international competition. Another example of interest-group influence is the placement of biscuit factories in the province of La Rioja. Although wheat is grown over one thousand miles away, which makes the production of biscuits in La Rioja infeasible and costly relative to factories located near the fields, the government allocated funds to build factories there (Diz 1992).[28]

The incoherence of economic policy making is most clear in the industrial promotion programs completely at odds with neoliberal prescriptions followed by the military government.[29] In general, neoliberal policies are intended to open domestic markets to international competition, eliminate protection and subsidies for industries, and reduce the size of the state. Industrial promotion programs, in contrast, provide subsidies for industries, increase the state sector, and aid industries that face bankruptcy under competitive conditions.

Even though industrial promotion programs were inconsistent with neoliberal policies, the military continued previously inefficient programs begun in 1972 and adopted new ones in La Rioja, San Juan, and Catamarca. Initially designed to subsidize poorer regions, programs to promote industrial development then spread to other more prosperous regions in the early 1980s, until the federal government subsidized nearly every province (Teijeiro 1992).

Some of these investments carried with them high economic costs. In Tierra del Fuego, the southernmost province in Argentina, the government attempted to create an electronics and television industry. While costs of skilled labor in this region are high, and parts are not made in the area, the government compensated for these deficiencies by providing businesses with large subsidies to invest there. Since Argentina did not have the parts to build televisions, the government contacted Japanese television manufacturers in an attempt to buy parts from them. The Japanese manufacturers would only sell the televisions whole, not the parts separately. Argentina bought the televisions from Japan, disassembled them in Miami and Panama, and then reassembled them in Tierra del Fuego to be resold in the domestic market (Llambias 1992). The military also considered creating a computer industry in much the same way as it manufactured televisions, but it never came on line.

Argentina also used two methods to protect the domestic television market. In the first instance, the government imposed high tariffs, placed specific values, i.e., high customs duties, on goods, or applied quantitative restrictions on imported televisions (Teijeiro 1992). In the second instance, the regime adopted a color television system that few countries used and thus would not work with most imported color television sets (Pessino 1992).

Other policies also strained the budget. The government provided generous subsidies to the electronics industry, constructed three new soccer stadiums, and protected basic industries—especially those controlled by the military through Fabricaciones Militares (FM). In the case of FM, for example, its survival required protection from external and internal competition in addition to state subsidies. Everything from steel and aluminum plants, to petrochemicals and oil, to car production and telecommunications received subsidies. These are just a few examples of the many inefficiencies promoted in the military period.

Uruguay

Effect of Economists on Military and Interest-Group Influence

The discussion of Uruguay (1973–84) mirrors the situation in Argentina. In Argentina and Uruguay, a low proportion of neoliberal economists worked in the policy-making positions. Moreover, although economic policy makers and military government leaders in Uruguay and Argentina's second military regime advocated orthodox policies,[30] in both cases, policy makers chose gradual policies which they failed to sustain (Végh 1975).

Beginning in 1974, President Juan María Bordaberry named Alejandro Végh Villegas, the best-known and most respected economist in Uruguay, as minister of economics and finance. With notable exceptions, however, few economists made up the rest of the economic team. Neoliberal economists represented only 11.3 percent of the economic policy makers (see chart 4.3) from 1973 through 1976. While Végh may have wanted to appoint more economists, military officers controlled or had the right of refusal over most appointments. Instead of economists, officers appointed fellow military personnel, without economics training, to work in policy-making positions. Indeed, Végh's subsecretary of economics in 1974, Valentín Arismendi, who later served as minister of economics and finance, was a former classmate of officers and not an econo-

Chart 4.3   Percent of Neoliberal Economists in Economic Policy
Making in Uruguay, 1973–1984

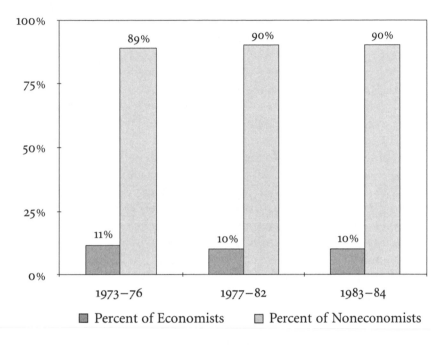

□ Percent of Economists   □ Percent of Noneconomists

Sources: Uruguayan central bank and planning office.
Note: Economic policy-making positions in Uruguay are: director and subdirector of SEPLACODI (the planning office), president, vice president, and director of the central bank, president, vice president, and director of the Banco de
la República, minister and subsecretary of economics and finance, and minister
of industry and commerce.

mist. His previous affiliation with the military eased the way for his selection (Tiribocchi 1992).[31]

Military officers also held prominent positions in the Banco de la
República and Banco Central, the two most important financial enterprises in Uruguay. In addition, an army general and air force general usually served in the top positions in SEPLACODI, the planning ministry
(Vaz 1992). These officers helped to block neoliberal programs (Bordaberry 1992). As Gillespie (1986) and Myers (1988) point out, the military

did not favor neoliberalism. The military's writings during this period and its communiqués announced in 1973 emphasized national security and national development and the important role of the state (*El Proceso Político* 1978).

An example of opposition to neoliberal policies comes from an officer's experience as head of ANCAP, the state-owned oil company, which also held concrete concerns. According to former president of the Banco Central Ramón Díaz (1992), the general in charge of the company would not consider privatizing the cement interests since he had not been appointed "to give away the wealth of the nation."

The economic policies introduced in 1974 reflected the antiorthodox views of the military. While the government, advised by Végh, initiated financial liberalization, cut tariff rates in half, and reduced price controls, tariffs continued at high levels and the government privatized almost no firms (Végh 1977; López Murphy, et al. 1988). When Végh resigned in 1976, the likelihood of initiating even more orthodox policies declined. The proportion of neoliberal economists in economic policy-making positions fell to only 10.0 percent from 1977 through 1982, which hampered efforts to put forward an all-encompassing neoliberal program. As Uruguayan economist Michele Santo (1992) stated, "To carry out a deep reform, one needs the right amount and quality of human capital." In the case of Uruguay, only around five economists advocated neoliberal policies, a number too small to support a reform (Caumont 1992; Viana 1992).

Similar to Argentina's military regimes, Uruguay's leader espoused orthodox policies, but different economic views held by members of the economic team in Uruguay made it difficult to convince themselves, let alone military officers, of the benefits of sustaining neoliberal policies. As in Argentina, this lack of a cohesive team enabled interest groups to influence policy choices (Caumont 1992; Protasi 1992).

In an example of interest-group influence, a Uruguayan textile manufacturer had supported tariff reductions for many years. The manufacturer favored lower tariff rates in order to import his inputs at lower cost. When informed that the government intended to lower tariffs on finished textile goods in the early 1980s, however, the manufacturer contacted the general in charge of the Ministry of Interior to issue an ultimatum. The manufacturer asserted that if the government reduced tariffs on products he manufactured, he would shift his operation from exporting to importing. The manufacturer claimed that he had placed an order for millions of dollars in Taiwanese imports and would close his plant that employed between one thousand and two thousand workers. Three days later, the general rescinded the reduction in tariffs on finished textiles (Vaz 1992).

Similarly, Finance Minister Végh attempted in 1975 to permit the importation of already-assembled vehicles. Once auto assembly executives and vehicle parts companies learned of Végh's intentions, they joined forces to lobby sympathetic military officials for their cause (Handelman 1981b). After six months, Végh gave up on his fight to import cars. In addition, Végh attempted to deregulate prices in the meatpacking and tanning industries and permit foreign ownership in meatpacking (Handelman 1981b). In both cases, interests from the meatpacking and auto industries cultivated military "protectors," who stopped the reform process. As Végh (1992a) would later say, "You can't win all your battles."

Summary

The data for the Southern Cone countries suggests the role of neoliberal economists for the initiation and sustaining of orthodox policies. The Chileans initiated orthodox neoliberal policies only after appointing a high proportion of "Chicago" economists in economic policy-making positions. Argentina and Uruguay applied less orthodox neoliberal policies and had lower proportions of neoliberal economists. The lack of coherence in the Argentine and Uruguayan teams also facilitated access to policy makers by interest groups opposed to reductions in tariffs and protection, which further impeded the initiation of orthodox policies.

If some military regimes promote orthodox policies, while others block them, this leads to questions about the relationship between orthodox policies and goals of the military. What effect do orthodox policies have on military officers and how do the beliefs of officers influence the ability of neoliberal economists to achieve their policy goals? The following chapter examines military interests by reviewing privatization and the opportunities for employment, patronage, and other benefits provided to officers.

FIVE

Privatization under Military Rule

A more important obstacle to introducing competition is the nature of the political process. Competition would benefit the general public. But the general public has no effective lobby.
—Milton Friedman, *An Economist's Protest*

The by-product argument, detailed in chapter 3, explained when military rulers are most likely to appoint neoliberal economists. Chapter 4 showed the effects of neoliberal economists for explaining, in general, different policy decisions. This chapter focuses on privatization of state-owned enterprises (SOEs), a critical element of most market-oriented programs, to assess the importance of neoliberal economists for a specific kind of policy choice. Attempts to privatize SOEs, as will become apparent, are consistent with expectations generated by arguments in chapter 4. In Argentina and Uruguay, fewer neoliberal economists worked in economic policy-making positions, which reduced their commitment to privatize. Policy makers also confronted strong opposition to privatization from officers who served as directors in SOEs and from officers inside the government. In Chile, by contrast, despite substantial opposition to privatization, neoliberal economists privatized many firms in the mid to late 1970s. Most of the largest SOEs, however, remained in the state's hands until the mid-1980s.

The Chilean economic team's inability to privatize the largest SOEs in the 1970s and its success in privatizing many of them in the mid-1980s suggests that the commitment of the economic team is one part of the puzzle for explaining privatization under military rule. A second part considers resistance to privatization from military personnel in SOEs, and their impact on decisions made by military leaders. This chapter demonstrates that leaders often use the appointment of officers to SOEs as part of a survival strategy to retain the loyalty and support of their troops. The conditions under which leaders overcome military and societal opposition to privatization while maintaining their survival are highlighted. The concluding summary and epilogue draw parallels and contrasts between Chile's privatization of SOEs in the mid-1980s and privatization in Argentina and Uruguay under democratic rule in the 1990s.

Background to Privatizing

Prior to the 1930s, many countries in the world subscribed to a minimalist state for economic development. Under this minimalist framework, the state's activities included: stimulating investment by the private sector through tax codes and minimal regulation; involving itself in economic enterprises that the private sector could not do on its own (such as utilities, heavy industrialization, and natural monopolies); providing for police, defense, and infrastructure; and protecting property rights. The state limited itself to areas that the private sector could not manage alone, and created incentives to promote private investment.

In the 1930s and 1940s, the state took a more active role in large-scale production. The Great Depression provided the impetus for countries to look inward, in an attempt to insulate their economies from external shocks (Thorp 1984). As part of this insulation, the state gained control in such vital sectors as petroleum, mining, electricity, aerospace, and telecommunications.

The Southern Cone countries also increased the state's role in the economy. Through Decree Law 6640, Chile created CORFO (Corporación de Fomento de la Producción)—a state-owned holding corporation and development bank—in 1939, which promoted state control of many important sectors of the economy.[1] Argentina's shift to a more active state began with the creation of Fabricaciones Militares in 1941. Juan Perón's presidential victory in 1946 and his subsequent nationalization policies further expanded the role of the state in development (Díaz-Alejandro 1970, 109).[2] In Uruguay, welfare state-oriented policies and state control of the economy preceded the Depression. In the early twentieth century, President José Batlle y Ordóñez advocated state ownership of the largest industries (Finch 1981, 12).[3] Following the Depression, a more activist state developed, as the state engaged itself in sectors formerly occupied by the private sector.

The increasing importance of the state in Argentina, Chile, and Uruguay complemented their choice of import substitution industrialization (ISI) policies.[4] ISI policies provided tariff protection for import-competing private firms from the 1940s through 1960s. Many state-owned industries also required the protection generated by ISI policies to "compete" in the domestic market. To insure supplies of inputs at subsidized rates, SOEs also created subsidiaries or backward linkages that increased the state's involvement in the economy.

As a result of ISI policies and the increasing influence of the state in import-competing industries, Southern Cone growth rates decreased in the 1950s and 1960s.[5] Ironically, during the same period, international trade expanded worldwide, as regions outside Latin America, including Southeast Asia, prospered through their adoption of export-oriented strategies. Prosperity in other regions and economic decline made policy makers in the Southern Cone countries begin to question the merits of ISI policies in the late 1960s and early 1970s (Ramos 1986). In fact, these countries (except Chile) adopted policies to promote export growth. Reforms that reduced the role of the state, however, received little notice.[6]

Given the time period, it comes as no surprise that policy makers made few attempts to denationalize the state. Unlike the late 1980s and early 1990s, when many countries considered and, in some cases, privatized most of their state portfolios, in the early 1970s, almost no country seriously broached selling off state assets (Hall 1989). Not many economists, let alone politicians, recognized the potential benefits of reducing the state sector.

Going against popular wisdom, however, policy makers in the Southern Cone openly pledged their support to privatize SOEs in the mid-1970s. The backing of policy makers and even some military leaders made it appear highly probable that these countries would initiate similar reforms that greatly reduced their state sectors. Instead, Argentina and Uruguay privatized few SOEs, while Chile privatized many SOEs in 1975 but waited ten years before privatizing most of its largest. Why did policy makers privatize extensively in some cases and not in others? What factors explain changes in the degree of privatization over time in Chile?

Theoretical Perspectives on Privatization

To understand the recent growth in state divestiture, researchers offer economic and political explanations. Most economic explanations are based on microeconomic or macroeconomic variables. The main microeconomic variable is the percent of total external debt caused by public enterprises. The inefficiencies of SOEs, and their contribution to increasing fiscal budget deficits and debts, motivate policy makers to sell off state assets (Vernon 1988, 4). The main macroeconomic variables include total external debt and inflation. High external debts or inflation rates, so the story goes, are positively associated with privatization efforts (Ramamurti 1996). Revenue generated from sales of SOEs reduces fiscal deficits and enables countries to repay their loans, which limits inflationary pressures.

Microeconomic and macroeconomic variables do not fully account for differences among the Southern Cone cases. As table 5.1 shows, the percent of total external debt caused by SOEs is virtually identical for Chile and Uruguay, and is slightly less for Argentina. Chile's SOEs were also in better economic shape than the SOEs in the other countries, providing less incentive for state divestiture. Indeed, the SOE balances before transfers in table 5.1 reveal that Chile's SOEs operated in the black, while Argentina's SOEs drained resources from the government's budget.

From a macroeconomic view, although the debt crisis encouraged the sale of state assets since the late 1980s, economic policy makers in the Southern Cone advocated privatization in the mid-1970s, years before the debt crisis (Martínez de Hoz 1991; Végh 1992a; *El Ladrillo* 1992). Inflation was also less fierce in Chile. As table 5.1 shows, Chile enjoyed the lowest median inflation, and its average level was far below Argentina's. The data raises questions about the effect of macroeconomic performance on state divestiture.

Alternatively, others use political factors including "policy bandwagoning" or the honeymoon hypothesis to explain differences in privatization. Some argue that bandwagoning or demonstration effects prompt countries to imitate "successful" policies that are initiated elsewhere. Policy makers mimic policies such as those adopted by Prime Minister Margaret Thatcher in Great Britain and President Ronald Reagan in the United States in the early 1980s that endorsed deregulation, privatization, and a shrinking of the state, in part because of visits from First World intellectuals (Drake 1998, 83). Others support the honeymoon hypothesis, which suggests that privatization occurs immediately after a change of government. Political leaders have more "freedom of political maneu-

Table 5.1   Effect of Microeconomic and Macroeconomic Variables
on Privatization (%)

Country	SOE in Total External Debt		Inflation (Consumer Price Index)		SOE Balances Before Transfers (Prop. of GDP)	
	Mean	Median	Mean	Median	Mean	Median
Argentina (1976–83)	13.0	12.8	208.6	170.2	−3.9	−2.7
Chile (1973–89)	14.6	14.8	110.8	26.4	7.6	7.7
Uruguay (1973–84)	14.5	14.7	57.3	54.5	1.2	1.4

Sources: For SOEs in total external debt and SOE balances before transfers, see World Bank (1995, 292–94, 308–10); for inflation figures in Chile, see Edwards and Edwards (1991, 40, A-2); for Argentina's inflation, see Di Tella and Dornbusch (1989, 328); for Uruguay's inflation, see Larraín (1986, A).

ver" immediately after taking power, as they can blame the outgoing government for its problems (cf. Williamson and Haggard 1994).

Although policies introduced by Reagan and Thatcher influenced the shift toward a more limited state, policy makers in the Southern Cone pledged their support for privatization in the 1970s. In fact, Chile went even further than Reagan and Thatcher by privatizing its social security system in 1981. The honeymoon hypothesis may explain Chile's privatization in 1975, but it does not account for Chile's privatization of most of its largest SOEs ten years later. Moreover, none of these theories explains why countries espousing the same goals differed in their ability to privatize.

Public Ownership and Survival

Attempts to privatize SOEs in military regimes face two distinct obstacles. One obstacle is locating support for privatization. Highly unpopular with many groups, placing privatization on the policy agenda is not easy for survival-minded politicians. The selection of neoliberal economic policy makers, who strongly endorse privatization, is important for increasing demand for state sell-offs. Resistance to privatization, especially from officers employed in SOEs, however, represents a second obstacle. The economic and political benefits that officers earn from SOEs motivate them to oppose privatization. This section examines the effects of policy makers and military personnel in SOEs on privatization under military rule.

Neoliberal Economists as Economic Policy Makers

As argued in chapter 3, who the military ruler selects to economic policy-making positions affects policy decisions including privatization reforms. The choice of many neoliberal economists is critical for the implementation of market-oriented reforms. Through their training and education, neoliberal economists share a commitment to the market and private ownership for promoting economic growth. This commitment inspires them to sell SOEs. It also helps them to persuade opposition forces about the potential benefits of privatization, which reduces the level of resistance to denationalizing.

Policy makers from diverse educational backgrounds, by contrast, share a weaker commitment to private enterprise and the market. These policy makers have difficulty convincing a reluctant population and especially state employees, who fear the loss of their jobs under private ownership, to support privatization. If military leaders appoint military officers and lawyers to economic policy-making positions—groups who in the past have held these positions—the demand for privatization declines.

Historically, the military has never endorsed policies that reduced the role of the state in development. Most officers perceive market-oriented policies and the influx of foreign investors and their monies as potential threats to the sovereignty, security, and economic well-being of the nation. Similarly, most lawyers have had limited experience with economic issues and do not understand the significance neoliberal economists attach to a reduced state role for development (Diz 1992). At a minimum, lawyers in political office are unlikely to use their limited political resources to sponsor a program that most oppose.

Based on their strong preferences, a team of neoliberal economists in economic policy-making positions provides the greatest opportunity for privatization to occur. These economists, however, do not guarantee the initiation of privatization reforms. Even as economists work to privatize SOEs, military officers may derail privatization of individual firms.

Officers in SOEs and Political Survival

In most cases, economic problems are the principal cause for military coups. The inability of democratic leaders to solve deteriorating economic conditions contributes to their overthrow. Because of these declining conditions, newly installed military governments are often forced to administer some kind of economic reforms to help to revive their economies. The question, of course, is which reforms are selected.

In any package of economic reforms, policy makers have many different ones to choose from. Policy makers, for instance, may adopt stabilization measures. Alternatively, policy makers may instead, or in addition to a stabilization program, privatize SOEs or promote trade liberalization.

To explain the policy choices made by military governments, it is necessary to examine how different reforms affect military interests. If we assume that military governments are committed to implementing economic reforms and they are given a choice between privatization versus stabilization or exchange rate reforms that reduce income levels for workers, I contend that the military will select the latter option. As Geddes (1991) argues, governments often find it easier to squeeze the working class than to privatize. These regimes can adopt salary reductions through exchange rate controls, hiding the immediate effects of wage reductions. If exchange rate devaluations are done in small increments, workers may not immediately recognize the effects of such devaluations. By squeezing the wages of the working class, the government also may attract strong support from employers. Moreover, given that the military sometimes blames the working class for the political and economic problems that preceded the military's intervention, military leaders are often less sympathetic to the plight of workers, and show less willingness to protect their interests. Most importantly, as long as military budgets (including salaries and equipment) are exempted from reductions in government expenditures that are usually associated with stabilization or exchange rate reforms, these reforms may not draw intense military opposition.

Privatization reforms, by contrast, may have direct repercussions for officers and their leaders. As argued in chapter 3, military leaders cater to officers in an effort to avoid military counter-coups. SOEs are gold mines for military leaders to deliver benefits to the military and to secure their tenure in office.[7] Military leaders can use SOEs as forms of patronage, delivering individual benefits to officers who threaten their survival. Officers in charge of SOEs earn additional salaries, travel excursions, a car and driver, the power and prestige of directing a company, and, in some cases, whatever they can pilfer from the firm. Even if officers do not make large salaries or engage in corrupt activities, the directing of these SOEs confers recognition on these officers, which may help them later for military promotions. Given these benefits, officers in SOEs usually want to retain their positions. With privatization, employers will hire the most qualified personnel, which probably will result in the layoff of officers. Leaders meting out these jobs and officers receiving them consequently oppose privatization.

Privatization may be seen as a collective good. While in some rare cases a majority of the population advocates privatization,[8] as no one can be excluded from its benefits, small groups who are negatively affected by privatization will lobby to maintain state ownership. Small groups, such as the military, who stand to gain a disproportionate share of societal income if SOEs remain in the state's hands, will lobby not to advance collective welfare but to maintain state control (Olson 1982). With respect to regulatory action, if the benefits are diffuse and the costs are concentrated on a limited number of individuals, a high probability exists that the action will not occur (Wilson 1980). Privatization imposes concentrated costs on officers, especially those who work in SOEs, and disperses benefits throughout the population. These high costs provide officers with incentives to halt privatization plans.

The public also may not recognize the advantages of privatization. The costs of state ownership are often so diffuse that the public sees only the benefits from state control, especially when SOEs subsidize the prices of staple goods and services. In some instances, however, the quality of essential services provided by SOEs may have deteriorated to such an extent that opinion polls document public support for privatization. In these cases, the public, which incurs the cost of not privatizing, has less capacity—especially in military governments—and less incentive than the directly injured parties, the military officers, to lobby for change and to punish their leaders (Stigler 1975). Thus, even in cases where neoliberal economists dominate economic policy-making positions and pursue privatization reforms, as long as officers serve in SOEs, strong limits are imposed on state divestiture.

Civilian Directors in SOEs and Political Survival

Although military rulers generally face stiff obstacles to privatization, there are instances where state reforms can occur. Such reforms require civilians to work in the capacity of directors of SOEs. Under military rule, civilian directors in SOEs are different than military directors. Military leaders usually allot benefits to officers before distributing them to civilians. Fear of military counter-coups and measures to consolidate power compel military leaders to use SOE appointments as forms of patronage for loyal officers.[9] The appointment of civilian directors under military rule, by contrast, is based on different criteria. Military leaders appoint civilian directors on the basis of their credentials that qualify them for the positions. Their background and training justifies their appointment to SOEs. Given their competence, civilian directors have less fear of losing their jobs under private ownership than military directors, which weakens their opposition to privatization.

Civilian directors also have less influence over military leaders than military directors. Given that civilians have less potential for mobilizing forces to commit a counter-coup compared to officers, civilians pose a lower threat to the survival of military leaders. Under this scenario, civilian directors may have less capacity to prevent privatization of the SOEs they manage. Thus, when neoliberal economists committed to privatization serve as economic policy makers and civilian directors operate SOEs, the likelihood for privatization increases.

This leads to the question of when military leaders will appoint civilian directors to SOEs. I argue that military leaders are most likely to replace officers with civilians when officers in SOEs no longer want to retain their positions. There are several factors that affect the desire of officers to remain in their positions. If, for instance, SOEs are managed on a competitive basis—meaning that SOEs are run as if they operated in a competitive market—this limits opportunities for corruption and excessive gains from employment. Exorbitant salaries that are typical for the highest-level positions in SOEs are less common in competitive situations, where costs are closely monitored by policy makers and their staffs. Officers who do not earn large benefits from their employment may not want the additional responsibilities that come with their positions in SOEs. Officers on active duty may also need to spend time in the field to receive military promotions. This creates incentives for military leaders to leave their SOE positions. In addition, military leaders may have consolidated their rule to the extent that they feel secure in their political positions. This provides leaders with more autonomy in their appointment strategies.

In short, supply-and-demand factors influence privatization. Much like democratic leaders, military rulers face steep roadblocks in their quest to reduce the state sector. But if military leaders are able to replace

officers in SOEs with qualified civilian directors, and if neoliberal economists committed to privatization serve in economic policy-making positions, this increases the likelihood for privatization of SOEs.

Privatization in the Southern Cone

The following sections examine the effect of supply and demand on privatization in the Southern Cone. They show that demand for privatization increases when neoliberal economists occupy economic policy-
making positions. Neoliberal economists by themselves are not the only
necessary factor for privatization. Civilian directors also need to serve in
the highest positions of SOEs. Table 5.2 illustrates the effect of demand
for privatization by policy makers and resistance to the sale of SOEs by
officers for the Southern Cone cases.

Chile

The history of state ownership of important industries is fairly long in
Chile. Dating from the creation of CORFO in the late 1930s through to
the early 1960s, Chile successively expanded the state's position in the
economy. In the late 1960s under President Eduardo Frei, the movement
toward greater state ownership increased, only to explode under President Salvador Allende. Even before Allende's arrival in 1970, the state sector controlled over 40 percent of GDP and accounted for 75 percent of
total gross domestic investment in fixed capital. In the 1960s, Frei introduced agrarian reforms that aided in the expropriation of farms by the
state and "Chileanization" of copper corporations.[10] During Allende's
presidency, the government intervened or expropriated many privately
owned firms to the point that the state owned or controlled nearly 600
firms (Hachette and Lüders 1993, 5). The state also regulated water rights
for agriculture and expropriated large land holdings. By 1973, the state
controlled much of Chilean industry, agriculture, mining, and finance.

Following Allende's overthrow, the military appointed officers to
SOEs as interventors whose job was to assess the condition of the bulging
state sector. The military soon discovered that many of the enterprises
were insolvent. They also learned that many former owners would not
want their expropriated firms returned to them in their current state.
This prompted the military to dissolve bankrupt firms and return others

Table 5.2 Demand for and Resistance to Privatization of SOEs

	Argentina		
	1966–73	*1976–80*	*1981–82*
Demand for Privatization	Low POE (35.8%)	Medium POE (51.9%)	Low POE (34.0%)
Resistance to Privatization	n.d.	High MSOE (67.9%)	High MSOE (74.6%)
	Chile		
	1974–79	*1980–85*	*1986–89*
Demand for Privatization	High POE (69.2%)	High POE (82.4%)	High POE (93.9%)
Resistance to Privatization	High MSOE (55.2%)	High MSOE (54.4%)	Medium MSOE (42.6%)
	Uruguay		
	1974–76	*1977–82*	*1983–84*
Demand for Privatization	Low POE (13.2%)	Low POE (10.0%)	Low POE (10.0%)
Resistance to Privatization	High MSOE (49.0%)	High MSOE (61.1%)	Medium MSOE (40.5%)

POE = Proportion of Economists in Economic Policy Making; MSOE = Proportion of Military Officers in State-Owned Enterprises;[a] n.d. = no data.
a. This table examines the top three positions of the largest SOEs in each country, including the president, vice president, and director. The specific enterprises studied are detailed in the footnotes to charts 5.1, 5.3, and 5.4.

to their original owners "on [the] condition that they would formally agree not to litigate against the state" (Hachette and Lüders 1993, 46).

Until 1975, however, many firms expropriated or intervened by Allende remained under state control. In 1975, large-scale changes occurred with General Pinochet's appointment of "Chicago Boys." These economists recognized the effects of severe fiscal deficits on the Chilean economy and reasoned that the sale of assets, and particularly of SOEs that operated at a loss, would fill the state coffers with badly needed reserves and relieve the state of fiscal burdens.

Following the appointment of neoliberal economists, privatization took off in many industries, including firms originally founded by the state under the auspices of CORFO. Economists returned more than 250 firms expropriated during the Allende government and privatized another 200 firms, including most financial institutions and many other smaller firms (Sigmund 1990, 347).[11] The largest and most important firms, however, remained in the state's hands. Economists favored privatization of large, traditional SOEs, but the state retained these firms until the mid-1980s (De Castro 1992).

The main obstacle to large-scale privatization came from the military.[12] From the onset of military rule, officers openly rejected privatization of firms they considered "strategic" (Kelly 1992). Officers opposed the sale of SOEs on moral grounds, arguing that the wealth of the nation and its assets needed to remain in the state's hands. The military even considered textile manufacturers as strategic, because of unemployment implications if the state privatized these firms (Léniz 1992). Many officers also had received appointments as directors, presidents, and vice presidents of SOEs (Montecinos 1988). In as much as officers are not experts in the managing of firms, officers faced the prospect of forfeiting monetary benefits and other perquisites if the state privatized these firms. Officers also acquired prestige and power by making SOEs run efficiently, which was especially important for retired servicemen (Matthei 1992).

Officers inside and outside SOEs opposed privatization of Corporacíon Nacional del Cobre de Chile (CODELCO), the state-owned copper company, because of the benefits it provided the military.[13] As a result of a reserve law (13.196) enacted in the legislature in 1958 and later modified under democratic rule, the military services shared 10 percent of the gross revenue from CODELCO's sales (Delano and Traslaviña 1989, 20). Officers feared that privatization of CODELCO might shrink the military's budget. To insure state control of CODELCO and ENAP, the state petroleum concern, the military inserted amendments into the 1980 constitution that virtually guaranteed state ownership of these firms.

Military opposition to privatization extended beyond the largest SOEs. In the late 1970s, Minister of Labor José Piñera designed a plan to privatize the state pension system as a first step toward a private social security system. Military officers, however, balked at efforts to privatize military pensions (Piñera 1991b). In 1980, when the government privatized the state pension system that went into effect in 1981, pensions for officers remained under state control.

Although General Pinochet favored privatization of SOEs, his appointment of pro-statist officers to SOEs was intended to promote his political survival. Like any military ruler, Pinochet needed the backing of officers. The use of particularistic benefits through SOE appointments helped retain officer loyalty to him. According to former commander in chief of the air force General Fernando Matthei (1992), while Pinochet made most decisions on his own, he could not completely ignore military interests. Former Minister of Finance Sergio de Castro (1992) concurred, arguing that Pinochet used appointments in SOEs as patronage to foster loyalty from the troops. Measures such as privatization of SOEs, which would provoke hostility among the armed forces, interfered with Pinochet's goal to remain in office. Pinochet decided to maintain military personnel in charge of SOEs, which enhanced their loyalty to him.

In the 1980s, changes occurred that created opportunities for privatizing. In 1982, large conglomerate holding companies known as *grupos*, who controlled a significant proportion of Chile's private sector activities, including many banks, suffered greatly from the world recession.[14] These *grupos* were highly leveraged with high debt-to-asset ratios. When foreign banks cut off external financing in the early 1980s, some of the largest of the conglomerates collapsed, with their banks failing to repay their loans. This forced the government to intervene many banks. The holdings within the *grupos*, which owed debts to insolvent creditor banks, became known as the "odd sector" because they legally belonged to the private banks that lent them money, but the government's intervention of these banks forced the state to manage these firms.[15] The government's intervention prompted an opposition economist to joke that the Chicago Boys had "followed the monetarist road to socialism" (Meller 1992).

Over the next two years, the government's attempts to resurrect the economy and to recapitalize enterprises in the odd sector worked against privatization of SOEs, as did the decline in the proportion of neoliberal economists in economic policy making. The new team of economic policy makers as well as many from the military questioned the merits of privatization. Military personnel contended that traditional SOEs had held up better during the economic recession than newly privatized firms and saw no need to promote privatization.

In 1985, changes occurred that supported privatization in the odd sector and traditional SOEs. Based on interviews with former finance ministers (Cáceres 1992; Lüders 1992a; De la Cuadra 1992) and central bank presidents (Seguel 1992; Errázuriz 1992), few doubted that the odd sector would be reprivatized. Privatization of traditional SOEs surprised many, though. In 1985, the state privatized firms in the odd sector and sold 30 percent stakes in traditional SOEs. Within two years, ownership of many traditional SOEs, including natural monopolies in electricity, telecommunications, and even some mining and oil interests, fell under private control. The members of the economic team that entered in 1985, some of whom had worked with the economic team of the 1970s, offer an explanation for state divestiture. Much like their economic predecessors, these economists headed by Finance Minister Hernán Büchi were strongly committed to privatization. Unlike economists in the 1970s, however, this team of economists encountered different constraints and adopted innovative policies to defuse resistance to privatization.

In the mid-1980s, a generational schism developed within the leadership of the military. Many older officers did not understand why the state should sell profitable enterprises when the state could secure the profits for itself (Reyes 1992). They also protested privatization of natural monopolies (Medina 1992). Many younger officers, who had earned advanced degrees in economics, backed privatization (Seguel 1992; Concha 1992; Martínez 1992).

More important than the generational schism, change occurred in the top positions of SOEs. In the 1970s, large SOEs employed a high proportion of officers who blocked privatization (see chart 5.1). From 1974 through 1979, officers held 55.2 percent of the top positions. The proportion of officers remained at almost the same level (54.4 percent) from 1980 through 1985. In the mid-1980s, however, when the regime privatized many firms, the proportion of military personnel in SOEs declined. The proportion of officers from 1986 through 1989 dropped to 42.6 percent. Moreover, as chart 5.2 indicates, when officers held top positions in SOEs (54.5 percent), the likelihood of privatization decreased. Firms privatized by the state, by contrast, held a much higher proportion of civilians (70.0 percent) in top positions, as did firms partially privatized by the state (54.7 percent).

Chart 5.1   Military Control in Chilean Public Enterprises, 1974–1989

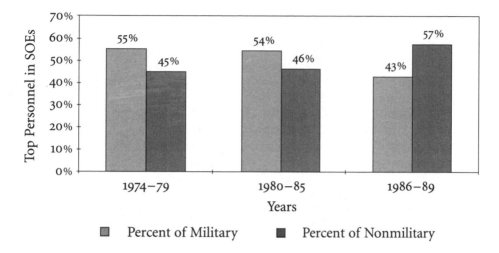

Years

☐ Percent of Military   ■ Percent of Nonmilitary

Sources: Memorias of the enterprises.
Note: This chart includes the following fifteen enterprises: CAP, Chilectra, Chilgen, Chilmetro, CODELCO, COPEC, CTC, EMEL, Emporchi, Empremar, Enami, Enap, Endesa, ENTel, and Ferrocarriles. The three positions reviewed are: president (or administrator general or interventor), vice president (or subadministrator general or subinterventor), and director (or vocal or manager). This study excludes the president of companies when the president is also a minister (e.g., the minister of mining is the president of CODELCO and Enami). This helps us distinguish between the role of ministers and individuals directly involved in the enterprise.

Economic incentives are one reason for officers occupying fewer SOE positions. Relative to other countries, top positions in Chile's SOEs provided less generous benefits. Through the advice of economic policy makers, the government introduced marginal-cost pricing in the 1970s, running SOEs as if they operated in a competitive market economy. Economists disallowed the central bank from financing SOEs, which forced SOEs to self-finance themselves (Larroulet 1992b, 12; Lüders 1992b, 133). The state also eliminated special privileges for SOEs, such as tax exemptions, tariff concessions, and subsidized credits. As a result, state firms operated more competitively, which contributed to a reduction in the number of employees in SOEs from 161,000 to 89,000 (Sigmund

Chart 5.2   Chilean Privatization of Public Enterprises, 1974–1989

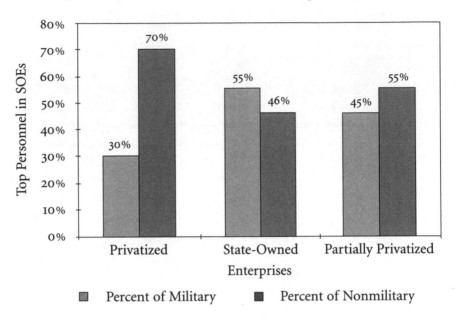

Sources: *Memorias* of the enterprises.

1990, 349). Setting price equal to marginal cost, that is, marginal-cost pricing, eliminates monopolistic rents (Tullock 1990). Reduced rents from state employment lowered incentives for officers to remain in these positions. Precisely at the moment of privatization of SOEs, these enterprises experienced a relative withdrawal of army officers and a complete withdrawal by the other services (Varas 1992).

Pinochet's political survival also affected appointments to SOEs. In 1980, Pinochet expressed an interest in privatizing large SOEs.[16] Having overwhelmingly won a constitutional referendum showing the public's support, Pinochet's survival in office seemed assured. However, prior to replacing military directors with civilians, economic depression in the early 1980s incited violent street protests and monthly riots that threatened Pinochet's survival. Weakened by economic crisis and protests, Pinochet knew that privatization of large SOEs only would aggravate military interests (Larroulet 1992a). Thus, he stayed with mostly military directors to maintain his rule. The decline in protests in 1985 showed that Pinochet had weathered the storm and reconsolidated his political position. With his survival no longer in doubt, Pinochet could pursue medium-term economic goals over short-term political ends.

Capitalismo popular also minimized opposition from workers in SOEs. As part of the privatization agreement, employees received between 5 and 10 percent of the stock of divested corporations, in exchange for an advance on their severance pay. The state offered stock from these corporations at low prices, with guarantees to repurchase stock once employees retired. The new private corporations also agreed to repay workers the value of their stock at the original purchase price if the stock fell in value (Larroulet 1992b, 13). In effect, workers purchased shares at below market prices, "without having to put up any money and without risking any loss" (Hachette and Lüders 1993, 61). These measures reduced resistance from managers and employees within SOEs (Baraona 1992; Larroulet 1992a).

Most firms that remained under state control held strong attachments to military interests. In addition to CODELCO, other firms including industries related to the sea (e.g., shipping and ports) received protection from privatization from the service chief of the navy, Almirante José Toribio Merino (Pérez de Arce 1992). While Almirante Merino backed 90 percent of the divestitures, he tied protection of the borders and sea traffic to national security interests (J. Fontaine 1992). The military also kept weapons manufacturing in the state's hands.

Argentina

Argentina's privatization experience contrasts sharply with Chile's. Like Chile, from the 1940s through the mid-1960s the size of the Argentine state and its influence in the economy grew. Unlike Chile, however, military regimes in Argentina privatized few state enterprises.

Following the military intervention in 1966, only a handful in Argentina considered policies to reduce the size or influence of the state in the economy a priority or even necessary. Indeed, the first economic team headed by Jorge Nestor Salimei initiated policies that expanded the state's role in the economy. As the economy worsened, Adalbert Krieger Vasena replaced Salimei as economic minister in late 1966. Although Krieger initiated policies to address weaknesses in the economy, privatization received minimal attention. Krieger (1992) maintained that the state produced goods efficiently and provided the population with reliable public services in the 1960s.[17] Enrique Folcini (1992), former secretary of finance, concurred with Krieger that economic policy makers did not perceive privatization as a vital issue.

Though the government sold off a few firms, Krieger and his policy-making team addressed rising public sector expenditures not through privatization, but by controlling wage growth in SOEs. In addition, few academics discussed the benefits of privatization. Privatization on the order of Chile in the 1970s and 1980s and Britain under Thatcher served as forerunners for privatization. The condition of public enterprises and economic ideas held by policy makers in Argentina and by most academics in the world reduced incentives for privatizing SOEs.

In March 1976, conditions emerged that prompted many policy makers to advocate state divestiture. From the early to mid-1970s, the state had expanded its role in the economy. Leaders under military and democratic rule attempted to attract more followers by offering jobs to loyal supporters and by distributing monies for public projects. These measures enlarged the state's positions in the economy and stretched the fiscal accounts of the state (Schenone 1991, 18–19). Under General Alejandro Lanusse, leader of the military government between 1971 and 1973, policy makers implemented industrial promotion programs that provided and guaranteed federal monies over a ten-year period for several provinces. Following the return of democratic rule in 1973, newly elected President Juan Perón and his party further expanded state participation in the economy, as did his successor, Isabel Perón. Of the one hundred largest companies in the 1970s, the state owned twenty of them (Schvarzer 1979, 46).

In addition to growth in the state sector, Chile's extensive privatizations drew the attention of Argentine policy makers. Chile's experience and concern over the burgeoning size of its state prodded many Argentine policy makers, including Economic Minister José Alfredo Martínez de Hoz, to proclaim their support for a "subsidiary" state and for sweeping privatization reforms (Memoria 1981; Martínez de Hoz 1981). Policy makers in the military *proceso*[18] (1976 through 1983) privatized peripheral areas of the economy and peripheral areas of the largest state enterprises.[19] Policy makers also returned one hundred twenty commercial or industrial companies to the private sector that the state had taken over in the past decade for various reasons (Martínez de Hoz 1990, 165). The largest SOEs, however, remained in the state's hands. The military also nationalized Italo, an electrical company, and Austral, an airline. In fact, the state sector diminished little between 1976 and 1978. Although the government announced that it had reduced public employment by one hundred thousand in 1979, the state accounted for about 50 percent of total investment and the gross public deficit remained at 40 percent of GDP (Smith 1980).

An important obstacle to extensive privatization came from the diversity of ideas held by economic policy makers. As discussed in chapter 4, the military appointed an economic team that satisfied various military factions. These appointments contributed to a policy-making team (especially in the first two years of military rule) that fought among themselves over the level of privatization (Solanet 1992). Martínez de Hoz and other policy makers disagreed with the ministers of commerce, industry, and energy over the intensity of neoliberal policies (Schvarzer 1983, 66). The lack of coherence among policy makers limited their commitment and resolve for privatization (Diz 1992; Estrada 1992).

Stiff resistance offered by officers also impeded privatization.[20] Based on their training, officers connected national security interests with control of the largest SOEs. More importantly, officers stood to lose great benefits if the state privatized the largest firms. Unlike Chile where the Chicago Boys pushed for marginal-cost pricing, the lack of coherence among Argentine policy makers hampered efforts to introduce self-financing mechanisms to keep down costs. As costs increased under state ownership, the state borrowed more from foreign creditors, which increased fiscal deficits and created opportunities for corruption in SOEs (Wehbe 1992).[21] The frequency of military coups in Argentina had enlightened officers about the benefits from managing SOEs (Teijeiro 1992).[22] These officers developed fiefdoms in SOEs and earned high salaries and trips abroad (Rock 1987, 371). As chart 5.3 indicates, of the three most important positions in each of the largest SOEs, officers held 67.9 percent of the positions from 1976 through 1980. In 1981 and 1982, the military controlled nearly 75 percent of the positions. It was not until 1983, during the democratic transition, that officers held fewer positions.

Military leaders also meted out top positions in SOEs to officers from the different military services to limit inter-service rivalries. The services staked out their claim to SOEs, dividing enterprises so that each service controlled one-third of all of the SOEs. The army took over the railroads and industries under Fabricaciones Militares (FM). The air force controlled the airlines and automobile and aluminum production, and the navy concerned itself with industries and areas related to the sea (Klein 1992; Poggi 1992). If, for example, the army had permitted privatization in its fiefdom, the navy would then have controlled a higher

Chart 5.3 Military Control in Argentine Public Enterprises, 1976–1983

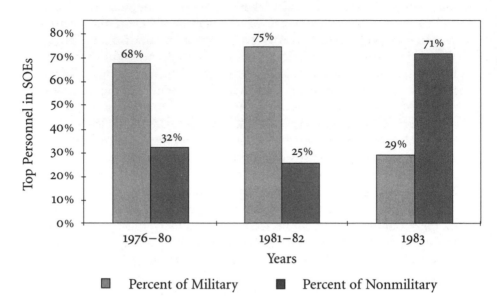

Source: Memorias of the enterprises.
Note: This chart includes the following seventeen enterprises: Aerolineas Argentinas, AGP, Aqua y Energia, DGFM, ELMA, Encotel, ENTel, Ferrocarriles, Gas, Hierro, Petro Bahia, Petro Mosconi, Petro Rio Tercero, SEGBA, Somisa, YCF, and YPF. The three positions reviewed are: president (or administrator general or interventor), vice president (or subadministrator general or subinterventor), and director (or vocal or manager). The government privatized most of the enterprises in 1991–92.

proportion of state enterprises. Competition and rivalry among the services, however, impeded this from happening.

These military rivalries hampered efforts to control deficits and privatize SOEs, especially in FM (Remmer 1991, 120). The military closely guarded industries under FM, as it served as a main source of financing for military projects. FM consisted of two types of activities. One part focused on mining and the extraction of primary materials. The other part manufactured arms, tanks, and armored vehicles (Martínez de Hoz 1991, 46). As the mining and extracting activities financed weaponry and armament production, officers opposed privatization of industries under FM.

Moreover, privatization or cutbacks in funding for FM would have threatened the careers of military engineers. Military engineers trained to work in FM industries. Privatization or reduced funding for FM jeopardized their professional horizon (Estevez 1992). As Martínez de Hoz (1990, 167) points out, "Some kind of professional distortion makes them (military engineers) more inclined to statism and more resentful of private enterprise. They themselves manage every important companies [*sic*] within the public sector." Officers thus hindered privatization for employment or corruption opportunities (López Murphy 1992).

In two cases, policy makers attempted to sell shares of stock from petrochemical firms (General Mosconi and Bahía Blanca) controlled by FM to the public. In both instances, officials from FM took action to block the sale of stock (Martínez de Hoz 1991, 47–48). Policy makers also planned to privatize Empresa Nacional de Telecomunicaciones (ENTel), Argentina's telephone company, but officers argued that privatization of ENTel threatened national security interests (Martínez de Hoz 1991, 76).

Officers in SOEs employed a fairly simple strategy to obstruct privatization. Officers in SOEs lobbied army secretaries, who in turn pressured the commanders in chief of the junta, the president, and the secretaries to the president (Solanet 1992). Officers also lobbied members of the Legislative Advisory Committee (LAC), composed of nine officers from the armed services, who could delay and change initiatives, such as privatization. Lobbyists from the military succeeded in gaining allies in the junta and the LAC to oppose privatization. As former junta leader Jorge Videla (1992) recalled, consensual agreement from members of the junta and from representatives of the LAC stalled efforts to privatize SOEs.

The fact that military leaders wanted to privatize SOEs leads to questions about the selection of nationalist officers to direct these enterprises. Threats to the leader's survival helps explain the choice of directors and the difficulties in changing directors. Policy makers, in fact, attempted to replace some military directors, as in the case of the director of SEGBA (Electrical Services of Greater Buenos Aires). But allies within the military backed directors who wished to retain their positions (Martínez de Hoz 1992). Military leaders in factionalized militaries feared any policy that aggravated tensions within the armed services, such as the replacement of officers.

Military factions also provided outlets for interest groups who opposed privatization or who wished to expand the role of the state in the economy. Some suppliers and contractors benefitted from subsidized prices on their inputs and from increased construction by the state under military rule. As Martínez de Hoz (1990, 166) contends, "Nobody wanted to lose anything when his or her interests were at stake, and lobbyists put up strong pressure." Beneficiaries of state ownership, including interest groups, lobbied sympathetic army secretaries, secretaries to the president, and economic ministers who impeded privatization.

Uruguay

Like Argentina and Chile, the role of the state in Uruguay expanded in the 1940s through 1960s. By the late 1960s, through its active ownership in enterprises and its use of economic instruments, such as price controls, the state controlled much of industry. High fiscal deficits, in part because of state ownership, marked the period preceding and at the inception of military rule.[23] One method for increasing fiscal revenues and reducing fiscal costs is to sell off SOEs. In spite of rising fiscal deficits and its awareness of privatizing reforms instituted by Chile, Uruguay sold off only a municipal bus company and an alcohol interest. SOEs in telecommunication, electricity, airlines, cement, and many other industries remained in the state's hands. In addition, the participation of the state in the economy increased by 17 percent in real terms between 1973 and 1978 (Lusiardo Aznarez 1981).

Lack of demand for selling SOEs created one obstacle to privatizing. As shown in chapter 4, neoliberal economists held few economic policy-making positions. In fact, officers with little basic training in economics or finance occupied prominent positions within the ministries and state banks commonly associated with economic policy making. Most officers, including those who held top positions in economic policy making, believed in a philosophy identified with former President José Batlle y Ordóñez, as did the general population. The philosophy of Batlle y Ordóñez feared foreign ownership and investment, and attached a high regard to public ownership and investment. *Batllistas* asserted that the state should take a prominent role in the managing and directing of the most important industries including, electricity, meatpacking, telecommunications, cement, railroads, and petroleum refining (Handelman 1981b, 241).

Generations grew up with Batlle's values and perceived the state in a paternalistic sense, as something that protected them (Anichini 1992). Military officers also supported state ownership and protection from foreign interests (Peirano 1992). General Pedro Aranco (1992), former director of the state planning office (SEPLACODI) concurred, stating the difficulty in trying to compete with "international monsters," a reference to competition from international airlines. Similarly, a former senator who served as the finance and economic minister six months prior to the military intervention, said that officers could not conceive of privatization and especially of foreign ownership, as this would be like "taking money from Uruguayan pockets" (Forteza 1992).

General Abdón Raimúndez, president of the Banco de la República in the 1970s, the agency along with the Banco Central that controlled the finances of SOEs, rallied against privatization. Raimúndez possessed the ability to give credit lavishly or sparingly to enterprises in the public and private sector based on his own personal and often peculiar interests (Díaz 1992). As an example of his peculiar interests, General Raimúndez stopped imports from some countries because he felt that the countries had harmed Uruguay in the past. Most other policy makers backed Raimúndez and opposed privatizing SOEs.[24]

Despite strong opposition, Végh tried to privatize meatpacking, cement manufacturing, and petroleum refining. Since Uruguayan business interests did not have sufficient capital, foreign investors and/or multinational corporations would have acquired assets in these enterprises (Handelman 1981b, 251). Végh's plans to privatize SOEs and to cultivate foreign investors, however, ran counter to General Raimúndez and others in the armed forces (R. Kaufman 1979, 183). Végh (1992a) contended that efforts to privatize would have resulted in a big fight that would have hampered other neoliberal reforms. Instead, Végh fought for liberalization of foreign exchange, of financial markets, and a greater opening of the economy—policies that appeared less contentious and battles he had a greater chance of winning. The lack of demand for privatization from a high proportion of economic policy makers inhibited the privatizing of SOEs.

A second obstacle to privatization emerged from the benefactors of SOEs—the personnel serving in the highest positions of SOEs.[25] Each armed service carved out its own fiefdom inside the SOEs, with officers from each service holding the highest positions (Gillespie 1991, 55). As chart 5.4 indicates, officers held 49.0 percent of the highest positions in SOEs from 1973 through 1976 and 61.1 percent from 1977 through 1982, when the military took greater control of all parts of the state. In 1983–84, the proportion of officers in SOEs declined sharply as the democratic transition began.

Chart 5.4   Military Control in Uruguayan Public Enterprises, 1973–1984

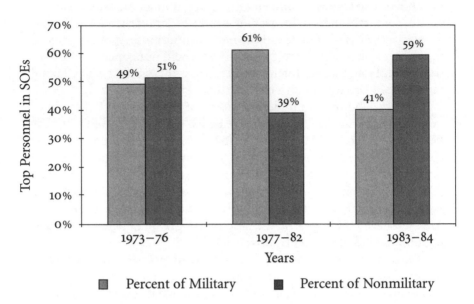

Source: Memorias of the enterprises.
Note: This chart includes the following nine enterprises: AFE, Ancap, ANP, ANTel, BHU, BSE, OSE, Pluna, and UTE. The three positions reviewed are: president (or administrator general or interventor), vice president (or subadministrator general or subinterventor), and director (or vocal or manager).

Officers working in these enterprises collected many benefits, including expensive cars and luxurious homes. The sight of military directors living lavish lifestyles is odd since most Uruguayan officers came from lower- or lower-middle-class backgrounds and received terrible salaries (Moore 1978).[26] Officers needed high salaries and opportunities for corrupt activities in SOEs if they wanted to live at such an exalted level. To maintain their new wealth, officers in SOEs lobbied many in Uruguay's collegial executive system, including the service chiefs and the president. Officers also consulted with the Junta de Oficiales Generales, made up of the twenty-one top generals, who the service chiefs and the president conferred with before making important decisions. These groups provided officers with several access points to derail privatization.

Summary

Neoliberal economists in economic policy-making positions are a necessary factor for explaining privatization of SOEs under military rule. Based on their commitment to reducing the size of the state in the economy, neoliberal economists increase the demand to privatize SOEs. For all-encompassing privatization of SOEs to occur, however, we also need to consider resistance to privatization, or the supply side of the equation. This chapter showed that military leaders appointed officers to top positions in SOEs in an effort to avoid military counter-coups and to consolidate power. The revenues from SOEs compelled officers to lobby against privatization.

Opportunities to privatize SOEs increased when few officers worked in SOEs. Under military rule, the appointment of civilians for SOEs reflected their expertise to direct firms. Given their expertise, civilian directors expected to retain their positions, even if the state privatized their firms. In addition, given their limited potential for mobilizing forces to commit a counter-coup compared to officers, civilians posed a lower threat to the survival of military leaders and had less capacity to prevent privatization of SOEs.

In comparisons of the Southern Cone, Chile suggested that strong demand elicited by neoliberal economists stimulated privatization of many SOEs in the 1970s. Officers working in the largest SOEs, however, blocked further privatization. Once Pinochet had consolidated his political position, he appointed civilian directors who contributed to the sell-off of most of Chile's largest SOEs in the mid-1980s. In Argentina and Uruguay, neoliberal economists held fewer economic policy-making positions relative to Chile, which reduced demand for privatization of SOEs. In addition, officers held a high proportion of top positions in SOEs and earned substantial benefits from their appointments. As such, officers lobbied junta members and fellow officers in order to retain their positions and prevent privatization.

Epilogue: Privatization under Democracy

The importance of neoliberal economists and civilian directors in SOEs has implications for privatization under democracy. In Argentina, privatization of SOEs began in 1989, with the majority of privatizations occurring after 1990. Not coincidentally, the proportion of neoliberal economists in economic policy-making positions jumped dramatically following Domingo Cavallo's appointment as economic minister in January 1991 (see chart 7.1). As Cavallo (1992, 23) argues, "[The] coherence of views within the economic policy team was a precondition for the comprehensive reform that the country needed."

Resistance to privatization also decreased in Argentina in the late 1980s.[27] Following his electoral victory, President Carlos Menem used his first two years in office to replace directors of SOEs with interventors, whose job was to prepare SOEs for privatization. Menem advocated privatization from the start, and he intended to carry out the "reform of the state," which included the privatization of almost all SOEs (Smith 1991, 54). Through his appointment of persons sympathetic to state sell-offs, and his choice of neoliberal economists, President Menem engineered extensive privatization reforms in the early 1990s. The effects of two hyperinflations also made Argentines more receptive to reform. In addition, deterioration in the quality of service of SOEs changed public sentiment toward privatization. While labor unions and state employees continued to oppose privatization, many in the private sector as well as public service customers vented their frustration over the declining quality of service.

In Uruguay, while former President Luis Alberto Lacalle backed efforts to reform the economy, including privatizing some of the largest SOEs, his policy-making team held a less strong commitment to privatization.[28] Uruguay's electoral system promotes cabinet appointments that appeal to interests from factions within the party, and sometimes members of the factions of the opposition parties. Satisfying various factions led to the appointment of few economists, which limited demand for privatization (see chart 7.4). Moreover, politicians and the public in Uruguay resisted efforts to privatize. Leaders under democratic rule historically have used directorships in SOEs to reward loyal supporters from the two main parties. Under the system of lemas (parties) and sublemas (factions within each party), intense competition exists between parties and factions within parties to garner as many votes as possible. It is not only important for the party to receive the highest proportion of the vote, but it is also critical that the faction within the party receives the most votes. Patronage, such as providing employment for loyal party officials in SOEs, is a common means for attracting votes for factions within each party (McDonald and Ruhl 1989, 98). The need for distributing benefits to many factions leads members from each party and within the parties to oppose privatization of SOEs.

In addition, Uruguay introduced coparticipation in SOEs in 1952, where seats on the boards of directors of SOEs are distributed among the majority and minority parties in a ratio of three to two (Finch 1981, 218). Even if the president advocates privatization, the executive controls a maximum of three seats. The president has no control over two persons who can lobby members of the legislature to block privatization. Alternatively, board members can mobilize employees from the enterprise to be privatized or the rank-and-file of unions, which represent other state employees who can protest attempts to privatize. The electoral system also enables voters to use referendums, as they did in 1992, to voice their displeasure of privatization (Mainhard 1992, 24). Low demand for privatization from economic policy makers and strong resistance from politicians and the public impeded efforts to privatize SOEs.

SIX

The Professionalization of Economists

We had no experience, China had no experts, the minister himself was an outsider, so we had to copy from foreign countries.
—Mao Tse Tung[1]

The people who are architects of economic reform all over the world are increasingly Ph.D. economists with fancy American training.
—Lawrence Summers, former U. S. Secretary of the Treasury[2]

The previous chapter showed that neoliberal economists affect demand for privatization. However, the policy preferences of neoliberals are not held universally by all economists. In fact, some economists build a whole research agenda, not to mention career, around opposing market-oriented reforms. In this chapter, we construct a comparative framework to explain differences among economists in their backing of neoliberal policies. Several similarities among the Southern Cone cases support such comparisons. First, many students in Argentina, Chile, and Uruguay studied economics in local universities, with most of the economics faculty at these universities favoring structuralist policies in the 1950s and 1960s. These countries, as we know, also operated for many years under military rule. In addition, the United States government, private foundations, and others provided scholarships for students in all three to study abroad. Despite these similarities, since the 1950s, the main ideas held in their economics professions have varied.

This chapter analyzes the interactions between political institutions in the United States and Latin America, and how these interactions affect the spread of economic paradigms in economics professions. Through their financing of Latin American graduate education, U. S. governmental and private agencies influenced the training of Latin American economists.[3] The first section provides a brief historical overview of Latin America's economics profession and the relatively late arrival of specialized economics training to the region. The second section builds on international arguments that emphasize economic assistance programs sponsored by U. S. government agencies and foundations to understand differences in the professions. It also examines the effect of domestic considerations on demand for economists trained abroad. Employment opportunities for U. S.-educated economists in their home countries affect whether future economists are trained by neoliberals or not. The concluding section compares the professions in Argentina, Chile, and Uruguay to stress the earlier and higher degree of U. S. influence in Chile relative to the others, and the recent growth of U. S. influence in Argentina.

History of the Economics Profession in Latin America

Economics as a specialized profession developed fairly late in Latin America. Growing out of the fields of accounting, commerce, and law, the profession formed near the beginning of the twentieth century. The formal teaching of economic sciences, however, only dates to the mid-1950s. Before this time, economics studies focused on "the nature of 'political economy' and came mostly within the province of historians, lawyers, public officials, politicians, or simply of cultured persons who were self-taught through reading the classical European texts" (Venezian 1982, 190). Latin American universities offered few economics courses, and most dealt with subjects that included economic thought, economic history, and political economy. Rarely did economics students engage in debates over narrow analytical issues. Instead, these students took a holistic approach to the study of economic problems that considered issues from a social, political, historical, and religious bent. As Venezian (1982, 191) writes, "The teaching of economics was very descriptive: learning current economic theories for general knowledge, rather than for their value as analytical tools for problem solving and policy purposes."

The lack of rigorous training meant that Latin American countries usually relied on technical assistance from "money doctors," i.e., foreign economists, or visiting professors mainly from the United States (Hirschman 1963, 165). These money doctors adhered to liberal doctrines of a limited state and notions of comparative advantage to promote economic prosperity. Latin American governments also "employed foreign advisers to improve their access to loans at reasonable rates" (Drake 1994, xiv). Their reputations as devout advocates of the free market certified the creditworthiness of Latin American administrations (Rosenberg and Rosenberg 1994, 71–73). Developed countries themselves also sent well-known money doctors, including Edwin Kemmerer and his students and friends, as security that Latin American officials adopted policies to help repay their debts (Kemmerer 1993; Seidel 1994, 89).

World economic disorder in the early 1930s tarnished the reputations of money doctors. The disruption of established patterns of trade because of the Great Depression and its precursor, World War I, worked against upholding liberal doctrine among many Latin American groups. Politicians, businessmen, military and labor leaders, and even some export-oriented landowners favored a break away from open-market policies and toward an activist and protectionist state. No longer reliant on the advice of money doctors, Latin America turned to members of its own tiny economics profession for policy guidance. Mirroring societal views, Latin American economists also shifted their economic beliefs from liberalism to protectionism.

As economics matured into a full-fledged profession in Latin America in the 1950s, new economics students advocated protectionist and nationalist policies popularized in the 1930s and favored by their faculty.[4] Most in the profession, including members of the United Nations' Economic Commission for Latin America (ECLA),[5] espoused a variant of structuralism, a school of economic thought highly popular in Europe. Based on the ideas of John Maynard Keynes, structuralists advocated state intervention and controls over the economy to stimulate demand and promote full employment. Latin America's version of structuralism held close ties to ECLA. Under the leadership of Argentine economist Raúl Prebisch, ECLA's main doctrine divided the world's economic system into an industrial center in the developed world and primary-product export periphery in the developing world. In this division, the developing world exported raw materials that experienced declining terms of trade and erratic prices relative to the industrial goods and expensive equipment they imported. ECLA theorists proposed a solution to this imbalance by having the state promote the domestic manufacture of higher-value-added, industrialized goods.[6] Through the propping up of protectionist barriers and generous subsidies to industrial sectors, the state intended to use import substituting industrialization (ISI) to improve its terms of trade and promote economic development. The doctrine also called for agrarian reforms and other measures to improve income distribution (Iglesias 1992, 11).

ECLA's development ideology, establishment of social and agrarian reform goals, definition of an industrial strategy based on ISI, and use of planning techniques resonated with most Latin American policy makers (Boeninger 1982, 264). Coming on the heels of market closing and the drying up of foreign loans as a result of World Wars I and II and the Great Depression, Latin American politicians and their policy makers favored an economic strategy that claimed to promote economic development but that protected their economy from world-market vicissitudes.[7]

Beyond its guiding economic development ideologies, ECLA developed close affiliations with nascent economics departments of most Latin American universities. In fact, ECLA officials taught courses at universities. Latin American economists also attended lectures and training seminars sponsored by ECLA that reinforced the structuralist view (Bruce 1980, 3).[8] ECLA also offered advisory missions to governments and research publications that propagated economic heterodoxy (Montecinos and Markoff 2001).

Despite the dominance of structuralism in Latin America's economics profession, rival economics schools of thought also existed. Neoliberalism represented the main intellectual rival for structuralism.[9] Although less popular in Latin America in the 1950s and 1960s, neoliberalism had many sponsors in the United States. Neoliberals espoused free trade and production and development based on comparative advantage to promote economic growth.[10] Rather than the state manufacturing goods itself or subsidizing inefficient producers, neoliberals contended that market mechanisms should determine which goods are produced. In addition, the state should allow the market to decide wealth considerations and not attempt to redistribute income.[11]

During the 1950s, private foundations, international organizations, and U.S. government agencies provided scholarships and other financial means to introduce neoliberalism into Latin American universities (Venezian 1982, 193). Strongly resisted by most economists in the region, neoliberalism slowly gained proponents in the profession. In fact, as Latin American economies struggled, in part because of economic policies backed by structuralist and ECLA economists in the 1970s, neoliberal economic theory attracted more followers.[12]

The experiences of Argentina, Chile, and Uruguay over the past half century reflect the changes in Latin America's economics profession. In these countries, most economists identified themselves with structuralism from the 1940s through the 1960s. Since the 1970s, neoliberal ideas have made inroads in the professions in all three. But there are variations among the countries in the level and timing of their support for neoliberalism. In Chile, the economics profession's support for neoliberal ideas arrived much earlier than in the others and the intensity of support reached much higher levels. The profession in Argentina grew to favor neoliberal ideas later than in Chile, but these ideas resonate in most economic discussions today. In Uruguay, many in its profession continue to sympathize with structuralism. Why do Latin America's economics professions vary in their support for neoliberalism?

The Rise of Neoliberalism in Latin America's Economics Professions

Several studies have attempted to explain the variations in economics professions. Some works focus the inquiry on economic factors. Analysts assert that the more serious the economic problems experienced under structuralist policies, the greater the likelihood that the profession would shift toward neoliberalism. Economic problems caused by ISI and other policies that expanded the state led a "consensus" of economists to reconsider their beliefs about economic development (Williamson 1994). According to Iglesias (1992, 52), "In recent years a considerable degree of consensus has been achieved in Latin America concerning the origins and solutions to the crisis it experienced in the eighties, a consensus that emerged from the lessons the Latin American countries learned at so high a cost." Although poor economic results converted some structuralists to back market-oriented policies, economic performance does not fully explain the variation among the cases. For instance, Argentina, Chile, and Uruguay experienced severe economic shocks in the early 1970s, but the profession changed only slightly in Argentina and Uruguay in these years, while most Chilean economists came to espouse neoliberal thought. Moreover, the ideas held by economists in Argentina and Uruguay began to shift in the late 1970s and 1980s, not when the economic difficulties first appeared.

Alternatively, others argue that domestic interest groups engineered the shift toward neoliberalism in the economics profession. Business groups, aware that economists trained abroad played a growing role in their firms, provided monies for students to earn graduate degrees in economics. These businesses also sponsored private educational institutes that favored market-oriented policies. Although some businesses hired economists trained abroad, and a few sponsored private institutes, most firms from the 1940s through 1970s favored protection and state subsidies for their industries (Dornbusch and Edwards, 1991). The private sector rarely supported neoliberal economists in these years, as most operated under an incentive structure based on closed markets and state protection. It is only since the 1980s that the private sector tends to advocate neoliberalism. Pluralist arguments also leave unexplained why Chile's profession changed earlier than the others.

Others contend that international incentives from U. S. government agencies and private foundations explain the growing influence of neoliberalism in Latin America's economics profession. Valdés (1995) contends that the earlier conversion of Chilean economists to neoliberalism resulted from a well-coordinated socialization effort by the U. S. government, the Department of Economics at the University of Chicago, and the Universidad Católica of Chile to challenge ECLA's supremacy in Latin America. As part of an agreement between the University of Chicago and Universidad Católica, Chilean students received graduate training and immersion in free-market philosophies at the University of Chicago. Following the completion of their studies, many Chileans returned as professors at Chilean universities to train another generation of economists in their way of thought.

The influence of international actors and socialization differentiates the training of economists. International actors including the International Cooperation Administration (ICA), its successor, the Agency for International Development (AID), along with the Ford, Fulbright, and Rockefeller Foundations granted varying amounts of financial resources for students to complete their advanced studies in the United States. Competition with Santiago-based ECLA to lessen support for structuralism in the region strongly influenced the allocation of more U. S. financial resources to Chile than to the other countries.

However, international training by itself does not explain some differences in the economics profession. In Argentina, for example, despite many of its economists having studied in the United States, the profession remained resistant to neoliberal ideas in the 1960s and 1970s. Part of the explanation for the resistance is that more than a few U. S.-trained economists failed to find work in universities at home, let alone returned to their homelands.

Argentina's experience compels a consideration of domestic factors, such as employment prospects for economists in their home countries. If U. S.-trained economists are not able to obtain full-time academic positions, they may accept fairly lucrative jobs from international organizations headquartered abroad, which affects their ability to socialize future generations of economists. Without these U. S.-trained economists, economics students are likely to take courses from professors who are less sympathetic to neoliberal theory and who assign course readings that bolster their own views. Students also receive less encouragement to study in the United States. As Boeninger (1982, 273) writes, "The perception of belonging to the same community of shared ideology, basic values, or religion generates a trust that facilitates transfer of products of social sciences from producers to users." In the end, if U. S.-trained economists decide not to return to their country, this inhibits the creation of a collegial or teamlike atmosphere among faculty members or economists toward neoliberal ideas.

Empirical Cases

The perception of growing U. S. influence in Latin America's economics profession merits a closer scrutiny of the professions in Argentina, Chile, and Uruguay. The following sections compare the effect of international donors on the development of coherent beliefs among economists. They consider whether U. S.-trained economists are returning to their home countries, and if those economists are finding academic positions that will enable them to train another generation of economists with ideas similar to their own.

Chile

From late in the nineteenth century until the mid-1950s, foreign experts played critical roles at crisis points in Chile (Hirschman 1963, ch. 3). From French economist Jean Gustave Courcelle-Seneuilin, to Edwin Kemmerer in the 1920s, to the Klein-Saks Mission in the 1950s, foreign experts provided Chile with economic advice.[13] In the mid-1950s, an agreement signed between the University of Chicago and Universidad

Católica in Santiago changed and enlarged the role of foreign experts in Chile and affected Chile's economics profession.

In the early 1950s, structuralists with a leftist orientation dominated the debate on development in Chile. At the prestigious Universidad de Chile, most faculty members in the economics department favored state intervention. ECLA, founded in 1948 and based in Santiago, also advocated greater state intervention and planning in the economy. Staff members at ECLA often served as part-time faculty for the Universidad de Chile and further influenced the university's School of Economics away from free-market dogma (Puryear 1994, 16).

The domination of Chile's economics profession by leftist economists, however, motivated U. S. officials to facilitate an agreement between the University of Chicago and Universidad Católica.[14] Following the onslaught of the Cold War, U. S. officials feared the spread of communism especially through universities. In an effort to stem potential support for communism, the U. S. created economic programs in the Third World that promoted economic development, political stability, and strengthened non-Communist forces (Packenham 1973, 109). U. S. officials used economic programs and foreign aid to advance its foreign policy objectives.

The agreement between the University of Chicago and Universidad Católica appeared to meet its foreign policy goals. Chile sent its best economics students to earn their graduate training in Chicago, in an intellectual atmosphere highly averse to Marxist economic teachings. Following the completion of their studies, these students returned to Chile as professors whose mission was to train a new generation of students in free-market economics.

The University of Chicago and Universidad Católica reached this agreement through the auspices of the U. S.'s International Cooperation Administration (ICA) and its Point Four Program,[15] precursor to the Agency for International Development (AID). According to Albion Patterson (1995), director of the ICA in Chile from 1953 through 1957, the idea for a technical assistance program that would send economists to the University of Chicago evolved through his conversations with Theodore Schultz, then chairman of the economics department at Chicago.

During the 1940s, Patterson worked in Paraguay, where he found almost no statistics on agriculture, health, and other social areas. Patterson recognized the importance of having basic research performed for improving agricultural performance. Once he arrived in Santiago in the early 1950s, Patterson met Schultz, who had recently received an $875,000 grant from the National Planning Association's Technical Assistance to Latin America Program to do research.[16] During their meetings, Schultz informed Patterson about the important role management, administration, and a thorough understanding of economics played in increasing national incomes (Flood 1979, 2). Schultz and his colleagues at Chicago had developed theories on human capital that demonstrated the benefits of education and training for economic growth and development. Schultz wanted to use Chile as a laboratory to test his theories.[17]

Following their discussions, Patterson proposed a joint project with the Universidad de Chile that would send Chilean students to earn advanced degrees at the University of Chicago. During his meetings with the rector of the Universidad, Juan Gómez Millas, however, Patterson learned that most of the economics faculty of the Universidad de Chile opposed the program (Patterson 1995). Chicago's reputation as staunch supporters of the free market clashed with the mostly leftist economics faculty at the Universidad de Chile, which inhibited acceptance for an agreement (Valdés 1989, 156–57).

The rector of the Universidad Católica, Monsignor Alfredo Silva Santiago, by contrast, solicited U. S. officials to develop programs with his university. Silva Santiago knew that through the funding of the ICA's "Food for Peace" program called Public Law 480—part of the U. S.'s Agricultural Assistance Act—Chile had accumulated large reserves.[18] Silva Santiago wanted to use these reserves to create a competitive economics department at the Universidad Católica (Valdés 1989, 58, 158–59).

After subsequent meetings with the monsignor, Patterson arranged a meeting between the University of Chicago and Universidad Católica. In June 1955, four members of the economics faculty from the University of Chicago, Theodore Schultz, Earl Hamilton, Simon Rottenberg, and Arnold Harberger, arrived in Santiago to meet with representatives from the Católica. On March 29–30, 1956, the two sides signed an agreement called Project Chile. The most important parts of the agreement included the recruitment of Chilean students for the University of Chicago's graduate program in economics and the assigning of faculty members from the University of Chicago to conduct research at the Católica (Hojman 1993, 23). As a result of the agreement, Chile sent students to Chicago from 1956 through 1964.

The ICA/AID provided initial resources to finance the education of students in Chicago. It allotted nearly one million dollars from 1956 through 1964 to Chilean graduate students (see table 6.1 for AID's financing

Table 6.1   Assistance and Grants from AID to Latin America, 1961–1970
Value as of June 30, 1970 (in $U.S. millions)

Year	Argentina	Chile	Uruguay
1961	0.8	22.9	0.1
1962	2.0	2.4	0.3
1963	2.9	5.4	1.9
1964	1.3	2.9	0.8
1965	1.5	2.5	0.9
1966	1.5	2.8	0.8
1967	1.3	2.8	1.6
1968	1.8	2.9	1.2
1969	1.8	2.7	1.3
1970	0.9	2.9	1.5

Source: Unión Panamericana (1972).

from 1961 through 1970). Additional funding for the program and for the Universidad de Chile came from the Ford and Rockefeller Foundations and the Organization of American States (OAS) (Puryear 1994, 16–17).

During its eight years in operation, Project Chile sent thirty students to Chicago (P. Silva 1991, 389). Once they arrived in Chicago, the Chileans quickly learned the importance of the free market for economic development (Pion-Berlin 1986, 320).[19] These students also developed cohort and social ties through the exchange program, which intensified the coherence of their economic ideas (Hecht Oppenheim 1993, 148). Having spent two years in courses that stressed the benefits of free-market economics, and having many occasions to interact with professors in formal and informal settings on the importance of free-trade policies and private ownership, most of these students devoutly espoused monetarism.[20]

After completing their studies in Chicago, more than a few of the Chileans returned to work as professors at the Universidad Católica. Unlike people in other countries, Chileans discovered many advantages to working in academia. For one, Chilean universities paid their faculties high-enough salaries so that they could earn a living without having to seek additional employment. Moreover, the political situation in Chile made employment in the universities attractive. Universities provided a professional atmosphere, largely free from governmental interference, where professors could do research and teach regardless of which party was in power. As Ascher (1975, 67) points out, "Because the universities [in Chile] were largely free from governmental interference and immune from external political manipulations, they were attractive sites for highly qualified technical professionals interested in political economy."

Once they returned as professors, these Chicago Boys taught Chilean undergraduates the same neoliberal ideas that they had learned in Chicago. Chicago Boys came to dominate the Católica almost as soon as they returned, with Sergio de Castro, one of the first students recruited into the program, taking over as dean of the economics faculty in 1965. In the mid-1960s, the Católica developed an economics program with "a well-trained faculty, a modern curriculum, and a growing capacity for carrying out research" (Puryear 1994, 16).

In addition to recruiting students, the University of Chicago created the Centro de Investigaciones Económicas at the Universidad Católica in 1956. Professors from Chicago conducted research at the Centro to demonstrate current research methods. Chicago designated three members of its faculty to serve at the Centro and to maintain responsibility over the program for a period of two years. Two additional faculty members worked in Chile but for shorter periods. Money accumulated in the Public Law 480 account helped to finance the Centro (Harberger 1995).

Even though funding for Project Chile dried up in 1964, the University of Chicago tapped into new resources that sustained the recruitment of Chilean students and built the University of Chicago's Latin American curriculum. Monies from the Ford Foundation, Organization of American States (OAS), and the planning ministry (ODEPLAN) and central bank in Chile financed the studies of Chilean students. The Ford Foundation also donated $750,000 over a ten-year period in 1965 to fund the Center for Latin American Economic Research at the University of Chicago.

The students who arrived in Chicago in the mid-1960s through 1970s also met the criteria of the original designers of Project Chile. Chicago alumni who worked at the Universidad Católica recommended Chilean candidates to study in Chicago, with economic orientations similar to their own being a consideration (Valdés 1989, 193). Using similar economic beliefs as criteria for entrance into the program provided some guarantee that the second generation of Chilean students embraced the theories that they learned in Chicago.

More than 150 students from Chile received their training in Chicago, some 30 to 50 of them as part of the exchange program through the early 1970s (Stenzel 1988, 332). The relationship with Chicago continued for at least three decades, with sponsorship coming from ICA/AID, the Ford and Rockefeller Foundations, and the OAS. In essence, once the program started, the flow of Chilean students never ceased (Harberger 1995).

Though most of the Chilean graduate students attended the University of Chicago, some studied at Columbia University, Harvard University, and M. I. T. While the ideological conviction toward neoliberal theory may not have been as strong as in Chicago, students at these other universities also found most of their professors questioning Keynesian policies. As former Chicago student Martin Costabal (1992) stated, while students trained at Chicago, M. I. T., and other universities in the U. S. might differ on narrow issues related to exchange rate policy, for example, they all held the same fundamental views.

In addition to academic positions, Chicago students discovered other job opportunities in Chile. Agustín Edwards, entrepreneur and publisher of the daily newspaper *El Mercurio*, and an early proponent of orthodox policies, created openings for economists returning from Chicago on the "influential Economic Page in *El Mercurio*" (O'Brien 1985, 146).[21] Other business owners followed and by the 1970s and 1980s some of the largest businesses in Chile employed foreign-trained economists in important positions in their companies or paid for their services as consultants (Hecht Oppenheim 1993, 131). Economists thus found employment opportunities not only in existing and newly created institutes and universities,[22] but also in business and finance.

Of course, not all economists in Chile subscribed to the strict neoliberal policies of the Chicago Boys. Indeed, most economists at ECLA, the Universidad de Chile, and elsewhere strongly rejected market-oriented policies in the 1950s. Many of these faculty members had earned advanced degrees in Europe and some had studied in East Coast universities in the United States in the 1940s and early 1950s, where Keynesianism had many followers. When the Chicago Boys returned to Chile in the 1960s, this created a polarized economics profession with Chicago Boys dominating the Católica and structuralists holding positions at other universities. Polarization, though, did not prevent some Chicago Boys from finding work at the Universidad de Chile, where they proceeded to indoctrinate students with their own ideas (Montecinos 1988, 422). Moreover, the split in the profession may have led the Chicago Boys to an "ideological escalation" of their views as they competed with their rivals.[23]

The military coup in 1973 strengthened the coherence of the economics profession. Following the coup, the military installed interventors in administrative positions at the universities. These interventors removed many leftists from the economics departments at Chilean universities, with others leaving out of sympathy for their colleagues. In fact, Spooner (1999, 89–90) claims that many of the left-wing professors at the University of Chile "had either been arrested or taken refuge. And right-wing academics were urging that remaining leftists on the faculty be fired, or, more ominously, that the military intervene and put the University of Chile under its administration." The inflow of a second generation of economists from Chicago made it easy to fill these slots.[24] In little time, Chicago Boys dominated the economics faculty at the Universidad de Chile.

Some opposition economists, in turn, created the think tank Corporación de Investigaciones Económicas para Latinoamérica (CIEPLAN) in 1975. While these economists wrote prolifically on their opposition to neoliberal economic policies, deep divisions in ideas did not separate the economists in Chile in the 1970s and 1980s. Based on a survey of articles in the principal academic journals, economists used the same research methods and techniques of analysis (Hojman 1993, 29). More importantly, economists at CIEPLAN magnified their differences with the Chicago Boys from an economic standpoint because the military government tolerated no other form of opposition (Ffrench-Davis 1992).

Argentina

The experience of Argentina's economic profession differs markedly from Chile's. Unlike Chile, full-scale economics training began much later in Argentina. Prior to the 1950s, the Universidad Nacional de Buenos Aires (UBA) created a doctorate in economic science in 1913 with a shorter course in accounting. For almost half a century, however, the doctorate covered only two courses in economics. Most economics students first took courses in accounting and then completed some courses in economics before earning their economics license. With few exceptions, Argentina had no "well-organized economic research groups using sophisticated techniques and modern equipment" (Dagnino Pastore 1989, 196).[25]

In the mid-1950s, the economics profession witnessed changes. In 1956 and 1957, as ECLA carried out a mission to examine Argentina's economy, it also sponsored a course in economics. This prompted UBA to offer sixteen new courses in economics and to create an economics department separate from accounting (Berlinsky 1994). New universities also emerged that offered courses in economics. This expansion of economics courses piqued interest in students to earn advanced economics degrees (Dagnino Pastore 1988, 3).

More changes in the economics profession occurred in the early 1960s. In an effort to reproduce Project Chile in other countries, AID created Project Cuyo in Argentina. With some of the same actors responsible for the agreement with Chile, Professor Arnold Harberger of the University of Chicago negotiated with Dr. Corti Videla, dean of the economics faculty at the Universidad Nacional de Cuyo in Mendoza, to establish a scholarly exchange program. The agreement, signed in 1961, included not only the Universidad de Cuyo and University of Chicago, but also the Universidad Católica in Chile.

As part of the agreement, which began in 1962 and ended in 1967, AID granted scholarships to twenty-seven Argentines to study in Chicago (Valdés 1989, 263). In addition, professors from the Universidad Católica in Santiago, who had studied in Chicago, arrived at Universidad de Cuyo to teach courses. Their commitment to Chicago ideas made them well suited to create a curriculum modeled after the University of Chicago. A "Chicago" curriculum also developed at the Universidad de Tucumán through the backing of Adolfo Diz, a former Chicago student. Moreover, the Ford Foundation, Fulbright Commission, OAS, and Rotary Club provided scholarships for Argentine economics students to study abroad (Sturzenegger 1994).

However, the results of these exchange programs differed from those in Chile. For one, AID provided less funding for Argentina than Chile, which impeded graduate study in the U.S. (see table 6.1). For another, the location of the universities influenced the exchange program. In Chile, once students completed their education at Chicago, they returned to Santiago—to the most favored city in the country—and found jobs at the best universities. In Argentina, around fifty students left the country for training in economics, but few returned. Because of the very low salaries at Argentine universities, many students chose to work abroad. Prior to 1989, a full-time professor at UBA might earn as little as $250 a month (Pessino 1994). These low salaries forced faculty members to hold down other jobs to supplement their income (García de Fanelli 1995, 6). Moreover, Buenos

Aires did not have many academic jobs. Academic positions could be found in such places as Mendoza and Tucumán, cities not as popular for professors who wanted the excitement of Buenos Aires.[26]

The disadvantages of university employment prompted many of the best Argentine students to accept positions abroad with international agencies such as the World Bank and International Monetary Fund. Others returned to Argentina to work in the private sector, in private consulting firms, or in the Consejo Nacional de Desarrollo (National Development Council) (De Pablo 1994). This left Argentina with fewer economists in Argentina's universities relative to Chile, and with less opportunity to train a new generation of neoliberal economists.

Fewer U.S.-trained economists also affected the coherence of ideas held by Argentine economists. In a study conducted by economist Juan Carlos de Pablo (1977), he asked questions fundamental to economic development to important economists in Argentina. The great differences in responses offered by these economists suggest the lack of congruence in Argentina's economic profession relative to Chile in the 1970s.

Other obstacles worked against the development of a consensus around neoliberal ideas in Argentina. In the early 1960s, Chicago-trained economists from Chile, sent to Mendoza as faculty members, had not received warm receptions from their colleagues at the Universidad de Cuyo. Ideological and personal disputes raged between Chilean and Argentine faculty members. These disputes interfered with the development of a coherent message and curriculum for economic students at Cuyo. Cuyo's remote location also limited its importance in national terms (Valdés 1989, 263).

Students at UBA also appeared unreceptive to neoliberal ideas. For instance, when AID and the Ford Foundation provided funds to send visiting scholars from Columbia University to UBA, students at UBA insisted on leftist scholars (Patterson 1995). Most professors at UBA and Universidad Católica in Buenos Aires also advocated structuralist views identified with Raúl Prebisch from the 1960s through the 1980s, in part because of Prebisch's personal influence (Canitrot 1994). Until the late 1970s, U.S. universities had little influence in Buenos Aires (Heyman 1994).

In the late 1970s and 1980s, however, changes occurred that brought about the founding of new institutes and universities more supportive of neoliberal policies. Spurred on by rising inflation in the mid-1970s, the private sector and government developed a growing interest in the role of economists (López Murphy 1992). These pressures prompted the opening of elite private institutes and universities in business and economics in the late 1970s and 1980s to meet the rising demand for economists and MBA students in the central bank and private sector (Rodríguez 1994).

The creation of elite private institutes and universities increased the number of new and better-paying jobs for scholars in the field (García de Fanelli 1995, 17). The high demand for trained economists allowed institutes and universities to charge significantly higher tuition than at public universities. Whereas UBA and other public institutions are virtually free for students, the cost of tuition in private schools can run into thousands of dollars per year. The need of companies for trained economists also enabled these institutes and universities to obtain corporate sponsorships and endowments. Sponsorships and higher tuition provided them with the ability to offer high-enough salaries to attract faculty members trained in the U.S. who might otherwise not work in academia or possibly live in Argentina.[27]

One of the first and most important of these new institutes is the Centro de Estudios Macroeconómicos de Argentina (CEMA). Founded in 1978 by former Chicago students, CEMA developed a postgraduate program in economics and an MBA program in the 1980s that helped to generate more neoliberal adherents to the profession. CEMA also funneled prospective doctoral students to the U.S. After completing their studies, many of these students returned to Argentina to train another generation of economists.

Other private universities and institutes created near the same time as CEMA, including the Universidad de San Andrés and Universidad de Belgrano, also are proliferating "Chicago" economics. The Universidad de San Andrés (whose faculty include Osvaldo Schenone and Mariano Tommasi) and the Universidad Torcuato Di Tella (whose rector, Gerardo della Paolera, and a faculty member, Juan Pablo Nicolini, are products of the University of Chicago) are increasing the number of neoliberal proponents to the profession.

The Instituto de Estudios Económicos sobre la Realidad Argentina y Latinoamericana (IEERAL) in Córdoba, an institute founded under the auspices of the Fundación Mediterránea by Finance Minister Domingo Cavallo, a Harvard-trained economist, adheres to its founder's vision on the importance of neoliberal ideas. This institute also contributes personnel for key economic governmental positions. Even institutes created in the early 1960s, like the Fundación de Investigaciones Económicas Latinoamericanas (FIEL), have UCLA- and Chicago-trained economists in director positions.

Uruguay

Like many other issues, the debate in the economics profession between structuralists and neoliberals arrived much later in Uruguay. In 1943, an independent career in economics separate from accounting began in Montevideo at the Universidad de la República, the main university in Uruguay.[28] The university offered economics courses in only three or four subjects, though. Most courses trained economists in accounting and business (Vaz 1994), and the professors that taught economics did not form part of an economics department (Caumont 1994). Economics and economists lagged in their development behind the school of law and other fields in Uruguay.

In 1966, an economics program separate from business and accounting began in the university. During the first three years of study, business and economics students took the same courses. In the last two years, economics students enrolled in courses focused on economic subjects. Although the separation of the business branch from economics provided economics students with better training in economic issues, Uruguay continued not to offer a graduate program in economics.

Structuralist theorists who supported dependency theory dominated the economics faculty. Although Marxist beliefs prevailed among many disciplines in the university, the economics department endorsed an ECLA point of view (Caumont 1994). One reason why most advocated ECLA's ideas is because many of these economists earned their postgraduate degrees abroad in the 1950s and 1960s, but not in the United States. AID offered little financial support in these years (see table 6.1). Many students earned their degrees in France, where the French structuralist movement—a blend of market and planned economics—carried the day (Vaz 1994). Others completed their course work in Latin America. ECLA, for example, offered short courses for Uruguayans beginning in the 1950s. Monetarist theory received little support from students and faculty of economics in Uruguay.

In the early 1970s, relations developed between schools in the United States and Uruguay. Following two decades of low economic growth, the military government requested assistance from abroad in order to develop economic reforms. The government invited Arnold Harberger and Larry Sjaastad from the University of Chicago and their team including former Chicago students from Argentina, Chile, and Brazil to reform Uruguay's tax system and commercial policy.

Over the course of their work, Harberger and Sjaastad met promising economics students trained at the Universidad de la República who needed to improve their technical skills. With money from AID and the Uruguayan government, the University of Chicago set up a program to recruit Uruguayan economics students for Chicago's graduate program (Caumont 1994). In 1974, Harberger and Sjaastad sent Uruguayans Jorge Caumont and Carlos Steneri to study at Chicago. Through 1981, AID provided many scholarships for Uruguayan students to study economics, principally in Chicago, though some attended universities in New York, Minnesota, and Los Angeles. After 1981, students interested in studying abroad applied for scholarships from organizations such as the Fulbright Commission and OAS.

In addition to graduate studies abroad, the central bank in Uruguay from 1976 through 1982 sponsored a program with Columbia University to create a master's degree in Montevideo. Headed by Professor Robert Mundell of Columbia University, professors from Columbia arrived two or three times per year to conduct courses that lasted nearly three weeks. After completing their training, officials at Uruguay's central bank hoped that these economists would possess technical skills necessary for handling the bank's operations.

Although many students earned advanced degrees in the United States or took short courses with U.S. professors, their influence on the economics profession in Uruguay is less than what it might otherwise have been. Many students decided not to return to Uruguay, in part because of poor job opportunities. While a few schools have opened in the last ten years, these schools tend to offer courses in business and computing and are of a very practical nature.[29] Economists trained in the U.S. who advocate neoliberal ideas also are not in high demand at other private institutes, including Centro Latinoamericano de Economía Humana (CLAEH), Centro Interdisciplinario de Estudios sobre el Desarrollo Uruguay (CIEDUR), and Centro de Investigaciones Económicas (CINVE). In fact, research conducted at these institutes often intends to show the flaws and limitations of neoliberal policies (Vaz 1995).

The Instituto de Economía Montevideo (IDEM) is an exception. IDEM attempts to train students in economics. With a staff of professors, many of whom earned postgraduate degrees in the U.S., IDEM provides employment for economists. But low salaries force faculty members to hold additional jobs outside of academia. Working multiple jobs and long hours for low pay may not appeal to U.S.-trained economists if other employment options are available abroad that offer higher salaries. Centro de Estudios de la Realidad Económica y Social (CERES) is another exception. Founded in the mid-1980s by the Uruguayan private sector and deemed as the think tank that promotes orthodox ideas, CERES, however, still cannot pay internationally competitive wages (Vaz 1995). In addition, though CERES continues to operate, it is no longer a research center. The Universidad de la República is another employment option, but very low salaries and older faculty less receptive to monetarist thought discourage job seekers in economics.

The diverse economics training received by many Uruguayans in the 1970s and 1980s also reduced the influence of U.S.-trained economists on the profession. Not all students during this time period attended universities in the U.S. Students earned advanced degrees in universities in Mexico (UNAM), Sweden (University of Götteborg), Belgium (Louvain), and even Cuba and the former Soviet Union. In general, students in these countries received training that sided more with structuralist thought than monetarism. The combination of U.S.-trained economists and structuralists mostly from European universities contributed to less coherence among economists and within the economics profession in Uruguay.

The lack of coherence or uniformity in the fundamental ideas of economists in Uruguay also affected efforts to train a second generation of economists. Unlike Chile and the Universidad Católica, where economists trained in the U.S. dominate the faculty and possess much the same economic philosophies, the Universidad de la República infuses students with diverse and divergent economic ideas. The prospects of a consensus developing among a second generation of neoliberal economists appears unlikely, as most U.S.-trained economists pursue decent-paying jobs abroad or work in Uruguay outside the university environment.

Conclusion

The influence of international organizations is an important factor for explaining differences in the economics professions. Based on the similar curriculum in U.S. universities, this chapter showed that the more students a country sent to the U.S. for economics training, the more likely that neoliberal ideas would affect the economics profession in the foreign country. It also demonstrated, however, that whether economists trained abroad chose to return to academia in their home country affected the economics profession.

In Chile, changes in the economics profession occurred as a result of the agreement signed between the University of Chicago and Universidad Católica in 1956. This agreement and programs funded by international organizations insured that a few hundred Chilean economics students earned graduate degrees in the U. S. After completing their studies, these students returned to Chile and found academic positions that enabled them to instill their beliefs in generations of economists.

In Argentina, in part because of less AID funding, fewer students studied economics in the U. S. from the 1950s through the 1970s. A lack of decent-paying academic positions also resulted in fewer U. S.-trained economists holding academic positions. Since the late 1970s, however, increased demand for well-trained economists by the private sector and the central bank led to the founding of private institutes and universities by U. S.-trained economists. Greater demand for economists allowed institutes and universities to charge high tuition and to secure corporate sponsorships and endowments that enabled them to offer competitive salaries to attract U. S.-trained faculty members. Through their teaching, faculty at these institutes and universities have produced another generation of economists who advocate neoliberal ideas.

In Uruguay, fewer economists studied in the U. S. relative to Chile and Argentina. In the 1950s and 1960s, most Uruguayan economists received their graduate training from ECLA and from European schools that favored structuralism. In the 1970s and 1980s, when international organizations sent students to the U. S. for training, many Uruguayans continued to study in Europe and Latin America. A scarcity of job opportunities for U. S.-trained economists also limited their opportunities to spread neoliberal theories. Many economists found positions in international organizations abroad, which further restricted their influence in the profession.

The increasing influence of the U. S. in Latin America's economics profession has far-reaching implications. As Latin American presidents, many of whom hold advanced economic degrees from U. S. universities, appoint more U. S.-trained economists for economic policy-making positions,[30] this affects economic policy choices and, ultimately, economic development in the Third World. Moreover, as U. S.-trained economists come to dominate the universities and professions in their home countries, this has the potential to extend U. S. influence in Latin America for generations. Finally, the employment of U. S.-trained economists in the private sector and as consultants in their home countries widens the reach of U. S. influence abroad.

SEVEN

The Strategic Role of Ideas under Democratic Rule

This book began with the following puzzle: why do military regimes that claim to advocate the same economic policies actually adopt different ones? In the Southern Cone, policy makers and some military rulers declared their support for market-oriented reforms. Despite their self-proclaimed neoliberal goals, policy makers varied in their policy choices. Differences between policy intentions and actual policy choices suggest that, contrary to conventional wisdom, most military regimes are highly susceptible to pressure, especially from within the military itself. It is only under exceptional circumstances, such as in Chile, that military rulers are able to adopt survival strategies that help to insulate economic policy makers from lobbying influences.

This chapter begins by summarizing the findings of the study. It briefly reexamines military regimes in Argentina, Chile, and Uruguay, as well as in Brazil and Peru, to explain the effect of institutions and ideas on appointment strategies and policy choice. This study also shows that the model crafted to explain appointment strategies of military rulers has implications for Latin American democracies. Building on the institutional work of Haggard and Kaufman (1995) and Mainwaring and Shugart (1997), the findings suggest the importance of neoliberal economists for market-oriented reforms under democracy. The conclusion examines how this research potentially complements other studies, furthering our understanding about policy choice.

Summary of the Case Studies

This study proposes an anchor for the ideational literature based on the strategic interests of government officials. It examines the appointment strategies of survival-minded military rulers to understand the interplay between ideas and institutions. In specific, it shows that differences in long-standing characteristics of the military and in the kinds of governing institutions installed by military leaders shape the appointment of policy makers. Leaders under one-man rule, whose military has little experience with factions, have more autonomy in their appointments than collegial governments or factionalized militaries that require consensual agreement. This autonomy enables leaders to follow medium-term appointment strategies based on technical merit rather than serving immediate political concerns. Technical merit criteria contribute to the appointment of ideologically committed policy makers, and especially neoliberal economists. The selection of a high proportion of neoliberal economists promotes the initiation and maintenance of market-oriented economic policies. Based on their training, neoliberal economists hold similar economic ideas. Their ideas enable them to create a buffer against societal interests, which helps them to implement their policy preferences.

To test the argument, this study examines military regimes in Argentina (1966–73; 1976–83), Chile (1973–89), and Uruguay (1973–84). In Chile, a less factionalized military and one-man rule enabled General Pinochet to appoint neoliberal economists in policy-making positions, as part of a strategy to thwart competitors and achieve his political ambitions. Following their appointment, these "Chicago" economists initiated orthodox, market-oriented reforms. This contrasts with appointment strategies chosen by military rulers in Argentina and Uruguay. While Argentina's first military government also operated under one-man rule, the history of factional disputes forced General Onganía to choose policy makers who satisfied various interests and appoint few neoliberal economists in an effort to prolong his tenure. Argentina's second military government not only had to placate military factions, but its institutional structure of power sharing among the junta leaders restricted the president's control over cabinet appointments. Like Argentina's junta government, Uruguay's less factionalized military and system of collegial rule with strict rotations fostered negotiation and consensual agreement among the service chiefs. Consensual agreement worked against the appointment of neoliberal economists. Because military rulers selected fewer neoliberal economists in Argentina and Uruguay, the coherence of their economic teams paled in comparison to that of Chile. The lack of coherence in their teams facilitated interest-group access to key policy makers. In the end, despite pledging their support for orthodox, market-oriented reforms, military rulers and policy makers in Argentina and Uruguay initiated gradualist policies, which they later abandoned.

Military rule in Brazil (1964–85) and Peru (1968–80) also suggests the importance of institutions and ideas for explaining policy choice. In Brazil, the presidential succession system provided multiple access points for officers and interest groups to influence policy. Because most officers and pluralists opposed market reforms, prospective military rulers promised more heterodox policies. Brazil's history of military factions also reinforced the need for consensual decision making from among the officer's corps, which reduced the chance of selecting neoliberal economists. In Peru, military factionalization and junta rule obliged consensus from among the military establishment. Like Brazil, factional pressures offered policy-making access to interest groups and officers, most of whom favored protectionism. As a result, survival-minded military rulers appointed few neoliberal policy makers to satisfy these interests.

Implications for Democratic Countries

Policy-Making Appointments and Political Survival

The findings in this study also have implications for democratic governments. In specific, the ideas and institutions framework used to explain policy choices under authoritarian regimes is applicable to democracies. Since the late 1980s most political leaders and policy makers in Latin American democracies have endorsed stabilization, privatization, and economic liberalism. The bankruptcy of the ISI model combined with the 1980s debt crisis forced these countries to consider alternative economic strategies, including market-oriented reforms.

Despite the abandonment of ISI policies by most Latin American governments in the 1980s, their policy choices differed. Some countries initiated extensive (or orthodox) market-oriented reforms while others initiated only partial reforms. Although democratic leaders and policy makers in Argentina, Mexico,[1] Uruguay, and Colombia proclaimed their support for market reforms as early as the 1980s, some were more successful than others in achieving their preferred goals. Why do countries whose policy makers and governmental leaders often claim to favor orthodox reforms differ in their policy choices?

Contemporary political economy offers several possible explanations. Many scholars focus on the importance of state autonomy and insulation for initiating more orthodox reforms. The basis for an insulated state relies on political survival strategies along with collective action issues. In the democracy literature, it is assumed that most leaders want to survive in office. Although they surely have additional interests, political survival—remaining in office—is paramount.[2] Subject to electoral constraints, leaders are compelled to institute policies that improve economic performance in the short-term.

The initiating and sustaining of unpopular orthodox reforms, the story goes, are considered politically suicidal for democratic leaders. Orthodox reforms that attempt to eliminate market imperfections and promote greater efficiency generate high short-term costs, including price hikes, high unemployment, and production decreases. Price hikes result from the lifting of price controls and introduction of exchange rate reform. High unemployment and production shortfalls are caused by the collapse of formerly protected industries. Although new industries geared to a competitive economy will emerge, rewards for these firms come mainly in the long term (Geddes 1995, 60). Individuals who face unemployment because of privatization usually form a relatively small and concentrated group. According to Olson (1965), small and concentrated groups are better able to organize against reforms (and resolve a collective action problem) compared to the more numerous and dispersed beneficiaries of reform.

To withstand the pressure generated by the more organized and vocal interests, political leaders and their policy makers require some form of insulation. Haggard and Kaufman (1995) contend that the successful initiation of orthodox reforms depends on centralized executive authority. Under centralized authority, the executive uses special constitutional provisions and emergency powers to bypass pluralist pressures usually hurt by extensive reforms. Centralized executive authority is also important for overcoming political stalemates, selecting and backing a cohesive policy-making team, and overriding bureaucratic and political opposition to policy initiatives.

Similarly, Mainwaring and Shugart (1997) argue that a "strong" executive facilitates the initiating of orthodox reforms. They also emphasize the need for the president and majority of the legislature to come from the same party during the initiation phase. The combination of a strong executive and the executive party's dominance in the legislature removes obstacles to initiating and consolidating reforms.

Designing a theoretical structure similar to that used for military rule, this study complements work by Haggard and Kaufman (1995) and Mainwaring and Shugart (1997). Once again, political leaders' survival strategies affect policy-making appointments, only this time under democratic rule. To understand appointment strategies of democratic executives, I examine governing institutions and characteristics of the legislature. Differences in governing institutions and party strength in legislatures influence the appointment decisions of political leaders. Political and institutional environments determine which policy makers will contribute most to the political survival of political leaders.

Similar to Haggard and Kaufman (1995), this study hypothesizes that centralized executive authority is important for introducing policy initiatives. It also bolsters work by Mainwaring and Shugart (1997). The study suggests that in countries where governing institutions confer much power on executives and where a majority of the legislature come from the same party as the executive, the executive has greater autonomy in the appointment of economic policy makers.[3] Like one-man rule and less factionalized militaries, a strong executive and legislatures dominated by the executive's party provide executives with more means to do whatever they want. Political survival strategies, based on different institutional settings, influence the executive's willingness to appoint economists.

Independent Variables

Centralized Executive Authority

I use many of Shugart and Carey's (1992, ch. 8) variables, including the power to issue executive decrees and veto decisions, and make and censure cabinet appointments, as well as the president's holding an electoral mandate, to operationalize centralized executive authority. Using these variables, we are able to create an executive strength scale. A score of two indicates that the executive has full powers for that particular category. A score less than two but above zero indicates that the executive has some power in that category; a score of zero shows that the executive has no control over that category.

Divided Government

To measure the effect of the executive's party holding a majority of seats in the legislature, I combined data primarily from the Center for Education and Social Research (several years), Mainwaring and Scully (1995), and

Mainwaring and Shugart (1997). A score below 50 percent indicates that the executive's party does not hold a majority of seats in parliament. A score above 50 percent indicates that the party holds a majority in the legislature.

Results

A review of democratic regimes in Argentina, Colombia, Mexico, and Uruguay over the past two to three decades shows the usefulness of the modified military model. The findings suggest the importance of central-ized executive authority and that the president and majority of the legisla-ture come from the same party for the executive to have greater autonomy in his policy-making appointments. Over the last ten years, governments in Argentina, Colombia, and Mexico have for the first time introduced orthodox policies. In the past, neoliberal economists almost never repre-sented more than half of the policy makers in these countries. Today, how-ever, a high proportion of their policy makers are neoliberal economists. In Uruguay, by contrast, President Luis Alberto Lacalle (1990–94) proclaimed his support for orthodox, market-oriented reforms, but appointed few neoliberal economists for policy-making positions and initiated gradual-ist policies. The appointment of neoliberal economists occurred under strong executives whose party held a majority in the legislature. These cases demonstrate that executive powers and the composition of legis-latures shape survival strategies and influence the choice of economic policy makers (see diagram 7.1).

Strong Executive with Majority Support in Legislature

Since the late 1980s, executives in Argentina, Colombia, and Mexico could issue executive decrees (in Colombia, especially prior to the 1991 constitu-tional reform), control most cabinet appointments, veto important legisla-tion, and had won electoral mandates (see table 7.1).[4] Recent elections in Argentina, Colombia, and Mexico also gave the executive's party a majority or near majority in their respective legislatures (see tables 7.2, 7.3, and 7.4).

In Argentina, President Carlos Menem's sizable electoral victory,[5] the swelling in the number of legislative seats held by his party that increased at midterm elections (see table 7.2), and the fall in seats held by the main opposition party provided Menem with much freedom in his economic appointments. Satisfying party factions and opposition parties in an

Diagram 7.1   Executive Strength and Party Composition in the Legislature

	Democratic Rule	
	Strong Executive	Weak Executive
Executive Party **Majority**	Argentina post-1989 Colombia post-1986 Mexico	Argentina pre-1989
Executive Party **Minority**	Colombia pre-1986	Uruguay

Legislature

Note: In Argentina, the executive's party did not hold a clear-cut majority in both houses of Congress in the 1980s and 1990s. However, in most cases, the party held a majority in one house and a near-majority in the other.

Table 7.1   Measurement of Executive Strength, 1985–1997

Country	Executive Decrees	Electoral Mandate	Cabinet Appointments/ Censure	Veto Powers	Total
Argentina	2	2	1.5	2	7.5
Colombia	2	2	2	2	8.0
Mexico	2	2	2	2	8.0
Uruguay	0	0	1	0.5	1.5

2 = the highest level of executive strength in each category; 0 = the lowest.

Table 7.2 Executive Party's Seats in Argentina's Senate and Chamber of Deputies, 1983–1997

President	Senate	% of seats	Chamber of Deputies	% of seats
			1997 (PJ)	45.9
	1995 (PJ)	55.6	1995 (PJ)	52.1
	1992 (PJ)	62.5	1993 (PJ)	50.2
1989 Carlos Menem (PJ)	1989 (PJ)	54.2	1991 (PJ)	50.2
			1989 (PJ)	50.0
	1986 (UCR)	39.1	1987 (UCR)	46.1
1983 Raúl Alfonsín (UCR)	1983 (UCR)	39.1	1985 (UCR)	51.2
			1983 (UCR)	50.8

Sources: 1997, Center for Education and Social Research (1998, 46); 1995, 1993, 1992, 1991, 1989, 1987, 1986, 1985, 1983, Jones (1997, 265–66).
PJ = Partido Justicialista; UCR = Unión Cívica Radical.

effort to consolidate democracy also played a less pressing role than it did for the first democratic government following military rule, which enhanced the president's autonomy.

During his presidential campaign in the spring of 1989, Menem stressed ideals commonly endorsed by previous Peronist leaders. He proposed state intervention in the economy and support for workers as keys to economic revitalization. His electoral victory, however, led the already faltering economy into a hyperinflation. Investor concerns over the decisions Menem might make once he took office contributed to capital flight and economic chaos.

In an attempt to calm investors, Menem appointed an economic team that consisted of business leaders from Bunge and Born along with some economists, who initiated a gradualist neoliberal strategy (Smith 1991). Menem's initial appointments also served to marginalize the institutionalization of the Justicialista Party (PJ). Menem, a former governor of La Rioja and political outsider, wanted to limit the institutionalization and organization of the PJ and redesign it in his own image. Menem reduced party influence by appointing "minor Peronist figures con-

Chart 7.1   Percent of Neoliberal Economists in Economic Policy Making in Argentina, 1984–1997

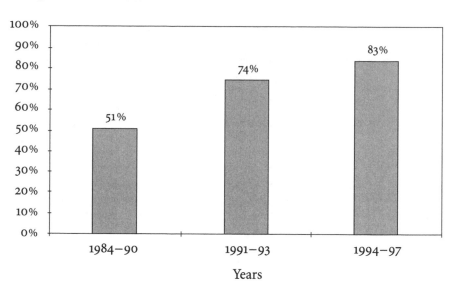

Sources: Argentine finance ministry, central bank, and planning office.
Note: Economic policy-making positions in Argentina are: secretary and subsecretary of finance, minister and subsecretary of the economy, secretary and subsecretary of SEPCE (the planning office), secretary and subsecretary of commerce, and president, first vice president and second vice president of the central bank.

nected personally to him or extraparty technocrats committed to liberalizing the economy" (McGuire 1995, 232).

In December 1989, Argentina experienced a second bout of hyperinflation. Menem selected another team to address these economic difficulties, but economists still did not dominate the economic ministries. Menem waited until January 1991, with his survival at stake,[6] to select Harvard-trained economist Domingo Cavallo as his new economic minister. Bringing with him "Cavallo Boys," economists from the IEERAL, an economic think tank he helped to launch, Cavallo assembled an economic policy-making team of neoliberal economists (Corrales 1997, 56). From 51 percent of economists holding policy-making positions from 1984 through 1990, the percent of economists rose to 74 percent from 1991 through 1993 and 83 percent from 1994 through 1997 (see chart 7.1).

Table 7.3   Executive Party's Seats in Colombia's Senate and House of Representatives, 1974–1994

President	Senate	% of seats	House of Reps.	% of seats
1994 Ernesto Samper (PL)	1994 (PL)	50.7	1994 (PL)	49.5
	1991 (PL)	52.5	1991 (PL)	50.9
1990 César Gaviria (PL)	1990 (PL)	58.5	1990 (PL)	59.1
1986 Virgilio Barco (PL)	1986 (PL)	49.3	1986 (PL)	47.7
1982 B. Betancur (PC)	1982 (PC)	41.2	1982 (PC)	43.0
1978 Julio Turbay (PL)	1978 (PL)	55.4	1978 (PL)	55.8
1974 López Michelsen (PL)	1974 (PL)	59.8	1974 (PL)	56.8

Sources: 1994, 1991, 1990, 1986, Archer and Shugart (1997, 150–51); 1982, 1978, 1974, Archer (1995, 193–94).
PL = Partido Liberal; PC = Partido Conservative.

Cavallo instituted sweeping and deep orthodox reforms. His team privatized nearly all state enterprises, opened markets to international competition through tariff reforms, reduced if not eliminated state subsidies to domestic producers, and liberalized prices and financial instruments.[7] Menem's appointment of Cavallo and his team suggests the significance of a strong executive and control of the legislature by the executive's party for autonomy in policy-making appointments. The willingness to appoint economists depended on earlier economic failures as well as Menem's attempt to marginalize the PJ's party leaders.

Like Argentina, Colombia is another case of a centralized presidential system (especially prior to the reforms of 1991)[8] and executive party control over the legislature. In late 1989, near the end of his presidency, Virgilio Barco increased the proportion of economists in economic policy-making positions. With his Liberal Party controlling a near majority of seats in the Senate and House of Representatives (see table 7.3), Barco had great freedom in his cabinet appointments. Barco ruled under a one-party government, with the opposition, the Conservative Party, "shut out of major government positions" (Martz 1992, 28).

Barco—who previously opposed orthodox policies and, in fact, blocked liberalization plans in May 1989—took measures to open domes-

Chart 7.2   Percent of Neoliberal Economists in Economic Policy Making in Colombia, 1970–1997

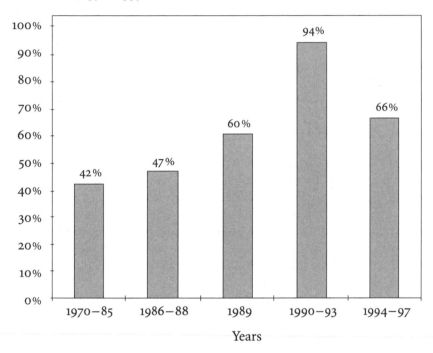

Years

Sources: Revista del Banco de la República (various years); *Agenda de la Comunicación Social* (various years); *Despachos Públicos* (various years).
Note: Economic policy-making positions in Colombia are: minister and viceminister of finance, minister and viceminister of agriculture, minister and viceminister of economic development, director and subdirector of national planning (DNP), minister and viceminister of external trade, and manager and assistant manager of the Banco de la República. The minister and viceminister of external trade were newly created positions and not part of the data for the entire period.

tic markets to international competition (Urrutia 1994). He reduced tariffs, devalued the peso, submitted plans to privatize important sectors of the economy, and introduced reforms in the financial and tax system. Prior to the initiation of neoliberal policies, the proportion of neoliberal economists increased in 1989 by 13 percent to 60 percent of economic policy makers (see chart 7.2). Barco's willingness to appoint these economists came as a result of his backing of an advisor and presidential candidate from the same faction in the Liberal Party (PL). While Barco may not have advocated a large proportion of neoliberal economists, as indicated by the proportion of economists from 1986 through 1989, his close advisor and future successor César Gaviria did (Urrutia 1994, 304).

Gaviria was not the Liberal Party's original presidential candidate. The assassination of the popular Luis Carlos Galán gave Gaviria his opportunity. Gaviria secured the party's nomination despite opposition from established party bosses who favored Hernando Durán Dussán, a longtime party stalwart, and Ernesto Samper of the Liberal left (Martz 1992, 37). Gaviria used his victory to initiate "more substantial liberalization than was supported by the [party] leadership or rank and file" (Geddes 1995, 71). Gaviria appointed economists to consolidate his power and marginalize the left wing of the party, especially Samper.

Gaviria also appointed neoliberal economists because of his earlier experience as finance minister and his economics training at La Universidad de Los Andes, which has an economics department filled with U. S.-educated economists. When President Gaviria entered office in 1990, his party held a majority of seats in the House (59.1 percent) and the Senate (58.5 percent), which provided him with some autonomy from his own party in policy-making appointments. Gaviria brought with him a large contingent of neoliberal economists. From 42 percent of the policy makers being economists from 1970 through 1985 (see chart 7.2), the proportion of economists rose to 94 percent from 1990 through 1993. The shift toward even more market-oriented policies also followed with Gaviria's term in office (Hallberg and Takacs 1992). Colombia's implementation of reforms under less than adverse economic circumstances also suggests that economic chaos is not a necessary condition for the adoption of market-oriented policies.

Like Colombia, Mexico is characterized by a strong presidential system and domination by the executive's party, in this case the Institutional Revolutionary Party (PRI), in the Senate and Chamber of Deputies (see table 7.4). And like Colombia, from the 1970s to the mid-1980s, Mexican leaders refused to implement orthodox policies. The proportion of economists prior to 1986 never exceeded 56 percent, and tended to fall below 50 percent for the whole period (see chart 7.3).

In late 1987, near the end of President Miguel de la Madrid's term, important policy changes occurred. De la Madrid introduced the Pact for Economic Solidarity, a stabilization and trade reform package with a

Table 7.4   Executive Party's Seats in Mexico's Senate and Chamber of Deputies, 1976–1997

President	Senate	% of seats	Chamber of Deputies	% of seats
	1997 (PRI)	59.4	1997 (PRI)	47.8
1994 Ernesto Zedillo (PRI)	1994 (PRI)	74.2	1994 (PRI)	60.0
	1991 (PRI)	95.3	1991 (PRI)	58.0
1988 Carlos Salinas (PRI)	1988 (PRI)	93.8	1988 (PRI)	52.0
	1985 (PRI)	100.0	1985 (PRI)	72.3
1982 M. de la Madrid (PRI)	1982 (PRI)	100.0	1982 (PRI)	74.8
	1979 (PRI)	98.4	1979 (PRI)	74.0
1976 López Portillo (PRI)	1976 (PRI)	98.4	1976 (PRI)	82.5

Sources: 1997, Center for Education and Social Research (1998, 610); 1994, Center for Education and Social Research (1997, 553); 1991, Center for Education and Social Research (1993, 543); 1988, Center for Education and Social Research (1991, 443); 1985, Center for Education and Social Research (1987, 383); 1982, Center for Education and Social Research (1982–83, 326); 1979, 1976, Craig and Cornelius (1995, 275). PRI = Partido Revolucionario Institucional.

commitment to fiscal austerity. Elements of the trade reform "included lowering maximum tariffs to 20 percent and the average to about 10 percent, as well as a sharp reduction in the coverage of QRs [quantitative restrictions], and the virtual elimination of official reference prices" (Kaufman, Bazdresch, and Heredia 1992, 1).

The initiation of orthodox policies followed the appointment of more neoliberal economists. From 55.8 percent in the 1983 through 1986 period, the proportion of economists jumped to 67 percent from 1987 through 1988.[9] De la Madrid's willingness to select neoliberal economists came on the advice of economists from the Banco de México, the ministry of finance, and the planning ministry, who allied with Carlos Salinas de Gortari,[10] de la Madrid's designated successor (Kaufman, Bazdresch, and Heredia 1992, 22).[11] De la Madrid selected Salinas, his former secretary of programming and budgeting, because Salinas came from the same technocratic faction of the PRI as de la Madrid. Factional pressures

Chart 7.3   Percent of Neoliberal Economists in Economic Policy Making
in Mexico, 1970–1997

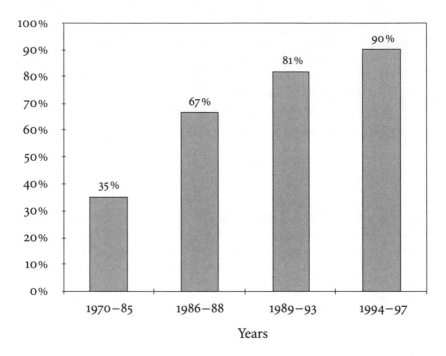

Sources: Diccionario Biográfico del Gobierno Mexicano (various years); *El Gobierno Mexicano* (various years).

Note: Economic policy-making positions in Mexico are: secretary and subsecretary of finance, secretary and subsecretary of programming and budgeting, subsecretary of development planning and budgeting, secretary and subsecretary of agriculture, secretary and subsecretary of external trade, subsecretary of industry (also called subsecretary of industry "A"), subsecretary of trade, director and subdirector of the Banco de México, secretary and subsecretary of national planning (1971–82), and subsecretary of income. Because of data limitations, some of the undersecretary positions are not reported for 1994–97.

in the PRI intensified in the mid- to late 1980s. Most leftist members in the PRI formed a dissident movement called the Corriente Democrática (CD). The CD, led by Cuauhtémoc Cárdenas, withdrew from the PRI and merged with another party in October 1987. Other divisions also existed in the PRI. By choosing Salinas, de la Madrid could reduce "to obsolescence and irrelevance" the nationalist-populist wing in the PRI (Craig and Cornelius 1995, 259).

Following his electoral victory, President Salinas also attempted to marginalize the left from his party and weaken the new rival leftist party. In 1988, Salinas won an election that was marred by claims of electoral fraud from former leftist PRI members who had formed the Democratic Revolutionary Party (PRD) only a few years earlier.[12] He also witnessed a bitter division within his own party between technocrats who favored greater economic and political liberalization and dinosaurs who advocated state-led economic development and resisted democratization. Salinas used economic policy-making appointments to marginalize the dinosaurs, the leftist PRD, and bolster his own faction. Market reforms reduced patronage options used primarily by dinosaurs and former PRI members.

Salinas's economic team initiated even more orthodox policies. Based on his economics training at Harvard[13] and previous experience as secretary of programming and budgeting, Salinas appointed personnel with strong neoliberal backgrounds as his policy makers. The proportion of neoliberal economists rose to 81 percent of the economic policy-making positions from 1989 through 1993 (see chart 7.3). Nearly all the economists in Salinas's government held doctorates from universities in the United States. Perhaps Salinas's support for the North American Free Trade Agreement, which opened Mexico to international competition, best demonstrates the shift in Mexico's economic policies. Salinas's successor, President Ernesto Zedillo, continued the marginalization of the PRI's left.

Weak Executive with Minority Support in Legislature

Governments with weak executives (as in fragmented governments), in contrast, whose party represents a minority within the legislature, tend to rely on coalition support. Like collegial leadership under a factionalized military, this institutional setting prompts the weak executive to negotiate with party members and the opposition in appointing policy makers that satisfy interests from factions within the party and from other governing parties. The need for political backing from the legislature reduces executive autonomy in policy-making appointments, as executives use appointments to secure short-term political support. Members of congress also may deny appointments in confirmation hearings, or censure or interpellate cabinet ministers.

In addition, legislative members usually have different constituencies than the executive. These members are accustomed to "distributive logrolling," wherein each legislator trades votes in order to gain legislative support for bills that affect his or her constituents.[14] Since protectionist policies and state-owned enterprises provide added opportunities for legislators to distribute resources selectively to their supporters, legislators are unlikely to favor appointments that limit these opportunities.[15] Legislators trade votes among themselves to block reforms and appointments that threaten the political machines that reward their supporters.

Uruguay exemplifies a government with a weak executive and minority position held by the executive's party in the legislature. With its history of a weak executive or quasi-presidentialism[16] and many factions (sublemas) within the main parties, Uruguay relies on coalition governments. Because of the double simultaneous vote,[17] primaries are in effect held at the same time as the presidential election itself, with no second round of voting. This leads to the winning presidential candidate earning a minority of the total poll, with no claim to a personal mandate (Finch 1989, 21). The weak executive is invariably forced to include members from his or her own party faction in the cabinet; other factions in the party; and sometimes opposition parties. Governments with participants from the two main parties contribute to compromise in policy-making appointments, as they can block the executive's selections.

Following Uruguay's return to democratic rule in late 1984, newly elected President Julio Sanguinetti appointed few economists to policy-making positions. His party needed the support of opposition parties, especially the Blanco Party, as his Colorado Party held only 41.4 percent of the seats in the Chamber of Deputies and 43.3 percent of the seats in the Senate (see table 7.5). The sharing of power forced compromise among the parties that reduced the opportunity to appoint many economists.[18] Sanguinetti's cabinet consisted of ECLA, neoliberal, and dirigiste (statist) tendencies (*Latin America Weekly Report*, February 15, 1985, 10).

In 1989 Luis Alberto Lacalle, a neoliberal proponent,[19] took over the presidency. However, he failed to initiate neoliberal policies. Despite his support for market reforms, Lacalle neglected to privatize state enterprises. He also failed to cut state spending and employment, and reform the social

Table 7.5   Executive Party's Seats in Uruguay's Senate and Chamber of Deputies, 1984–1994

President	Senate	% of seats	Chamber of Deputies	% of seats
1994 Julio Sanguinetti (PC)	1994 (PC)	33.3	1994 (PC)	34.3
1989 Luis Lacalle (PN)	1989 (PN)	40.0	1989 (PN)	39.4
1984 Julio Sanguinetti (PC)	1984 (PC)	43.3	1984 (PC)	41.4

Sources: 1994, for the Senate and Chamber of Deputies: Latin American Data Base, December 2, 1994; 1989, for the Senate: *Keesing's Record of World Events* (1989, 37039), and for the Chamber of Deputies: Center for Education and Social Research (1993, 909); 1984, Center for Education and Social Research (1989, 676).
PN = Partido Nacional, PC = Partido Colorado.

security system. The low proportion of neoliberal economists (16 percent) in policy-making positions from 1990 through 1994 worked against the adoption of orthodox policies (see chart 7.4). These policy makers disagreed among themselves about which policies promoted economic development, making them susceptible to powerful interest-group lobbying.[20]

The institutional setting explains Lacalle's appointments. Because opposition parties outnumbered his Blanco Party in the legislature (see table 7.5), Lacalle formed a coalition government that included opposition members in the cabinet.[21] Although Lacalle wanted to appoint many economists, his weakness relative to the legislature and his faction's dependence on other factions in the Blanco Party and on factions in opposition parties forced compromise.

Weak Executive with Executive Party Majority

Similar arguments apply to weak executives where the majority of legislators come from the same party as the executive. A weak executive with a legislature dominated by the executive's own party implies a high degree of control by the executive party's leaders in congress. Junior party legislators generally express loyalty to their senior leaders in congress, something akin to a less factionalized military under collegial leadership. A weak executive whose party dominates the legislature functions as if in a

Chart 7.4 Percent of Neoliberal Economists in Economic Policy Making in Uruguay, 1985–1997

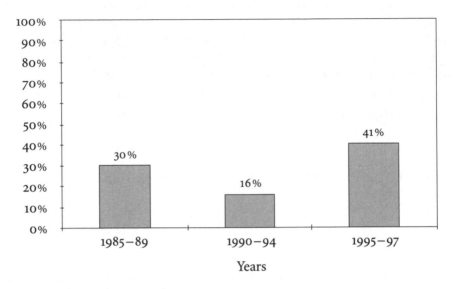

Years

Sources: Uruguayan central bank and planning office.

Note: Economic policy-making positions in Uruguay are: director and subdirector of SEPLACODI (the planning office), president, vice president, and director of the central bank, president, vice president, and director of the Banco de la República, minister and subsecretary of economics and finance, and minister of industry and commerce.

parliamentary system, with the executive forced to respond to various factions within the party. Satisfying various factions leads to appointment strategies that reduce the executive's autonomy.

Although Argentina's experience with strong presidential rule and domination by the executive's party in the legislature is well-documented, particularly with the dictatorial powers acquired by Juan Perón and his party in the 1940s and 1950s, the executive possessed fairly weak powers in the early 1980s. The debacle with authoritarian governance ruled out strong executive powers during the democratic transition. Despite President Raúl Alfonsín's party holding a majority of seats in the Chamber of Deputies, and a strong "contingent [in the Senate] that could construct agreements from a position of relative strength" (see table 7.2), Alfonsín needed to satisfy interests within his party and the opposition (Jones 1997, 267). Fear of democratic rule not being consolidated, or worse, of a return to military rule, was Alfonsín's prime concern. This fear, complemented by weak executive powers, prompted Alfonsín to appoint a diverse group of policy makers in 1984 that reflected compromise among the parties.[22]

Over the next year, Alfonsín's economy minister, Bernardo Grinspun, proclaimed his program to reflate the economy and promote equitable income distribution.[23] This program led to economic disaster, causing Alfonsín to replace old-time party stalwarts with extraparty technocrats in 1985 (McGuire 1995, 230). Pressures from interests in the Radical Party and from opposition Peronists restricted his selection of economists (see chart 7.1). Alfonsín also personally opposed orthodox policies.[24] These economic policy makers attempted to implement gradualist reform policies, including privatization of SOMISA, the state steel corporation, and Fabricaciones Militares. The policy makers succeeded in their efforts to deliver stabilization programs. However, many reforms, such as privatization and cuts in state spending, required legislative approval. Opposition from Alfonsín's own party and the Peronist-dominated Senate blocked these reforms (Rock 1987, 400). In addition, the Radical Party's loss of many seats in 1987 midterm elections stole any momentum Alfonsín might have had with introducing privatization policies.

Strong Executive with Executive Party Minority

A strong executive by itself does not guarantee the executive autonomy in policy-making appointments. A government with a strong executive and legislature not dominated by the executive's party—also known as a divided government—forces the executive to accommodate the majority party in the legislature in most policy and appointment decisions. Satisfying opposition party members generally limits the executive's autonomy in cabinet appointments.[25]

An example of a strong executive and an executive party in the minority of the legislature is the administrations in Colombia prior to the Barco government. From 1958 to 1974—a period known as the National Front—the government consisted of bipartisan coalitions, with each party controlling exactly half of the appointments (Hartlyn 1989, 292). Under coalition rule, the parties attempted to satisfy various coalition players, which limited the executive's autonomy in cabinet appointments. In addition, until 1968 passage of legislation required a two-thirds vote, assuring that all bills met with the approval of both parties.

After the collapse of the National Front, parties earning the second highest number of votes still received "adequate and equitable" representation in the government between 1974 and 1986 (Hartlyn 1994, 236). Although presidents appointed finance ministers and other top officials, providing the opposition with cabinet appointments reduced the executive's autonomy. In 1982, for example, when Belisario Betancur won the presidency, the opposition Liberal Party held a majority of seats in the legislature (see table 7.3). Domination by the Liberals blocked legislation favored by Betancur (Archer 1995, 196). This forced Betancur "to negotiate more with the congress on legislation and to offer more in the areas of patronage and brokerage than he might otherwise have been willing to do" (Hartlyn 1994, 232). Efforts to reach an accommodation with Liberals in congress led to changes in Betancur's cabinet.

Moreover, bipartisan clientelism that marked the National Front, and that would continue until 1986, affected cabinet appointments. Rewarding ardent loyalists with favors, including resources and rewards of the national government, remained an important tool of the political leadership of both parties (Martz 1992, 31). The appointment of neoliberal economists who wanted to reduce the size of the state and, by consequence, decrease the resources available to reward party loyalists seemed unlikely for parties competing for support. Economists held less than half of the positions in economic policy making during this period (see chart 7.2).[26] Fewer economists may explain why Colombia implemented fewer market-oriented reforms than other countries in the region in the 1970s and early 1980s.

Argentina, Colombia, and Mexico suggest that a strong executive in combination with a legislature dominated by the executive's party facilitate the selection of neoliberal economists. The willingness of executives to appoint neoliberal economists depends mainly on their attempts to survive politically given their institutional settings. Uruguay, by contrast, exemplifies a case where the president may prefer to appoint neoliberal economists, but strong legislative forces tied his hands. Uruguay's government under Lacalle shares many similarities with military regimes in Argentina, Peru, and Uruguay. Some military rulers in these regimes proclaimed their support for neoliberal economists as policy makers, but because of the need to reach consensual agreements, they sought compromise in their appointments.

These cases also suggest that the correlation between neoliberal economists and orthodox market-oriented policies is not spurious. As neoliberal economists in economic policy-making positions favor similar policy views and are able to form a team, it comes as little surprise that the appointment of neoliberal economists precedes the implementation of orthodox policies. In the past, when policy makers in these countries applied less orthodox economic policies, only a small proportion of trained economists served as economic policy makers. Today, by contrast, a high proportion of these policy makers have received their advanced training in economics either in the United States or in local universities from professors who studied in the United States.

In addition, prior opposition to orthodox policies by leaders in Chile (Pinochet), Argentina (Menem), Colombia (Barco), and Mexico (de la Madrid), who later introduced orthodox policies, and the inability of leaders in Argentina (Videla) and Uruguay (Bordaberry and Lacalle), who supported orthodox policies but failed to initiate these policies, further suggest the importance of neoliberal economists for policy choices. While leaders possess policy choice strategies that affect policy choices, their ability to initiate these policies also depends on the background and commitment of their policy makers.[27]

These cases also show that military governments do not guarantee more orthodox neoliberal policies. In Argentina, a democratic government proved more successful than both military regimes and its democratic predecessors in instituting policy reform. The higher proportion of neoliberal economists in economic policy-making positions suggests an important difference between the government in 1991 that first enacted the all-encompassing reforms and its predecessors. Moreover, the initiation of orthodox policies under civilian governments in Colombia and Mexico demonstrates the significance of economists for policy choices and the limited role military regimes play in promoting orthodox policies.

Potentially Complementary to Other Studies

This study attempts to demonstrate the significance of appointment decisions made by military and democratic leaders to explain economic policy choices. The main concepts introduced here build on theories developed in the interest-group, state autonomy, ideas, and institutions literatures. Indeed, the argument presented here borrows heavily on these literatures. This section intends to show how this study complements and possibly extends these literatures.

Interest Groups

As demonstrated in our findings, powerful economic interest groups are often able to lobby policy makers or military leaders to modify or abandon policy decisions. In military regimes in Argentina, Uruguay, Brazil, and Peru, and in Uruguay's democratic government, interest groups helped to shape policy choice. Powerful interest groups received various forms of protection, including the maintenance of high tariffs, import bans, industrial promotion, and other subsidy schemes. This protection enabled inefficient producers to flourish. On the basis of interviews with policy makers in Argentina and Uruguay, and secondary accounts in the other countries, powerful interest groups often affect policy choice. In demonstrating that interest groups influence policy, this study concurs with interest-group arguments that a careful examination of powerful interests helps to describe, explain, and predict policy choice.

This study, however, goes a step further in explaining when interest groups will influence policy choice and when they will not. Clearly, there are examples in history where powerful interest groups had little effect on policy choice. In Chile under Pinochet, and in democratic governments in Argentina, Colombia, and Mexico, some powerful economic interest groups suffered as a result of orthodox policies. Powerful groups advocated protection for their industries, and policy beneficiaries appeared only after the initiation of reforms. In Chile, rarely did policies designed by the Chicago Boys favor powerful interests.

Most interest-group arguments fail to consider that policy makers sometimes are autonomous from interest-group pressures. These arguments ignore the possibility that military rulers can restrict interest-group access to policy makers through different governing institutions. These arguments also ignore that the appointment of similarly trained economists in economic policy-making positions limits access points for interests to lobby. By showing that the likelihood of interest groups affecting policy depends on institutional structures and the ideology of policy makers, this study complements interest-group arguments.

State Autonomy

In addition to showing when interest groups are most or least likely to influence policy, this research documents when governments are most autonomous in policy decisions. As suggested above, sometimes policies are implemented that go against the interests of powerful pressure groups and classes. Attempts to explain such policy choices on the basis of state autonomy, however, have stimulated calls to bring the state back out. Despite policy choices not always appearing to reflect the demands of interest groups, some have questioned whether the state, and the "baggage" that comes with it, is useful for explaining policy decisions.

This study builds on work by Geddes (1994) in its focus on individual state actors and the incentives they confront. Focusing mainly on military rulers in military regimes, I show that one-man rule and a less factionalized military provide military leaders with greater autonomy in their policy decisions and policy-making appointments. Military leaders, of course, are never fully autonomous from societal pressures. But differences in governing institutions and characteristics of the military insure greater autonomy for some than others. Executive policy-making appointments can also enhance the autonomy of the state and its policy makers from pressure groups. Policy makers who share the same ideas on economic policy choice and dominate policy-making positions minimize access points for societal interests to influence policy. On the other hand, if policy makers fight among themselves over which economic policies to initiate, the number of access points increases.

Ideas

In the ideas literature, analysts attempt to show how ideas by themselves, or in combination with interest groups, influence policy choice. Ideas are important for creating or devising new ways to approach problems. In some instances, interest groups are necessary for bringing these ideas to the attention of policy makers. In others, the ideas of experts, who work together to resolve problems, have direct influence on decision makers who can institute policy changes.

Much criticism of the ideas literature focuses on its inability to demonstrate concretely how ideas shape policy choice. Some also ridicule it for not addressing where ideas come from. This study, however, shows both how ideas affect the initiation and implementation of economic policy and where ideas come from. By examining the background and training of economic policy makers, we can predict the policies that are initiated. Knowing who the policy makers are that make policy decisions is critical for understanding issues related to economic development. To predict which policies economic policy makers favor, we need to evaluate the training of policy makers. If most economic policy makers earned degrees at virtually the same schools and share similar beliefs with regard to economic policy, we can establish a close connection between the ideas of policy makers and the policies they initiate. Rather than claim that ideas matter with little supporting evidence, we can examine the educational background of policy makers to understand how ideas and ideology influence policy choice.

In the cases under review, countries that initiated orthodox economic policies had economic policy-making teams dominated by neoliberal economists—mostly trained in the United States or in foreign universities with much of the faculty holding degrees from U.S. institutions. Countries that initiated and sustained orthodox policies included Chile under military rule and Argentina, Colombia, and Mexico in the late 1980s and early 1990s under civilian leadership. Countries that initiated gradual neoliberal policies but abandoned these policies included Argentina, Uruguay, Brazil, and Peru under military rule and democratic governments in Argentina, Colombia, Mexico, and Uruguay before the late 1980s. In these cases, neoliberal economists almost never represented more than half of the economic policy makers.[28]

Institutions

This study also supplements work in the institutions literature. Various writers detail the effects of political institutions on the making of economic policy. Researchers usually examine institutions such as electoral rules and party systems in democratic governments, but rarely do they investigate institutions under military rule. Some may argue that electoral rules or party systems have little or no significance in a military government. But other institutions, which mirror ones found in party systems or electoral rules in democracies, exist in military regimes. Long-standing characteristics of military institutions act much like party systems. In both cases, these institutions provide a strong indication of the loyalty or support government leaders are expected to receive. Like disciplined parties, wherein the party faithful usually back the party leader, militaries that have historically remained outside politics and obeyed the orders of their superiors grant leaders more autonomy in their decisions.

Similarities in the governing institutions of democratic and military governments also exist. Democracies operating under collegial executives function in ways similar to military regimes managed by juntas. In both, executives must seek consensual agreements.[29] Parliamentary rule also shares features with advisory committees or other quasi-legislatures made up of large groups of generals. In both cases, formal ties are established between legislative and executive branches, with legislative or advisory committees granted voting rights and vetoing or delaying privileges on important legislation.

The role of institutions in shaping the incentives of executives in both civil and military regimes is demonstrated by their similar responses to their respective institutional environments. These institutional structures influence their appointment decisions. As suggested by this research, certain institutional structures facilitate the appointment of neoliberal economists to policy-making positions. Examining these different kinds of institutions under democratic or military governments helps to determine the appointment strategies of executives.

NOTES

One.   The Effects of Institutions and Ideas on Policy Choices

1. On the advantages of authoritarian regimes in coping with economic concerns, such as mass poverty, see Andreski (1968, 206).

2. Although Tocqueville's main concerns about democracies are on the conduct of foreign relations, his views are applicable to economic development questions. For contrasting interpretations about Tocqueville's foreign policy position, see Clinton (1988) and Joffe (1988).

3. For studies that consider the strengths of authoritarian and military rule for supporting austerity policies that promote economic growth, see Huntington (1968), Skidmore (1977), Marsh (1978), Weede (1983), Callaghy (1993), Olson (1982), and Kaufman (1986).

4. See Jowitt (1971), who makes a similar argument for the autonomy from societal interests of Leninist regimes to carry out unpopular policies.

5. These regimes also have the capacity to use repression as a means for initiating and sustaining their policy choices. See Nelson (1990, 22), who compares regime type and policy choice.

6. Although many western journalists criticized the Pinochet regime for its human rights abuses and lack of political liberties, they also praised it as a model for economic development in the developing world in the early 1990s. In particular, articles in the *Economist* (1/28/95; 6/17/95), *Wall Street Journal* (12/19/89; 1/6/95), *New York Times* (10/8/90; 10/6/94), *Newsweek* (2/6/95), *Washington Post* (8/23/91), and *Business Week* (6/9/97) suggested that Russia, among others, might adopt Pinochet's model. The *Moscow News* (9/17/93; 6/3/94) also discussed Pinochet's model for Russia. In fact, twenty-five economists from the former Soviet Union attended a Chilean conference in 1992 on the regime's economic model (Spooner 1999, 266).

7. In the mid-1990s, many in Russia including General Alexander Lebed considered adopting the Chilean model for economic and political reasons. Lebed foresaw himself as Russia's next Napoleon or Pinochet with unlimited governmental powers. A stimulating debate has also emerged among researchers about the adoption of the Chilean model, and military rule more generally, for economic development. See, for instance, Przeworski (1991), Maravall (1995), Heller, Keefer, and McCubbins (1998), and Piñera (2000).

8. Ironically, during the first phase of independence, "most African governing elites [under authoritarian rule] evinced statist propensities" (Chazan and Rothchild 1993, 182).

9. See, for instance, Sheahan (1980), Remmer (1986, 1990), Haggard (1986), Haggard and Kaufman (1989), Huntington (1987), Kohli (1986), and Bresser Pereira (1993).

10. See Haggard and Kaufman (1995), Nelson (1990), Stallings and Kaufman (1989), Frieden (1991), Naím (1993), and Remmer (1991).

11. Some exceptions that compare economic policy choice in the Southern Cone include Corbo and de Melo (1985), Ramos (1986).

12. President Carlos Menem in Argentina and President Luis Alberto Lacalle in Uruguay chose more orthodox economic policies than did military governments.

13. As Loveman (1998, 116) states, "Popular beliefs, expectations, and experiences do not preclude military rule nor military mediation of policy making; the historical weight of institutions, political culture, and the recent past ('path dependence') make military coups and authoritarian government thinkable and make institutionalizing democracy in the region difficult."

14. Moreover, a cottage industry has formed in the economics literature around criticizing the use of ISI policies to redistribute wealth. See, for example, the classic article by Baer (1972).

15. This consensus is sometimes referred to as the "Washington consensus," which Williamson (1994, 17) defines as a convergence of ideas among the powers that be in Washington about which measures are necessary for policy reform.

16. It is also plausible that the military could employ far-left economists, as well. The Peruvian military during the late 1960s and early 1970s is a case in point where military regimes can adopt more populist economic thinking as a guidepost for policy. Indeed, there is no necessary relationship between militaries and rightist economics.

17. See Haggard (1990), who also argues for the need to develop a theory about the incentives facing political actors.

18. Ames (1987) actually tries to show not just that the political survival assumption is plausible, but that it is true.

19. Even political ideologues recognize that they need to be in power to implement their policies, which suggests that getting electing precedes ideological goals.

20. The fact that the main interest of leaders is the maintenance of office does not preclude them from having substantive preferences that go beyond staying in power. However, the need for short-term survival imposes a constraint on military leaders' efforts to achieve those preferences.

21. Although the military recognizes the threat that permanent, direct military governance might have on the military as an institution, and will want to relinquish power and return to the barracks, military governments usually attempt to do so on their own terms and when circumstances dictate that it is in their interest (Stepan 1988).

22. Exceptions are leaders who take over the presidency to oversee transitions who understand that their rule is short-term.

23. This discussion of appointment strategies builds on a framework developed by Geddes (1994).

24. On the vulnerability of military regimes to economic crisis, see Haggard and Kaufman (1998).

25. The use of Plato's "philosophers as kings" metaphor does not imply that economists are noble, uncorrupted, and willing to learn every kind of knowledge. It does suggest that economists appear most competent and knowledgeable in the realm of economic policy making.

26. Although extreme divisions may develop in militaries over issues of strategy, weapons, and national security, divisions over such issues are less common in Latin American militaries. The influence of the Monroe Doctrine in restricting warfare between neighbors and reducing the urgency of security issues is a possible explanation for this.

27. As Remmer (1991), O'Donnell (1981), Fontana (1986, 1987), and others in personal interviews have pointed out, a majority of officers in the Southern Cone did not support neoliberal policies. Even in Chile, most officers opposed neoliberal policies prior to the coup (Fontaine 1988; Garretón 1986, 157). This may not be true of military forces in advanced industrialized countries whose training generally rejects dependency ideologies.

28. See Milner (1997), who also shows the effect of increasing the number of actors on policy decision making.

29. See Haggard and Kaufman (1995, 37–44), who also stress reduced factionalism within the government and increased cohesion for successful economic adjustments.

30. One-man rule can have negative consequences, as shown by authoritarian regimes under Ferdinand Marcos in the Philippines, Joseph Mobutu in Zaire, Jean-Claude Duvalier in Haiti, and Idi Amin in Uganda.

31. This does not suggest that neoliberal economists will automatically lead to adequate economic performance. Rather the assumption is that they have more knowledge about the policies necessary to produce economic growth than those without economic training do.

32. See Garritsen de Vries (1986, 54–57), who shows that neoliberal econo-mists make up nearly all the staff and the board of the IMF.

33. See Haas (1992), especially the articles therein by Peterson (1992), Drake and Nicolaïdis (1992), Ikenberry (1992), and Hopkins (1992).

34. The importance of economists has not gone unnoticed. A 1993 confer-ence in Washington, D. C., sponsored by the Institute for International Economics, focused on the role of economists in policy making. The *Economist* and the *Wall Street Journal* have also documented the importance of economists for policy changes in Chile. For other excellent studies about the role of economists in eco-nomic policy making, see Centeno and Silva (1998), Domínguez (1997), Conag-han and Malloy (1994), Schneider (1991), Montecinos (1988), Centeno (1994), and Valdés (1995).

35. According to Piñera (1991a, 7), economists trained at any American uni-versity after the 1950s share this commitment to open-market policies because of the use of Samuelson's textbook in introductory economics courses. Amsden (1992, 353) also acknowledges that between 1953 and 1991 free-market theory tri-umphed both intellectually and politically within the economics profession in the United States.

36. See Callaghy (1993, 473), who connects coherence among policy makers with effective economic performance in Africa.

37. Rueschemeyer and Evans (1985, 55) similarly argue that a coherent team may act as a barrier to outside forces.

38. Like Williamson (1994, 480), I argue that the initiation of economic reforms needs a coherent economic team with sufficient political support.

39. This does not imply that neoliberal economists agree on all economic policy choices. But similar economic training contributes to strong coherence among economic policy makers and increases the likelihood that policy makers espouse similar economic policies.

Two. Economic Policy Choices in the Southern Cone

1. Advice Argentine President Juan Perón gave to Chilean President Carlos Ibáñez in 1953 (cf. Hirschman 1979, 65).

2. Foxley (1986, 14) also argues that Chile applied the most orthodox poli-cies in the most consistent way, as compared to Argentina and Uruguay.

3. In some exceptional years, Latin America abandoned liberal policies. During World War I, for example, when developed countries shipped relatively few goods and closed off markets to nonstrategic, Latin American exports, countries in the Western Hemisphere engaged in an unconscious ISI strategy.

4. This does not imply that no protection existed. The level of protection, however, skyrocketed in the 1930s. On Chile's maintenance of an export-led strat-egy of development from the late nineteenth century until the 1930s, see De la

Cuadra and Hachette (1985, 1988) and Cortés Douglas, et al. (1981). On Argentina's support for an export-oriented economy, see Rock (1987). For Uruguay's economic policies prior to the Depression, see Handelman (1981b) and Anichini, et al. (1977).

5. For data that documents the fairly equal living standards and literacy rates among Argentina, Chile, and Uruguay, see various editions of the *Statistical Abstract of Latin America*.

6. For the effect of the Depression on Chile's exports, see De la Cuadra and Hachette (1985, 17) and Corbo (1983, 3). For its effect in Argentina, see Díaz-Alejandro's (1970) classic study; and for Uruguay, see Finch (1981, 125–26).

7. In addition to the Great Depression, the specific crises in trade during World Wars I and II also helped to inspire the shift toward inward-oriented economic development (Schneider 1999, 284).

8. On the successful wave of state interventions in both developed and developing countries, see Bresser Pereira, Maravall, and Przeworski (1993, 5).

9. Drake (1978, 21) documents Chile's urban migration from the 1930s through the 1950s. Van Niekerk (1974, 137) details Argentina's urban population surge following the Depression. Handelman (1981b, 244) claims that by the turn of the century, 80 percent of Uruguay's population already lived in cities.

10. Each country periodically attempted to eliminate or minimize ISI policies. Argentina's policies from the 1940s through the 1960s resembled a pendulum, swinging between populist stimulus and orthodox contraction (Mallon and Sourrouille 1975). Chile launched three stabilization programs in the 1950s and 1960s and invited economic policy makers from the United States, as part of the Klein-Saks mission in the late 1950s, to address problems caused by ISI (Edwards and Edwards 1991, 5). In Uruguay, the rural-based Blanco Party won its first election in the twentieth century in the late 1950s and attempted to shrink the public sector (Gillespie 1991).

11. For a general discussion of the disadvantages of ISI policies, see Baer (1972) and Hirschman (1968). For a review of Chile's experience with ISI policies, see Ffrench-Davis (1973). On Uruguay's economic problems because of ISI, see Anichini, et al. (1977) and Macadar (1982). For Argentina's ISI-related economic problems, see Díaz-Alejandro (1970) and O'Donnell (1978).

12. R. Kaufman (1979, 224–28) also documents many similarities among these countries.

13. Stabilization measures include government expenditure reductions, decreases in the growth of the money supply, and domestic currency devaluation (Foxley 1983).

14. For details about Chile's economic policies, see Edwards and Edwards (1991).

15. In terms of its export promotion policy, the state provided no subsidies or special incentives to exports (De la Cuadra and Hachette 1988, 88).

16. Stallings (1990, 130) argues that Carlos Cáceres, the finance minister appointed in 1983, shared the same basic approach as policy makers who preceded

him. Corbo and Fischer (1994, 40) also claim that the government adhered to the main thrust of its policies. In addition, Foxley (1986, 29–30), who wrote prolifically in opposition to the economic policies initiated in the 1970s and early 1980s, argued that despite the crisis, policy makers maintained orthodox policies.

17. As Maynard (1989, 170) suggests, variation in beef prices also contributed to high inflation. Depressed beef prices in the late 1960s encouraged cattle farmers to slaughter their cattle and deplete the herd. Once the process reversed itself and beef prices rose, farmers held back their herds in order to fatten the cattle, which stimulated inflation.

18. See Dornbusch and Edwards (1991) for details about populist policies in Latin America.

19. The monthly rate of inflation for March 1976 was 54 percent (Martínez de Hoz 1991, 15).

20. As Sjaastad (1989, 254) puts it, "It has been frequently remarked that Argentina never became more liberal than Yugoslavia."

21. On the problems of economic speculation during the transition, see Schvarzer (1983, 95–96).

22. Végh (1977, 34) used mini-devaluations to demystify the exchange rate and promote exports.

23. Tax reforms included the elimination of personal income and inheritance taxes, a reduction in corporate taxes, and a widened application of the value-added tax (Fernández Vaccaro 1978, 42).

24. Even Végh (1977, 33) concedes that the program emphasized gradualism over shock treatment. López, et al. (1988, 24) also stress the gradualist nature of the program.

25. On the negative fiscal impact of public enterprises in Uruguay, see the World Bank (1978).

26. Beneficiaries of protection included the automobile industry and companies related to car production.

Three.   The Effects of Institutions on Policy-Making Appointments

1. For a brief description about the effect military characteristics and governing institutions have on appointment strategies, see Biglaiser (1999).

2. In fairness to Frieden, he argues that classes overrode sectoral pressures in Chile. However, he also contends that classes overrode sectoral pressures in Argentina.

3. See Rabkin (1993, 7), who also cites the financial crash of 1982 as evidence that many powerful pluralist groups did not benefit from military rule.

4. Building on Hirschman's (1970) classic study, Bates and Lien (1985) argue that the exit option used by liquid asset holders has a more powerful effect on policy making than lobbying by specific asset holders.

5. The effect of bureaucratic insulation on economic development issues is also stressed in the developmental statist literature (Pempel 1999, 146).

6. Because it lacks legitimacy, a military government may attempt to use elections, plebiscites, and even constitutional conventions to demonstrate its popular support. However, as Loveman (1998, 121) argues, "No modern political ideology, not even fascism and other variants of corporatism, provides a legitimating myth that supports permanent military rule."

7. Unlike East Asian countries including Japan and South Korea that are well known for their professional, meritocratic bureaucracies, Latin America has a tradition of making political, and not meritocratic, appointments (Woo-Cummings 1999, 13; Schneider 1999, 291–93).

8. Although these three factors can contribute to military factionalization, the goal of this research is not to explain what causes factionalization. Our goal is to show that these three factors, which minimally are indicators of factionalization, have predictable effects on policy-making appointments.

9. Class and educational differences among services also exacerbate inter-service rivalries.

10. See Spooner (1999, 150), who argues that the absence of a tradition of coups in Chile "meant that Pinochet, who came to power in one himself, would be unlikely to ever be ousted in one."

11. Class backgrounds in each military branch may also affect appointments. The fact that naval officers usually come from upper-middle-class backgrounds, while army officers come from lower-middle-class backgrounds, influences their receptivity to policy makers (Potash 1980).

12. This does not suggest that economists in policy-making positions will automatically lead to adequate economic performance. Because of their training, however, economists have more knowledge about the policies necessary to produce economic growth than those without such training do.

13. For literature on the Chilean military, see Valenzuela and Valenzuela (1986), Valenzuela (1989, 1991), Constable and Valenzuela (1991), Agüero (1989), Arriagada (1988), Remmer (1988, 1989, 1991), Loveman and Davies (1989), and Varas (1987); for Uruguay, see Gillespie (1986, 1991), Rial (1984, 1986, 1989), Perelli (1990), and Handelman (1981a); for Argentina, see Lewis (1992), Pion-Berlin (1985, 1989), O'Donnell (1973, 1976, 1988), Rouquié (1981), Potash (1980), Fontana (1984, 1986, 1987), and Waisbord (1991); for South America, see Stepan (1971, 1973, 1988) and Rouquié (1987).

14. Because Brazil and Peru are not the main countries under study, their economic policies were not detailed in chapter 2. For the sake of clarity, the discussion of these cases will elaborate on their policy choices, the model's applicability to the cases, and the effect of different appointment strategies on policy choice, a subject that is addressed for the Southern Cone cases in chapter 4.

15. According to Spooner (1999, 19), "In a continent not noted for military professionalism, the Chilean armed forces stood out as a rare exception; the

country could boast that its military had never suffered defeat. Adding to this pride was the fact that the Chilean military had kept almost completely out of government since independence, leaving the business of running the country to civilians." Also see Haggard and Kaufman (1998, 109) about the absence of factions in Chile's armed forces.

16. In fact, on September 4, 1974, Pinochet asserted, "I am Chilean, and I know our idiosyncrasies, which do not permit someone to perpetuate himself in power" (cf. Spooner 1999, 83).

17. Leigh's more polished and articulate demeanor and wider popularity among officers in comparison to Pinochet also made many Chileans expect him to lead the junta (Valenzuela 1991, 30). Moreover, the fact that Leigh had served as one of the originators of the military coup, while Pinochet committed himself only forty-eight hours prior to the coup, conferred greater prestige on Leigh among officers (Arriagada 1986; Valenzuela 1991). Indeed, some did not expect Pinochet to participate in the coup. Allende's widow, Hortensia Bussi, when told of the military uprising on September 11, 1973, exclaimed, "And what will become of poor General Pinochet?" (cf. Spooner 1999, 270).

18. On the human rights abuses committed by members of DINA, see Spooner (1999, ch. 4).

19. Leigh subsequently formed the Commando Conjunto, a new group led by air force intelligence officials, as the air force equivalent of DINA.

20. Even Barros (1996, 22), who contends that no single service or individual made decisions in the Chilean military government, concedes that Pinochet used various machinations to institute an absolute dictatorship. See Spooner (1999, 103) about Leigh's outrage to D. L. 527.

21. Although, as Barros (1996, 27) suggests, D. L. 527 intended that all government appointments receive junta agreement—much like the 1925 constitution required democratic governments to obtain senate approval for nominees—in reality, Pinochet controlled most appointments. Under D. L. 527, civil servants would "keep their posts as long as they enjoy[ed] the President's trust," suggesting that Pinochet could sack appointees at will (Arriagada 1986, 130).

22. These new appointment powers complemented Decree Law 33 (September 21, 1973), which gave Pinochet exclusive control over promotions and retirements in the army for one year. For a thorough account of Pinochet's use of promotions to consolidate his rule, see Arriagada (1986).

23. See chapter 4 for details on the composition of the economic team and their policy choices under military rule in Chile, Argentina, and Uruguay.

24. Pinochet's opposition to orthodox policies is reflected in his writings (Pinochet 1974), and in interviews with his colleagues (Matthei 1992; Frez 1992) and policy makers (De Castro 1992).

25. As an example of his weakened position within the junta, Leigh complained about the suppression of ministerial councils and his exclusion from

government affairs (Varas 1979, 33). Also see Rabkin (1993, 7), who discusses the Chicago Boys' victories in their debates with opposition economists and nationalist military leaders.

26. The regime also faced an outflow of funds "as it negotiated compensation packages with ITT, Anaconda Company, Cerro Corporation, and Kennecott Copper Corporation for holdings nationalized during the Allende administration" (Spooner 1999, 95).

27. Even in the early 1980s, when most other countries in Latin America battled with international financial organizations like the IMF to renegotiate their debt, Chile and the IMF still shared the same point of view (Delano and Traslaviña 1989, 110).

28. See Vergara (1985) and E. Silva (1991) for a discussion of disagreements between corporate and entrepreneurial interests and "Chicago" economists. See also Pion-Berlin (1986, 320), who argues that the business community kept its distance from economists.

29. For military expenditures under military governments, see Scheetz (1991, 1992), Portales and Varas (1983), and Carranza (1983). For figures on the expansion of the officer corps under Pinochet, see Arriagada (1988, 157). Although some officers preferred not to expand the officer corps, most officers felt grateful to Pinochet for creating the circumstances by which they could rise through the ranks more quickly.

30. See Haggard (1988) for his description of President Ferdinand Marcos's similar use of patronage in the Philippines in order to bolster his survival.

31. For an overview on military interventions, see Potash (1980), Rouquié (1981), Little (1984), and Wynia (1978).

32. According to Wynia (1986, 73–74), the politicization of military officers preceded Perón's rule. In 1916, President Hipólito Yrigoyen's reimbursement of salaries for military officers who earlier were forced to retire as punishment for their affiliation with the Radical Party began the politicization of the armed forces. Whitaker (1968, 138) identifies 1930 as the first source of discord in the military, when military officers served as decision makers for the first time. In any case, factions widened during Perón's presidency.

33. On the rise in inter-service rivalries in the 1950s and 1960s, see Carranza (1983) and O'Donnell (1978, 1988).

34. The power of the navy should not be minimized. At the beginning of the twentieth century, the highly professional, British-trained navy acquired many resources.

35. Azules, however, supported military intervention when imminent danger threatened the country's national security.

36. Intra-military confrontations also occurred in 1955 and 1961.

37. While military factions formed along paternal, liberal, and national lines, Onganía appointed civilian representatives of the respective factions.

38. Rock (1987, 370) discusses a third faction, headed by General Carlos Suárez Masón and General Luciano Menéndez, who opposed economic policies associated with Videla.

39. Business groups found allies among more nationalist officers, such as the military engineers (Epstein 1985, 30–31).

40. According to Rock (1987, 376), "Striking against enemies had become the regime's primary instrument for containing popular opposition and unifying the armed forces."

41. The number of generals increased to twenty-six in 1981.

42. Even before Végh's appointment, the authorities could not agree on a finance minister, which led to a series of individuals filling the position on an acting basis (R. Kaufman 1979, 183).

43. See Valenzuela (1991) for Bordaberry's support of restricted democracy.

44. For an informed account of the factors that contributed to the failed plebiscite and the eventual transition to democratic rule, see Gillespie (1991).

45. Moreover, when the military finally selected an officer as president, they chose a retired general (Gregorio Alvarez) with restricted power and influence over the armed forces.

46. However, prior to 1964, the military never assumed governing power in the twentieth century.

47. For a rich discussion about democratic breakdown in Brazil, see Stepan (1978).

48. Castello Branco's government also included hard-liners and right-wing nationalists (Ames 1987, 141).

49. The availability of neoliberal economists in Brazil is an issue. From the early 1950s until at least the late 1960s, structuralist views of Raúl Prebisch and the Economic Commission for Latin America (ECLA) "had almost no competition as an interpretation of Brazilian reality and the possibilities for action" (Leff 1968, 141). Economists who advocated neoliberal or monetarist ideas represented only 15 percent of Brazil's economists, while structuralists (70 percent) and nationalists (15 percent), who shared similar ideas with regard to ISI and basic industries, made up the other 85 percent (Leff 1968, 148). A majority of the economics profession favoring neoliberal policies, however, is not necessary for the initiation of such policies. In Chile, in spite of being in the minority in the economics profession in the 1970s, neoliberal economists dominated policy-making positions.

50. Fishlow (1973, 82) adds that the choice of a successor forced the military to consider the desirability of austerity policies.

51. Although the Congress formally selected Costa e Silva by indirect election, Costa e Silva ran unopposed (Roett 1972, 151).

52. According to Schneider (1987, 50), the absence of action taken by the SNI in blocking nominations or firing officials is because personnel "who rose to the top two or three levels of ministries and state enterprises likely shared the

politics and ideology of the military regime to such an extent that SNI surveillance was largely superfluous."

53. The senior officers polled to nominate a successor for Costa e Silva included approximately 118 army generals, 60 admirals, and 61 air force brigadiers (Roett 1972, 163).

54. According to Skidmore, "Delfim was continuously subject to direct instruction from the military. There was no question who held the ultimate power" (cf. Schneider 1987, 242).

55. For example, the regime offered rural credit at negative real interest rates, resulting in a substantial transfer of real income to agriculture (Ames 1987, 156).

56. The SNI seems to have been induced to join the coalition by the offer of the next presidential term to its leader, General João Baptista Figueiredo.

57. Some of these basic inputs included the building of power plants and mining to provide energy sources, production of fertilizers, and metallurgy of nonferrous materials (Rabello de Castro and Ronci 1991, 163).

58. See McClintock (1989) for a discussion about the history of military interventions in Peru.

59. See also McClintock (1983) and Abugattas (1987) for more details about military factionalization in Peru.

60. The military particularly opposed the IMF because of its demand for a cut in arms purchases (Stallings 1983, 171).

Four.   The Effects of Neoliberal Economists in Economic Policy Making

1. See the fine edited works by Hall (1989), Haas (1992), and Goldstein and Keohane (1993).

2. For essays about the influence of experts on policy choices, see Peterson (1992), Drake and Nicolaïdis (1992), Haas (1992), Ikenberry (1992), and Hopkins (1992).

3. In a general sense, the role of neoliberal economists borrows from the work of Goldstein and Keohane (1993), who argue that ideas held by many people have implications for human action.

4. For Britain's experience with Keynesian policies, see Skocpol and Weir (1985).

5. As mentioned in endnote 35 of chapter 1, Piñera (1991a) argues that economists trained at any American university after the 1950s shared many similar orthodox philosophies because of the use of Samuelson's *Economics* textbook in introductory economics courses.

6. The countries' histories with policy failures, such as populist ideas and import substitution industrialization (ISI) policies in the cases under study, reinforced this commitment to their ideas.

7. As Nelson (1988, 82) points out, internal political pressures and politicians' fears of such pressures are the most common reasons for policy failure. Also see Rueschemeyer and Evans (1985, 55) for a similar argument on coherence as a barrier to outside forces.

8. The inability of the opposition to present a coherent policy package backed by an alternative economic team also spurred personnel changes (Cortázar 1989).

9. To determine if the economic policy makers were neoliberal economists or not, I consulted several economists in each country and reviewed publications (including "Who's Who") to obtain individual backgrounds about the policy makers. This is not a perfect measure of the influence of neoliberal thought. There is the problem of those who changed their ideological background over their lifetime. Nevertheless, based on the comments of economists in Argentina, Chile, and Uruguay, it is clear that the vast majority of policy makers categorized as neoliberal economists in this study were American-trained or studied under others trained in the U.S. In the exceptional cases where some structuralist economists also served as economic policy makers (e.g., Chile in 1984, Argentina in 1970–73), their appointment supports the findings of this study.

10. On the technocratic character of the military period, see P. Silva (1991) and Fontaine (1988).

11. If we separate neoliberal economists trained in the U.S. or Santiago's Universidad Católica from economists educated in other Chilean universities and outside the U.S., the proportion of "Chicago" economists falls even more.

12. See chapter 6 for a detailed discussion of the Chicago Boys and their training.

13. *El Ladrillo* (1992), a book written by Chicago Boys prior to the coup and published several years later, signifies the coherence of ideas among the economic policy makers. The policy makers saw this book as their blueprint. Moreover, in over twenty personal interviews conducted with former policy makers (July through September 1992), they all spoke of the coherence of the group and its ideas. See also Evans (1992, 151–66), who discusses classmate and interpersonal relations that promoted coherence in the Japanese, South Korean, and Taiwanese bureaucracies.

14. See Montecinos (1988, 178), who learned about the coherence of ideas held by Chilean economists through her interviews.

15. For a detailed account of the pressures faced by Pinochet in 1983, see Constable and Valenzuela (1991), Spooner (1999, ch. 7).

16. Although Pinochet faced intense political discontent in mid-1984, uncertainty within the opposition of its own direction strengthened his political position (Spooner 1999, 198).

17. One reason Pinochet decided to replace Jarpa and Escobar was because of the disappointing performance of the economy (Edwards and Edwards 1991,

214). Another was that Pinochet still believed in the orthodox economic model (Stallings 1990, 36; Walker 1992).

18. Members in the cabinet of Finance Minister Hernán Büchi (1985–89) claimed that their predecessors enhanced the policy freedom they later enjoyed (Larroulet 1992a; J. Fontaine 1992).

19. Although Pinochet's replacement of neoliberal economists in some policy-making positions in 1984 may suggest his lack of commitment to neoliberal policies, it should be recalled that Pinochet maintained orthodox policies and the economists tied to these policies despite double-digit levels of unemployment and widespread bankruptcies in 1982 through mid-1983. It was not until riots broke out in the streets, protests occurred on a monthly basis, and Chileans almost unanimously called for the heads of the Chicago Boys that Pinochet removed these economists from office (Pérez de Arce 1992). Within a year, however, neoliberal economists, some of whom were members of the earlier team, retook these economic policy-making positions and reinstated orthodox policies.

20. Kast's admirers credit him with a sincere concern for the country's poor. His detractors "found him pompous and out of touch with social realities" (Spooner 1999, 108).

21. Kast later held the positions of labor minister and president of the central bank. He died from cancer in 1982 at the age of thirty-five.

22. President Pinochet's calls for a 1978 referendum and 1980 constitutional reform demonstrate approaches used by military regimes for gaining legitimacy. For a discussion of the 1980 plebiscite, see Sanders (1981, 371).

23. The importance of television as a propaganda tool should not be underestimated. By 1982, for example, as a result of tariff reductions, nearly 78 percent of Chilean households owned a television set, a sixfold increase from 1970 figures (Constable and Valenzuela [1991, 155]).

24. See chapter 6, which examines the training of economists from the 1950s through 1990s.

25. According to one account, Onganía met Salimei, who was unfamiliar to nearly everyone, while on a spiritual retreat (*Latin American Regional Reports: Southern Cone,* March 7, 1980, 7).

26. Wynia (1982) claims that Martínez de Hoz's concern about the power of labor also encouraged a gradual approach to economic liberalization.

27. As noted earlier, General Videla (1992) favored liberal policies.

28. See also Epstein (1985, 23) for reversals in original governmental decisions, as brought about by private interests.

29. See Artana (1988) and Nogues (1988) for a discussion of industrial promotion in Argentina.

30. According to Bordaberry (1992), he and Minister of Economics and Finance Alejandro Végh Villegas agreed on economic policy and the need to impose orthodox measures. Their disagreements were on political liberalization and democratic values.

31. Even Bordaberry (1992) stated that the team did not have enough "players," referring to the lack of economists in economic policy-making positions to carry out orthodox reforms.

Five. Privatization under Military Rule

1. For a review of growing state intervention in the Chilean economy and CORFO's role in facilitating state expansion, see Lüders (1992b).

2. See Rock (1987, 263–64) for a discussion of hydroelectric plants, oil pipelines, shipbuilding, and other industries developed by the government.

3. For more details on Batlle y Ordóñez's policies, see Hanson (1938).

4. On the rise of ISI in Latin America, see Hirschman's (1968, ch. 3) classic study.

5. For a thorough account of economic policies and economic growth statistics in the Southern Cone from the 1940s through the 1990s, see Papageorgiou, et al. (1991).

6. A large literature has grown around privatization. For general sources on privatization, see Vernon (1988), Foglesong and Wolfe (1989), Marsh (1991), Massey (1992), and Ramanadham (1993, 1994). For privatization in Latin America, see the various articles in Glade (1991), Latin Finance (1991), Ramamurti (1992), Boeker (1993), and Baer and Birch (1994).

7. See Bates (1981) and Krueger (1974) for similar arguments in the rent-seeking literature.

8. Only rarely does the public organize itself as an interest group in favor of selling off state enterprises (Kelly 1996, 241). In the 1990s, however, many Chileans questioned why the state did not privatize more SOEs including CODELCO— the large copper interest (Meller 1993, 95).

9. Pinochet claimed that "generals in the cabinet tended to challenge his position more than civilians" (Spooner 1999, 109).

10. "Chileanization" of the copper mines implied that the Chilean government acquired 51 percent ownership of the largest mines (Larraín and Meller 1991, 177).

11. The state also liquidated many SOEs or merged them with other public enterprises, which further reduced the number of firms under state control (Marshall and Monte 1988, 290). For a historical account of privatization in Chile between 1973 and 1978 and the events that preceded privatization, see CORFO (1979).

12. For details on military opposition to privatization, see Delano and Traslaviña (1989, 82).

13. See *Latin America Weekly Report* (May 16, 1989, 8) for a discussion about strategies military generals used to prevent the privatization of CODELCO.

14. For an informed report on concentration of private sector activities, see Dahse (1979).

15. For a critical account of privatizations in the 1970s, see Marshall and Monte (1988).

16. Policy makers also planned to privatize large SOEs.

17. As a study conducted by FIEL (1988) documents, public sector expenditures represented a small percentage of GDP relative to the 1980s.

18. *Proceso* is short for "El Proceso de Reorganización Nacional," the phrase coined by the military to identify its goals during the intervention.

19. For example, policy makers privatized the transportation of petroleum from refineries to local markets and the selling of gas by local merchants.

20. Smith (1980) also identifies efforts to sell state-owned enterprises to private investors that met with resistance from military quarters.

21. On the relationship between increasing fiscal deficits and spending in public enterprises in the 1970s and 1980s, see Gerchunoff and Guadagni (1987, 43).

22. In one case, a retired naval captain living on a modest pension recalled how a captain from his same class had become a millionaire. The millionaire's involvement in the World Soccer Games in 1978 and his part in Argentina's choice of color television systems helped to line his pockets.

23. Végh (1977, 34) estimates the public sector deficit at 20 percent in 1974.

24. The few policy makers who favored privatization included Minister of Finance and Economics Alejandro Végh Villegas, President of the Banco Central José Gil Díaz, and some U.S.-trained economic advisors on policy matters. Végh's successor as minister of finance and economics, Valentín Arismendi, also advocated greater private initiative and a reduced role for the state (*Búsqueda* 1977, 4–9).

25. For a discussion about opposition to privatization by military officers in SOEs, see various issues of the magazine *Búsqueda* (including *Búsqueda* 1979, 1).

26. As Edy Kaufman (1979, 56) argues, "Lack of prestige, low salaries, and negligible political corporative influence placed army officers on a relatively low social level."

27. For an interesting account about Argentine President Raúl Alfonsín's efforts to privatize in the 1980s, see González Fraga (1991).

28. Unlike most policy makers, Ramon Díaz, former president of the Banco Central, strongly favored privatization. For his view on privatization, see Díaz and Sayagues (1985).

Six.   The Professionalization of Economists

1. Cf. Halpern (1993, 94).

2. Cf. Cassidy (1996, 52).

3. For a brief history about economists in the Southern Cone, see Biglaiser (2002).

4. See Balán (1982, 213), who argues that social-science teaching and research programs in Latin American universities are largely a post–World War II phenomenon.

5. The Spanish translation for ECLA is CEPAL (Comisión Económica para América Latina).

6. For a discussion of the economic ideas identified with ECLA, see Prebisch (1947), Mitchell (1967), and Iglesias (1992).

7. On the Great Depression and World War II serving as preconditions for postwar policies, see Sikkink (1991, 41).

8. See Pinto and Sunkel (1966, 82), who also discuss ECLA's efforts to spread its "practical" theories to policy makers in the region.

9. In the 1950s, few used the term *neoliberal* to identify economists who favored ideas reflective of the University of Chicago. During that time and even today, these economists are sometimes referred to as monetarists. Analysts popularized the term *neoliberal* to describe free-market economics in the 1970s and 1980s. Some Latin Americans also subscribed to a third economic school, namely Marxism.

10. For a discussion about the conflicts between structuralists and monetarists, see P. Silva (1991). For a thorough account about the different perspectives held by policy makers and economists on policies necessary for economic development, see Hirschman (1968).

11. For a review of neoliberal economic ideas, see Johnson (1975) and Friedman (1975).

12. On the collapse of the Keynesian consensus and neoliberalism's conquering of the universities, governments, and multilateral agencies in the First World, see Bresser Pereira, Maravall, and Przeworski (1993, 5–6).

13. For an in-depth discussion of the Klein-Saks Mission, see Correa (1985, 121–46).

14. For useful insights on the agreement, see Valdés (1989); Correa (1985); P. Silva (1991); O'Brien (1983).

15. For more details about the onset and functions of the Point Four Program, see Packenham (1973, 43–49).

16. Much of the funding for the National Planning Association's Technical Assistance Program probably came from the Ford Foundation.

17. For a discussion of the human capital "experiment" in Chile, see Valdés (1989, 57–58, 130).

18. As part of its agricultural assistance, the U. S. gave Chile its surplus of wheat or cotton at no cost, which Chile could then sell and place the proceeds of its sales in a P. L. 480 account (Patterson 1995). For more details on P. L. 480, see Bruce (1957, 8–9).

19. Although most Chicago Boys endorsed neoliberal policies, in a few cases economists who earned doctorates in Chicago (e.g., Ricardo Ffrench-

Davis and Carlos Massad) questioned some policies identified with the Chicago school. Still, all favored the use of market forces and limited government intervention to promote economic development.

20. In countless interviews conducted in Santiago from July through September 1992, former Chicago students remarked fondly on their experiences at Chicago and the attention and devotion given to them by the faculty, and in particular by the graces of Al Harberger and his Chilean wife, Anita.

21. A Chilean economist from Chicago also founded the influential weekly magazine *Qué Pasa,* which provided additional employment opportunities for economists (O'Brien 1982, 3).

22. Probably the most important of these new institutes is the Centro de Estudios Públicos, established in 1980 by neoliberal economists (P. Silva 1991, 395).

23. See Hirschman (1963, 241) for more insights about ideological escalation.

24. See chapter 4 for a discussion of Miguel Kast's efforts to recruit Chilean students to pursue graduate studies in the United States.

25. This does not imply that Argentina had no economists during the first half of the twentieth century. Economists including mathematician Julio Olivera at UBA and Oreste Popescu at the Universidad Nacional de La Plata conducted research and published original ideas. In addition, a few Argentine economists earned advanced degrees abroad.

26. The politicization of the universities also discouraged interest in academic employment.

27. The case of Argentina is not unique. In fact, Mexico shows a similar pattern of long-held support in the profession for structuralism giving way to neoliberalism in the late 1970s. Swelling enrollment and corporate sponsorship at expensive private universities contributed to increased demand for U.S.-trained economists.

28. The university first proposed to offer economics courses and seminars in 1931 (Rodríguez and da Silveira 1984, 35).

29. Schools such as the Universidad Católica and Universidad ORT Uruguay, which have taught courses in management at the bachelor's and master's levels for several years, are now considering the creation of a new career in economics (Vaz 1994).

30. In the past, presidents appointed lawyers or accountants, and not economists, for policy-making appointments.

Seven.   The Strategic Role of Ideas under Democratic Rule

1. The inclusion of Mexico in a study of democratic cases is perhaps controversial. However, Mexico's 2000 presidential election—which was won by the National Action Party (PAN) candidate and broke the seventy-year stranglehold

on the presidency held by the Institutional Revolutionary Party (PRI)—and the PRI's losing control of the Chamber of Deputies in 1997 are evidence of Mexico's democratic transition.

2. Some may argue that reelection is less important in Latin America, since most presidents are not allowed to hold consecutive terms. But decisions ratified recently in Argentina, Brazil, Peru, and Venezuela enable their presidents to serve consecutive terms. Moreover, in Uruguay and Venezuela, presidents have held office for more than one term, despite not serving consecutive terms. These examples suggest that executives are interested in surviving in office and advancing their careers.

3. While constitutions confer on executives the ability to select their own cabinet, political considerations and pressures affect their choices. Strong executive powers and legislatures dominated by the executive's party, however, may shield executives from these pressures.

4. Despite not having official decree powers, the president is the decision-making center of the Mexican system. The president serves as chief of state, head of government, de facto boss of the dominant political party, chief legislator, and ultimate decision maker (Gabbert 1992).

5. Menem garnered over 47 percent of the vote in 1989, while his nearest competitor won barely 32 percent.

6. Mounting corruption scandals against high officials and signs of another hyperinflation made Menem's survival appear in jeopardy. Indeed, speculation surfaced from high-placed members of his government that Menem might be eased out of the presidency before his term expired (*Latin American Regional Reports: Southern Cone*, March 14, 1991, 1).

7. As Estrada (1992) put it, in an analogy about Cavallo and his team, some policy makers sweep dirt under the rug, others put it in a corner, whereas Cavallo removes the dirt.

8. On the implications of Colombia's constitutional reforms in 1991, see Hartlyn (1994).

9. As described in the *Latin America Weekly Report* (January 10, 1986, 4), under de la Madrid, "economists outnumber lawyers in key positions, for the first time."

10. According to the *Latin American Regional Reports Mexico and Central America* (October 29, 1987, 6), "Since the beginning of the de la Madrid administration, Salinas has been credited with—and blamed for by the opposition—the authorship of the present economic policy, being considered responsible for the government's drive to streamline the state machinery and open up the economy."

11. Under the PRI's presidential nominating system, the incumbent president designated (*dedazo*) his successor.

12. See Camp (1999) for details on the 1988 election.

13. Salinas earned his doctorate in business administration.

14. Problems related to distributive logrolling for the executive are magnified when the opposition party holds a majority of seats in the legislature. Generally, executives share more similar views with members of their own party, which limits distributive logrolling.

15. For more details on distributive logrolling and differences between executive and congressional constituencies, see Lohmann and O'Halloran (1994).

16. See Gillespie and González (1994), who define Uruguay as quasi-presidentialist because of its affinity to traits associated with parliamentary rule.

17. Uruguay switched to a primary system under presidential rule in 1996.

18. Whether Sanguinetti would have appointed many neoliberal economists is also debatable, as he had never before advocated orthodox policies.

19. Examples of Lacalle's support for orthodox policies include his introduction of a tough economic adjustment program in his first days in office, attempts to privatize state enterprises, and efforts to reform the social security system through private pensions.

20. Other forces including popular referenda, court decisions, and negative congressional votes also blocked Lacalle.

21. In 1992, he even invited leftist parties in his cabinet, who promptly rebuffed his offer.

22. There is no guarantee that Alfonsín would have appointed economists if faced with different circumstances. I argue that leaders have greater autonomy in their appointments under certain governing institutions and legislative compositions, not that they will automatically choose neoliberal economists.

23. Members of the central bank also favored Grinspun's expansionist policies (Canitrot 1994).

24. In 1983, Alfonsín campaigned on a platform "advocating a strong economic role for the state and protection of domestic industry from foreign competition" (McGuire 1995, 223).

25. An exception is if the executive's ideological views are closer to the opposition party's.

26. Economists holding 40 to 50 percent of the economic policy-making positions is not low, but it is in comparison to Barco's last year in office and Gaviria's presidency.

27. To understand why leaders who want to select economists are unable to, see the discussion in chapter 3 about constraints leaders face in their appointments.

28. Mexico between 1983 and 1986 is an exception. Economists held nearly 56 percent of the positions in this period, but this percentage increased dramatically after 1986.

29. One-man military rule and a unitary executive under democracy also possess similarities.

REFERENCES

Abugattas, Luis A. 1987. "Populism and After: The Peruvian Experience." In James M. Malloy and Mitchell A. Seligson, eds., *Authoritarians and Democrats: Regime Transition in Latin America,* 121–44. Pittsburgh: University of Pittsburgh Press.

Agüero, Felipe. 1989. "Autonomy of the Military in Chile: From Democracy to Authoritarianism." In Augusto Varas, ed., *Democracy under Siege: New Military Power in Latin America,* 97–114. New York: Greenwood Press.

Agüero, Fernando. 1992. Interview of August 18 with the former president of the National Association of Manufacturers.

Alemanzar, General Augusto. 1992. Interview of December 9 with the former director of Fabricaciones Militares.

Alisky, Marvin. 1969. *Uruguay: A Contemporary Survey.* New York: Praeger.

Ames, Barry. 1987. *Political Survival: Politicians and Public Policy in Latin America.* Berkeley: University of California Press.

Amsden, Alice H. 1992. "The Globalization of the Crisis in American Economic Education." *The Journal of Economic Education* 23 (4): 353–56.

Andreski, Stanislav. 1968. *Military Organization and Society.* Berkeley: University of California Press.

Anichini, Juan José. 1992. Interview of October 5 with the former director of the planning office.

Anichini, Juan José, et al. 1977. *La Política Comercial y la Protección en el Uruguay.* Montevideo: Banco Central del Uruguay.

Arancibia, General Fernando. 1992. Interview of September 3 with the former vice minister of foreign affairs.

Aranco, General Pedro. 1992. Interview of October 21 with the former director of the planning office.

Archer, Ronald P. 1995. "Party Strength in Colombia's Besieged Democracy." In Scott Mainwaring and Timothy R. Scully, eds., *Building Democratic*

Institutions: Party Systems in Latin America, 164–99. Stanford: Stanford University Press.

Archer, Ronald P., and Matthew Soberg Shugart. 1997. "The Unrealized Potential of Presidential Dominance in Colombia." In Scott Mainwaring and Matthew Soberg Shugart, eds., *Presidentialism and Democracy in Latin America*, 110–59. New York: Cambridge University Press.

Arriagada Herrera, Genaro. 1986. "The Legal and Institutional Framework of the Armed Forces in Chile." In J. Samuel Valenzuela and Arturo Valenzuela, eds., *Military Rule in Chile: Dictatorship and Oppositions*, 127–43. Baltimore: Johns Hopkins University Press.

———. 1988. *Pinochet: The Politics of Power*. Translated by Nancy Morris with Vincent Ercolano and Kristen A. Whitney. Boston: Unwin Hyman.

Arriazu, Ricardo. 1992. Interview of November 27 with the Argentine economist.

Artana, Daniel. 1988. "Tax Policy and Resource Allocation in Argentina." Ph. D. dissertation, UCLA.

Arteaga, Domingo. 1992. Interview of September 8 with the former president of the National Association of Manufacturers.

Ascher, William L. 1975. "Planners, Politics, and Technocracy in Argentina and Chile." Ph. D. dissertation, Yale University.

Baer, Werner. 1972. "Import Substitution and Liberalization in Latin America." *Latin American Research Review* 7 (1): 95–122.

Baer, Werner, and Melissa H. Birch, eds. 1994. *Privatization in Latin America: New Roles for the Public and Private Sectors*. Westport, Conn.: Praeger.

Balán, Jorge. 1982. "Social Sciences in the Periphery: Perspectives on the Latin American Case." In Laurence D. Stifel, et al., eds., *Social Sciences and Public Policy in the Developing World*, 211–47. Lexington, Mass.: Lexington Books.

Banco Central del Uruguay. 1986. *Boletín Estadístico*. Montevideo: Banco Central del Uruguay 86 (July).

Baraona, Pablo. 1992. Interview of August 5 with the former minister of the economy.

Bardon, Alvaro. 1992. Interview of August 11 with the former president of the central bank.

Baretta, Silvio R. Duncan, and John Markoff. 1987. "Brazil's Abertura: A Transition from What to What?" In James M. Malloy and Mitchell A. Seligson, eds., *Authoritarians and Democrats: Regime Transition in Latin America*, 43–66. Pittsburgh: University of Pittsburgh Press.

Barros, Robert J. 1996. "The Constitution of the Exception: Defining the Rules of Military Rule." Ph. D. dissertation, The University of Chicago.

Bates, Robert H. 1981. *Markets and States in Tropical Africa: The Political Basis of Agricultural Policies*. Berkeley: University of California Press.

Bates, Robert H., and Da-Hsiang Donald Lien. 1985. "A Note on Taxation, Development, and Representative Government." *Politics and Society* 14: 53–70.

Berlinsky, Julio. 1994. Interview of March 28 with the Argentine economist.

Bhagwati, Jagdish N., et al. 1984. "DUP Activities and Economic Theory." *European Economic Review* 24: 291–307.

Biglaiser, Glen. 1999. "Military Regimes, Neoliberal Restructuring, and Economic Development: Reassessing the Chilean Case." *Studies in Comparative International Development* 34 (1): 1–24.

———. 2002. "The Internationalization of Chicago's Economics in Latin America." *Economic Development and Cultural Change* 50 (2): 269–86.

Boeker, Paul H. 1993. *Latin America's Turnaround: Privatization, Foreign Investment, and Growth.* San Francisco: International Center for Economic Growth.

Boeninger, Edgardo. 1982. "Application of the Social Sciences to Public Policies: Producers, Consumers, and Mechanisms of Mediation." In Laurence D. Stifel, et al., eds., *Social Sciences and Public Policy in the Developing World,* 251–76. Lexington, Mass.: Lexington Books.

Bordaberry, Juan María. 1992. Interview of September 29 with the former president of Uruguay.

Bresser Pereira, Luiz Carlos. 1993. "Economic Reforms and Economic Growth: Efficiency and Politics in Latin America." In Luiz Carlos Bresser Pereira, et al., eds., *Economic Reforms in New Democracies: A Social-Democratic Approach,* 15–76. Cambridge: Cambridge University Press.

Bresser Pereira, Luiz Carlos, José María Maravall, and Adam Przeworski, eds. 1993. *Economic Reforms in New Democracies: A Social-Democratic Approach.* Cambridge: Cambridge University Press.

Bruce, David C. 1980. "The Impact of the United Nations Economic Commission for Latin America: Technocrats as Channels of Influence." *Inter-American Economic Affairs* 33 (4): 3–28.

Bruce, David K. E. 1957. *South America (Peru, Chile, Argentina, Uruguay, and Brazil) Report on United States Foreign Assistance Programs.* Washington, D. C.: United States 85th Congress.

Búsqueda. 1977. "El Paternalismo Estatal Adormece al Empresario." 59 (May): 4–9.

———. 1979. "Editorial: Plebiscitar la Privatización de Ancap." 81 (June): 1.

Cáceres, Carlos. 1992. Interview of August 14 with the former minister of finance.

Callaghy, Thomas M. 1993. "Political Passions and Economic Interests: Economic Reform and Political Structure in Africa." In Thomas M. Callaghy and John Ravenhill, eds., *Hemmed In: Responses to Africa's Economic Decline,* 463–519. New York: Columbia University Press.

Camp, Roderic Ai. 1999. *Politics in Mexico: The Decline of Authoritarianism.* 3rd ed. New York: Oxford University Press.

Campero, Guillermo. 1991. "Entrepreneurs under the Military Regime." In Paul W. Drake and Iván Jaksic, eds., *The Struggle for Democracy in Chile, 1982–1990,* 128–58. Lincoln: University of Nebraska Press.

Canitrot, Adolfo. 1994. Interview of March 28 with the director of the Institute di Tella.

Cardoso, Fernando H., and Enzo Faletto. 1979. *Dependency and Development in Latin America*. Berkeley: University of California Press.

Carranza, Mario Esteban. 1983. "The Role of Military Expenditures in the Development Process: The Argentine Case, 1946–1980." *Ibero-Americana* 12 (1–2): 115–66.

Cassidy, John. 1996. "The Decline of Economics." *The New Yorker* (December 2): 52.

Caumont, Jorge. 1992. Interview of September 22 with the former advisor to the ministry of economics and the planning ministry.

———. 1994. Interview of March 24 with the former advisor to the ministry of economics and the planning ministry.

Cavallo, Domingo. 1992. "Argentina's Economic Revolution." In Pedro Aspe, Andres Bianchi, and Domingo Cavallo, eds., *Sea Changes in Latin America*, 21–25. Washington, D.C.: Group of Thirty.

Cavarozzi, Marcello. 1986. "Political Cycles in Argentina since 1955." In Guillermo O'Donnell, Philippe C. Schmitter, and Laurence Whitehead, eds., *Transitions from Authoritarian Rule: Latin America*, 19–48. Baltimore: Johns Hopkins University Press.

Centeno, Miguel A. 1994. *Democracy within Reason: Technocratic Revolution in Mexico*. University Park: Pennsylvania State University.

Centeno, Miguel, and Patricio Silva, eds. 1998. *The Politics of Expertise: Technocratic Ascendancy in Latin America*. London: Center for Latin American Studies (CEDLA), Macmillan Press.

Center for Education and Social Research. Various years. *Political Handbook of the World*. Binghamton: Center for Education and Social Research, State University of New York.

Chazan, Naomi, and Donald Rothchild. 1993. "The Political Repercussions of Economic Malaise." In Thomas M. Callaghy and John Ravenhill, eds., *Hemmed In: Responses to Africa's Economic Decline*, 180–214. New York: Columbia University Press.

Cleaves, Peter S., and Henry Pease García. 1983. "State Autonomy and Military Policy Making." In Cynthia McClintock and Abraham F. Lowenthal, eds., *The Peruvian Experience Reconsidered*, 209–44. Princeton: Princeton University Press.

Clinton, David. 1988. "Tocqueville's Challenge." *The Washington Quarterly* 11 (1): 173–89.

Conaghan, Catherine M. 1992. "Capitalists, Technocrats, and Politicians: Economic Policy Making and Democracy in the Central Andes." In Scott Mainwaring, Guillermo O'Donnell, and J. Samuel Valenzuela, eds., *Issues in Democratic Consolidation: The New South American Democracies in Comparative Perspective*, 199–242. Notre Dame: University of Notre Dame Press.

Conaghan, Catherine M., James M. Malloy, and Luis A. Abugattas. 1990. "Business and the 'Boys': The Politics of Neoliberalism in the Central Andes." *Latin American Research Review* 25 (2): 3–32.

Conaghan, Catherine M., and James M. Malloy. 1994. *Unsettling Statecraft: Neoliberal Coalitions in the Central Andes.* Pittsburgh: University of Pittsburgh Press.

Concha, General Manuel. 1992. Interview of August 26 with the former minister of the economy.

Constable, Pamela, and Arturo Valenzuela. 1991. *A Nation of Enemies: Chile under Pinochet.* New York: W.W. Norton.

Corbo, Vittorio. 1983. *Chile: Economic Policy and International Economic Relations since 1970.* Santiago: Pontificia Universidad Católica de Chile, Instituto de Económia 86 (3).

———. 1985. "Reforms and Macroeconomic Adjustments in Chile during 1974–84." *World Development* 13 (8): 893–916.

Corbo, Vittorio, and Jaime de Melo, eds. 1985. "Overview and Summary." *World Development* 13 (8): 863–66.

Corbo, Vittorio, and Stanley Fischer. 1994. "Lessons from the Chilean Stabilization and Recovery." In Barry P. Bosworth, et al., eds., *The Chilean Economy: Policy Lessons and Challenges,* 29–80. Washington, D.C.: The Brookings Institution.

CORFO. 1979. *Privatización de Empresa y Activos,1973–1978.* Santiago: CORFO Gerencia de Normalización de Empresa.

Corrales, Javier. 1997. "Why Argentines Followed Cavallo: A Technopol between Democracy and Economic Reform." In Jorge I. Domínguez, ed., *Technopols: Freeing Politics and Markets in Latin America in the 1990s,* 49–93. University Park: Pennsylvania State University Press.

Correa, Sofía. 1985. "Algunos Antecedentes Históricos del Proyecto Neoliberal en Chile (1955–1958)." *Opciones* 6: 106–46.

Cortázar, René. 1989. "Austerity under Authoritarianism: The Neoconservative Revolution in Chile." In Howard Handelman and Werner Baer, eds., *Paying the Costs of Austerity in Latin America,* 43–63. Boulder: Westview Press.

Cortés Douglas, Hernán, et al. 1981. "Proteccionismo en Chile: Una Visión Retrospectiva." *Cuadernos de Economía* 54–55: 141–94.

Costabal, Martin. 1992. Interview of September 2 with the former minister of finance.

Cotler, Julio. 1978. "A Structural-Historical Approach to the Breakdown of Democratic Institutions: Peru." In Juan J. Linz and Alfred Stepan, eds., *The Breakdown of Democratic Regimes,* 178–205. Baltimore: Johns Hopkins University Press.

———. 1986. "Military Interventions and 'Transfer of Power to Civilians' in Peru." In Guillermo O'Donnell, Philippe C. Schmitter, and Laurence Whitehead, eds., *Transitions from Authoritarian Rule: Latin America,* 148–72. Baltimore: Johns Hopkins University Press.

Craig, Ann L., and Wayne A. Cornelius. 1995. "Houses Divided: Parties and Political Reform in Mexico." In Scott Mainwaring and Timothy R. Scully, eds., *Building Democratic Institutions: Party Systems in Latin America,* 249–97. Stanford: Stanford University Press.

Dagnino Pastore, José María. 1988. *Cronicas Económicas: Argentina, 1969–1988.* Buenos Aires: Editorial Crespillo.

———. 1989. "Argentina." In Joseph A. Pechman, ed., *The Role of the Economist in Government: An International Perspective,* 195–212. New York: Harvester Wheatsheaf.

———. 1990. "José María Dagnino Pastore." In Guido di Tella and Carlos Rodríguez Braun, eds., *Argentina, 1946–83: The Economic Ministers Speak,* 104–10. Oxford: Macmillan Press.

Dahse, Fernando. 1979. *El Mapa de la Extrema Riqueza: Los Grupos Económicos y el Proceso de Concentración de Capitales.* Santiago: Editorial Aconcagua.

De Castro, Sergio. 1992. Interview of September 1 with the former minister of finance.

De Cecco, Marcello. 1989. "Keynes and Italian Economics." In Peter A. Hall, ed., *The Political Power of Economic Ideas: Keynesianism across Nations,* 195–230. Princeton: Princeton University Press.

De la Cuadra, Sergio. 1992. Interview of July 31 with the former minister of finance.

De la Cuadra, Sergio, and Dominique Hachette. 1985. *The Timing and Sequencing of a Trade Liberalization Policy: The Case of Chile (First Part).* Santiago: Pontificia Universidad Católica de Chile, Instituto de Economía, 98 (July).

———. 1988. *The Timing and Sequencing of a Trade Liberalization Policy: The Case of Chile.* Santiago: Pontificia Universidad Católica de Chile, Instituto de Economía, 113 (August).

Delano, Manuel, and Hugo Traslaviña. 1989. *La Herencia de los Chicago Boys.* Santiago: Ornitorrinco.

De Melo, Jaime, et al. 1985. "Microeconomic Adjustments in Uruguay during 1973–81: The Interplay of Real and Financial Shocks." *World Development* 13 (8): 995–1015.

De Pablo, Juan Carlos. 1977. *Los Economistas y la Economía Argentina.* Buenos Aires: Ediciones Macchi.

———. 1994. Interview of March 29 with the Argentine economist.

Díaz-Alejandro, Carlos. 1970. *Essays in the Economic History of the Argentine Republic.* New Haven: Yale University Press.

Díaz, Ramón. 1992. Interview of September 28 with the president of the central bank.

Díaz, Ramón, and Alberto Sayagues. 1985. *Las Empresas Públicas.* Montevideo: Tradinco S.A.

Di Tella, Guido. 1989. "Argentina's Economy under a Labour-based Government, 1973–6." In Guido di Tella and Rudiger Dornbusch, eds., *The Political Economy of Argentina, 1946–83*, 213–53. Oxford: Macmillan Press.

Di Tella, Guido, and Rudiger Dornbusch, eds. 1989. *The Political Economy of Argentina, 1946–83.* Oxford: Macmillan Press.

Di Tella, Guido, and Carlos Rodríguez Braun, eds. 1990. *Argentina, 1946–83: The Economic Ministers Speak.* Oxford: Macmillan Press.

Diz, Adolfo. 1992. Interview of November 25 with the former president of the central bank.

Domínguez, Jorge I., ed. 1997. *Technopols: Freeing Politics and Markets in Latin America in the 1990s.* University Park: Pennsylvania State University Press.

Donoso, Alvaro. 1992. Interview of July 28 and August 31 with the former head of ODEPLAN.

Dornbusch, Rudiger. 1989. "Argentina after Martínez de Hoz." In Guido di Tella and Rudiger Dornbusch, eds., *The Political Economy of Argentina, 1946–83*, 286–315. Oxford: Macmillan Press.

Dornbusch, Rudiger, and Sebastian Edwards, eds. 1991. *The Macroeconomics of Populism in Latin America.* Chicago: The University of Chicago Press.

Drake, Paul W. 1978. *Socialism and Populism in Latin America, 1932–52.* Urbana: University of Illinois Press.

———. 1998. "The International Causes of Democratization, 1974–1990." In Paul W. Drake and Mathew D. McCubbins, eds., *The Origins of Liberty: Political and Economic Liberalization in the Modern World*, 70–91. Princeton: Princeton University Press.

———, ed. 1994. *Money Doctors, Foreign Debts, and Economic Reforms in Latin America from the 1890s to the Present.* Wilmington, Del.: Scholarly Resources, Inc., Jaguar Books on Latin America, number 3.

Drake, William J., and Kalypso Nicolaïdis. 1992. "Ideas, Institutionalization: Trade in Services and the Uruguay Round." In Peter Haas, ed., "Knowledge, Power and International Policy Coordination." *International Organization* 46 (1): 37–100.

Dupuy, Trevor N. 1972. *The Almanac of World Military Power.* 2nd ed. New York: R. R. Bowker Co.

Edwards, Sebastian, and Alejandro Cox Edwards. 1991. *Monetarism and Liberalization: The Chilean Experiment.* Chicago: The University of Chicago Press.

Einaudi, Luigi R., and Alfred C. Stepan III. 1971. *Latin American Institutional Development: Changing Military Perspectives in Peru and Brazil.* Santa Monica: Rand.

El Ladrillo: Bases de la Política Económica del Gobierno Militar Chileno. 1992. Santiago: Centro de Estudios Públicos.

El Proceso Político: Las Fuerzas Armadas al Pueblo Oriental Tomo II. 1978. Montevideo: República Oriental del Uruguay Junta de Comandantes en Jefe.

Epstein, Edward C. 1985. "Inflation and Public Policy in Argentina." Presented at the annual meeting of the American Political Science Association, New Orleans.

Errázuriz, Hernan Felipe. 1992. Interview of August 24 with the former president of the central bank.

Estevez, Gonzalez. 1992. Interview of November 17 with the former subsecretary of commerce and industry.

Estrada, Alejandro Manuel. 1992. Interview of November 19 with the former secretary of commerce.

Evans, Peter B. 1979. *Dependent Development: The Alliance of Multinational, State, and Local Capital in Brazil*. Princeton: Princeton University Press.

———. 1992. "The State as Problem and Solution: Predation, Embedded Autonomy, and Structural Change." In Stephan Haggard and Robert R. Kaufman, eds., *The Politics of Economic Adjustment: International Constraints, Distributive Conflicts, and the State*, 139–81. Princeton: Princeton University Press.

Falcoff, Mark. 1989. *Modern Chile, 1970–1989: A Critical History*. New Brunswick, N. J.: Transaction Publishers.

Faroppa, Luis A. 1982. *Politicas para una Economía Disequilibrada: Uruguay, 1958–1981*. Montevideo: Ediciones de la Banda Oriental.

Favaro, Edgardo, and Pablo T. Spiller. 1991. "Uruguay." In Demetris Papageorgiou, et al., *Liberalizing Foreign Trade: Argentina, Chile, and Uruguay*, 328–407. Vol. 1. Cambridge, Mass.: Basil Blackwell.

Fernández, Julio A. 1976. "Political Immobility in Argentina." *Current History* (February): 73–86.

Fernández Vaccaro, Pablo. 1978. *La Economía en el Quinquenio, 1973–1978*. Montevideo: Acali Editorial.

Ferrer, Aldo. 1990. "Aldo Ferrer." In Guido di Tella and Carlos Rodríguez Braun, eds., *Argentina, 1946–83: The Economic Ministers Speak*, 111–16. Oxford: Macmillan Press.

Ffrench-Davis, Ricardo. 1973. *Políticas Económicas en Chile, 1952–1970*. Santiago: Editorial Nuevas Universidad.

———. 1988. "An Outline of a Neo-structuralist Approach." *CEPAL Review* 34 (2): 37–44.

———. 1992. Interview on July 23 with the Chilean economist.

FIEL. 1988. *El Gasto Público en la Argentina 1960–1988*. Buenos Aires: Fundación de Investigaciones Económicas Latinoamericanas.

Finch, M. H. J. 1981. *A Political Economy of Uruguay since 1870*. London: Macmillan Press.

———, ed. 1989. *Contemporary Uruguay: Problems and Prospects*. Liverpool: Institute of Latin American Studies.

Finer, S. E. 1962. *The Man on Horseback: The Role of the Military in Politics*. New York: Praeger.

Fishlow, Albert. 1973. "Some Reflections on Post-1964 Brazilian Economic Policy." In Alfred Stepan, ed., *Authoritarian Brazil*, 69–118. New Haven: Yale University Press.

Flood, David B. 1979. Personal correspondence between Mr. Flood and Ronald G. Hellman on July 23, made available through Albion Patterson.

Foglesong, Richard E., and Joel D. Wolfe. 1989. *The Politics of Economic Adjustment: Pluralism, Corporatism, and Privatization.* Westport, Conn.: Greenwood Press.

Folcini, Enrique. 1992. Interview of October 28 with the former minister of the economy.

Fontaine, Juan Andres. 1992. Interview of August 10 with the former chief economist at the central bank.

Fontaine Aldunate, Arturo. 1988. *Los Economistas y el Presidente Pinochet.* Santiago: Empresa Editora Zig-Zag, S.A.

Fontaine Talavera, Arturo. 1992. "Sobre el Pecada Original de la Transformación Capitalista Chilena." In Barry B. Levine, ed., *El Desafío Neoliberal: El Fin del Tercermundismo en América Latina*, 93–140. Bogotá: Editorial Norma S.A.

Fontana, Andrés. 1984. *Fuerzas Armadas, Partidos Políticos y Transición a la Democracia en Argentina.* Buenos Aires: Centro de Estudios de Estado y Sociedad.

———. 1986. "Armed Forces and Neoconservative Ideology: State Shrinking in Argentina, 1976–1981." In William P. Glade, ed., *State Shrinking: A Comparative Inquiry into Privatization*, 62–74. Austin: Institute of Latin American Studies.

———. 1987. "Political Decision Making by a Military Corporation." Ph.D. dissertation, University of Texas, Austin.

Forteza, Francisco. 1992. Interview of October 6 with the former minister of the economy and senator.

Foxley, Alejandro. 1983. *Latin American Experiments in Neoconservative Economics.* Berkeley: University of California Press.

———. 1986. "The Neoconservative Economic Experiment in Chile." In J. Samuel Valenzuela and Arturo Valenzuela, eds., *Military Rule in Chile: Dictatorship and Oppositions*, 13–50. Baltimore: Johns Hopkins University Press.

Foxley, Juan. 1992. Interview of July 27 with the former manager of financial intermediation for CORFO.

Frez, General Gaston. 1992. Interview of August 31 with the former head of CORFO and CODELCO.

Frieden, Jeffry A. 1991. *Debt, Development, and Democracy: Modern Political Economy in Latin America.* Princeton: Princeton University Press.

Friedman, Milton. 1975. *An Economist's Protest.* Glenridge, N.J.: T. Horton.

Gabbert, Jack B. 1992. "The Mexican Chief Executive." In Taketsugu Tsurutani and Jack B. Gabbert, eds., *Chief Executives: National Political Leadership in the United States, Mexico, Great Britain, Germany, and Japan*, 66–110. Pullman: Washington State University Press.

Gabriel Leyba, Carlos Raúl. 1990. "Carlos Raúl Gabriel Leyba." In Guido di Tella and Carlos Rodríguez Braun, eds., *Argentina, 1946–83: The Economic Ministers Speak,* 120–38. Oxford: Macmillan Press.

García de Fanelli, Ana María. 1995. "Institutional and Program Differentiation in the Argentine Higher Educational System: The Outcome of the Public Policies in the 1980s." Presented at the annual meeting of the Latin American Studies Association, the Washington, D. C., Sheraton Hotel.

Garretón, Manuel Antonio. 1986. "Political Processes in an Authoritarian Regime: The Dynamics of Institutionalization and Opposition in Chile, 1973–1980." In J. Samuel Valenzuela and Arturo Valenzuela, eds., *Military Rule in Chile: Dictatorship and Oppositions,* 144–83. Baltimore: Johns Hopkins University Press.

Garritsen de Vries, Margaret. 1986. "The International Monetary Fund: Economists in Key Roles." In A. W. Coats, ed., *Economists in International Agencies: An Exploratory Study,* 53–66. New York: Praeger Special Studies.

Geddes, Barbara. 1991. "Political Institutions and Economic Policy or How Politicians Decide Who Bears the Cost of Structural Adjustment." Presented at the American Political Science Association Meetings, Washington, D. C.

———. 1994. *Politician's Dilemma: Reforming the State in Latin America.* Berkeley: Series on Social Choice and Political Economy, University of California Press.

———. 1995. "Challenging the Conventional Wisdom." In Larry Diamond and Marc F. Plattner, eds., *Economic Reform and Democracy,* 59–73. Baltimore: Johns Hopkins University Press.

Gerchunoff, Pablo, and Alieto Guadagni. 1987. *Las Regulaciones en la Argentina: Elementos para una Reformulación Económica del Estado.* Buenos Aires: 5 Anual de Bancos Privados Nacionales.

Gillespie, Charles Guy. 1986. "Uruguay's Transition from Collegial Military-Technocratic Rule." In Guillermo O'Donnell, Philippe C. Schmitter, and Laurence Whitehead, eds., *Transitions from Authoritarian Rule: Latin America,* 173–95. Baltimore: Johns Hopkins University Press.

———. 1991. *Negotiating Democracy: Politicians and Generals in Uruguay.* Cambridge: Cambridge University Press.

Gillespie, Charles Guy, and Luis Eduardo González. 1989. "Uruguay: The Survival of Old and Autonomous Institutions." In Larry Diamond, Juan J. Linz, and Seymour Martin Lipset, eds., *Democracy in Developing Countries: Latin America,* 159–206. Boulder: Lynne Rienner Publishers.

———. 1994. "Presidentialism and Democratic Stability in Uruguay." In Juan J. Linz and Arturo Valenzuela, eds., *The Failure of Presidential Democracy: The Case of Latin America,* 225–52. Baltimore: Johns Hopkins University Press.

Glade, William, ed. 1991. *Privatization of Public Enterprises in Latin America.* San Francisco: International Center for Economic Growth.

Goldstein, Judith, and Robert O. Keohane, eds. 1993. *Ideas and Foreign Policy: Beliefs, Institutions, and Political Change.* Ithaca: Cornell University Press.

Gómez-Lobo, Andrés, and Sergio Lehmann. 1991. "Sobretasas Arancelarias en Chile: 1982–1991." *CIEPLAN Notas Tecnicas* 144 (11): 5–39.

González Fraga, Javier A. 1991. "Argentine Privatization in Retrospect." In William Glade, ed., *Privatization of Public Enterprises in Latin America*. San Francisco: International Center for Economic Growth.

Grindle, Merilee, and John Thomas. 1991. *Policy Choices and Policy Change: The Political Economy of Reform in Developing Countries*. Baltimore: Johns Hopkins University Press.

Guadagni, Alieto Aldo. 1989. "Economic Policy during Illia's Period in Office." In Guido di Tella and Rudiger Dornbusch, eds., *The Political Economy of Argentina, 1946–83*, 147–61. Oxford: Macmillan Press.

Haas, Peter, ed. 1992. "Knowledge, Power and International Policy Coordination." *International Organization* 46 (1).

Hachette, Dominique, and Rolf Lüders. 1993. *Privatization in Chile: An Economic Appraisal*. San Francisco: International Center for Economic Growth.

Haggard, Stephan. 1986. "The Politics of Adjustment: Lesson's from the IMF's Extended Fund Facility." In Miles Kahler, ed., *Politics of International Debt*, 157–86. Ithaca: Cornell University Press.

———. 1988. "Privatization in the Philippines." In Raymond Vernon, ed., *The Promise of Privatization: A Challenge for U.S. Foreign Policy*. New York: Council on Foreign Relations.

———. 1990. *Pathways from the Periphery: The Politics of Growth in the Newly Industrializing Countries*. Ithaca: Cornell University Press.

Haggard, Stephan, and Robert R. Kaufman. 1989. "The Politics of Stabilization and Structural Adjustment." In Jeffrey D. Sachs, ed., *Developing Country Debt and Economic Performance*, 263–74. Chicago: The University of Chicago Press.

———. 1995. *The Political Economy of Democratic Transitions*. Princeton: Princeton University Press.

———. 1998. "The Political Economy of Authoritarian Withdrawals." In Paul W. Drake and Mathew D. McCubbins, eds., *The Origins of Liberty: Political and Economic Liberalization in the Modern World*, 92–114. Princeton: Princeton University Press.

Hall, Peter. 1989. *The Political Power of Economic Ideas: Keynesianism across Nations*. Princeton: Princeton University Press.

Hallberg, Kristin, and Wendy E. Takacs. 1992. "Trade Reform in Colombia: 1990–94." In Alvin Cohen and Frank R. Gunter, eds., *The Colombian Economy: Issues of Trade and Development*, 259–99. Boulder: Westview Press.

Halpern, Nina P. 1993. "Creating Socialist Economies: Stalinist Political Economy and the Impact of Ideas." In Judith Goldstein and Robert O. Keohane, eds., *Ideas and Foreign Policy: Beliefs, Institutions, and Political Change*, 87–110. Ithaca: Cornell University Press.

Handelman, Howard. 1981a. "Military Authoritarianism and Political Change." In Howard Handelman and Thomas G. Sanders, eds., *Military Government and the Movement toward Democracy in South America,* 215–36. Bloomington: Indiana University Press.

———. 1981b. "Economic Policy and Elite Pressures." In Howard Handelman and Thomas G. Sanders, eds., *Military Government and the Movement toward Democracy in South America,* 237–84. Bloomington: Indiana University Press.

Hanson, James, and Jaime De Melo. 1985. "External Shocks, Financial Reforms, and Stabilization Attempts in Uruguay during 1974–83." *World Development* 13 (8): 917–40.

Hanson, Simon Gabriel. 1938. *Utopia in Uruguay: Chapters in the Economic History of Uruguay.* New York: Oxford University Press.

Harberger, Arnold. 1992. Interview of April 30 with the professor of economics at UCLA.

———. 1995. Interview of February 16 with the professor of economics at UCLA.

Hartlyn, Jonathan. 1989. "Colombia: The Politics of Violence and Accommodation." In Larry Diamond, Juan J. Linz, and Seymour Martin Lipset, eds., *Democracy in Developing Countries: Latin America,* 291–334. Boulder: Lynne Rienner Publishers.

———. 1994. "Presidentialism and Colombian Politics." In Juan J. Linz and Arturo Valenzuela, eds., *The Failure of Presidential Democracy: The Case of Latin America,* 220–53. Baltimore: Johns Hopkins University Press.

Hecht Oppenheim, Lois. 1993. *Politics in Chile: Democracy, Authoritarianism, and the Search for Development.* Boulder: Westview Press.

Heller, William B., Philip Keefer, and Mathew D. McCubbins. 1998. "Political Structure and Economic Liberalization: Conditions and Cases from the Developing World." In Paul W. Drake and Mathew D. McCubbins, eds., *The Origins of Liberty: Political and Economic Liberalization in the Modern World,* 146–78. Princeton: Princeton University Press.

Heyman, Daniel. 1994. Interview of March 29 with the Argentine economist.

Hirschman, Albert O. 1963. *Journeys toward Progress: Studies of Economic Policymaking in Latin America.* New York: Twentieth Century Fund.

———. 1968. "The Political Economy of Import-Substitution Industrialization in Latin America." *Quarterly Journal of Economics* 82: 1–32.

———. 1970. *Exit, Voice, and Loyalty: Responses to Decline in Firms, Organizations, and States.* Cambridge, Mass.: Harvard University Press.

———. 1979. "The Turn to Authoritarianism in Latin America and the Search for its Economic Determinants." In David Collier, ed., *The New Authoritarianism in Latin America,* 61–98. Princeton: Princeton University Press.

———. 1989. "How the Keynesian Revolution Was Exported from the United States and Other Comments." In Peter A. Hall, ed., *The Political Power of Economic Ideas: Keynesianism across Nations,* 347–59. Princeton: Princeton University Press.

Hojman, David E. 1993. *Chile: The Political Economy of Development and Democracy in the 1990s.* Pittsburgh: University of Pittsburgh Press.

Hopkins, Raymond F. 1992. "Reform in the International Food Aid Regime: The Role of Consensual Knowledge." In Peter Haas, ed., "Knowledge, Power and International Policy Coordination." *International Organization* 46 (1): 225–64.

Huntington, Samuel P. 1968. *Political Order in Changing Societies.* New Haven: Yale University Press.

———. 1987. "Political Change in the Third World." In Samuel P. Huntington and Myron Weiner, eds., *Understanding Political Development,* 3–32. Boston: Little, Brown and Co.

Iglesias, Enrique. 1992. *Reflections on Economic Development: Toward a New Latin American Consensus.* Washington, D.C.: IDB.

Ikenberry, G. John. 1992. "A World Economy Restored: Expert Consensus and the Anglo-American Postwar Settlement." *International Organization* 46 (1): 289–322.

———. 1993. "Creating Yesterday's New World Order: Keynesian New Thinking and the Anglo-American Postwar Settlement." In Judith Goldstein and Robert O. Keohane, eds., *Ideas and Foreign Policy: Beliefs, Institutions, and Political Change,* 57–86. Ithaca: Cornell University Press.

The International Institute for Strategic Studies. 1978. *The Military Balance, 1977–1978.* London: The International Institute for Strategic Studies.

International Monetary Fund. Various years. *International Financial Statistics Yearbook.* 1945–1996. Washington D.C.: IMF.

Jacobsen, John Kurt. 1995. "Much Ado about Ideas: The Cognitive Factor in Economic Policy." *World Politics* 47 (January): 283–310.

James, Harold. 1989. "What is Keynesian about Deficit Financing? The Case of Interwar Germany." In Peter A. Hall, ed., *The Political Power of Economic Ideas: Keynesianism across Nations,* 231–62. Princeton: Princeton University Press.

Janowitz, Morris. 1977. *Military Institutions and Coercion in the Developing Nations.* Chicago: The University of Chicago Press.

Joffe, Josef. 1988. "Tocqueville Revisited: Are Good Democracies Bad Players in the Game of Nations?" *The Washington Quarterly* 11 (1): 161–72.

Johnson, Harry G. 1975. *On Economics and Society.* Chicago: The University of Chicago Press.

Johnson, Kenneth F. 1982. "Military Government in Uruguay: Prospects for the 1980s." In Robert G. Wesson, ed., *New Military Politics in Latin America,* 117–30. New York: Praeger.

Jones, Mark P. 1997. "Evaluating Argentina's Presidential Democracy: 1983–1995." In Scott Mainwaring and Matthew Soberg Shugart, eds., *Presidentialism and Democracy in Latin America,* 259–99. New York: Cambridge University Press.

Jowitt, Kenneth. 1971. *Revolutionary Breakthroughs and National Development: The Case of Romania, 1944–1965.* Berkeley: University of California Press.

Kaufman, Edy. 1979. *Uruguay in Transition: From Civilian to Military Rule.* New Brunswick, N. J.: Transaction Books.

Kaufman, Robert R. 1979. "Industrial Change and Authoritarian Rule in Latin America: A Concrete Review of the Bureaucratic-Authoritarian Model." In David Collier, ed., *The New Authoritarianism in Latin America,* 165–253. Princeton: Princeton University Press.

———. 1986. "Democratic and Authoritarian Responses to the Debt Issue: Argentina, Brazil, and Mexico." In Miles Kahler, ed., *The Politics of International Debt,* 187–218. Ithaca: Cornell University Press.

———. 1990. "Stabilization and Adjustment in Argentina, Brazil, and Mexico." In Joan Nelson, ed., *Economic Crisis and Policy Choice: The Politics of Adjustment in the Third World,* 63–111. Princeton: Princeton University Press.

Kaufman, Robert R., Carlos Bazdresch, and Blanca Heredia. 1992. "The Politics of the Economic Solidarity in Mexico: December 1987 to December 1988." Prepared for the World Bank Project on the Political-Economy of Economic Reform, Washington, D. C., July 29.

Kaufman, Robert R., and Barbara Stallings. 1991. "The Political Economy of Latin American Populism." In Rudiger Dornbusch and Sebastian Edwards, eds., *The Macroeconomics of Populism in Latin America,* 15–43. Chicago: The University of Chicago Press.

Keesing's Record of World Events. 1989. London: Longman.

Kelly, Janet. 1996. "One Piece of a Larger Puzzle: The Privatization of VIASA." In Ravi Ramamurti, ed., *Privatizing Monopolies: Lessons from the Telecommunications and Transport Sectors in Latin America,* 241–77. Baltimore: Johns Hopkins University Press.

Kelly, Roberto. 1992. Interviews of August 7 and 21 with the former head of ODEPLAN.

Kemmerer, Donald Lorenzo. 1993. *The Life and Times of Professor Edwin Walter Kemmerer, 1875–1945, and How He Became an International 'Money Doctor'.* S.l.: S. N.

Keynes, John Maynard. 1964. *The General Theory of Employment.* New York: Harcourt Brace Jovanovich.

Klein, Guillermo Walter. 1992. Interview of November 2 with the former secretary of state of economic planning and coordination.

Kohli, Atul. 1986. "Democracy and Development." In John P. Lewis and Valerianna Kallab, eds., *Development Strategies Reconsidered,* 153–82. New Brunswick, N. J.: Transaction Books.

Krieger Vasena, Adalbert. 1988. *El Programa Económico Argentino, 1967/69.* Buenos Aires: Academía Nacional de Ciencias Económicas.

———. 1990. "Adalbert Krieger Vasena." In Guido di Tella and Carlos Rodríguez Braun, eds., *Argentina, 1946–83: The Economic Ministers Speak,* 85–103. Oxford: Macmillan Press.

———. 1992. Interview of October 28 with the former minister of the economy.

Krueger, Anne O. 1974. "The Political Economy of the Rent-Seeking Society." *American Economic Review* 64: 291–303.

Lancaster, Carol. 1988. *U.S. Aid to Sub-Saharian Africa: Challenges, Constraints, and Choices.* Washington D. C.: Center for Strategic and International Studies.

———. 1990. "Economic Reform in Africa: Is it Working?" *The Washington Quarterly* 13 (1): 115–28.

Larraín, Felipe. 1986. *Financial Liberalization in Uruguay: Success or Failure.* Santiago: Instituto de Economía, Universidad de Católica.

Larraín, Felipe, and Patricio Meller. 1991. "The Socialist-Populist Chilean Experience: 1970–1973." In Rudiger Dornbusch and Sebastian Edwards, eds., *The Macroeconomics of Populism in Latin America,* 175–214. Chicago: The University of Chicago Press.

Larroulet, Cristían. 1992a. Interview of August 19 with the former chief of staff of the minister of finance.

———. 1992b. "Impact of Privatization: The Chilean Case, 1985–1989." Working paper.

Latin American Data Base. 1997. *NotiSur—Latin American Affairs,* 7.

Latin Finance. 1991. "Privatization in Latin America: A Supplement to Latin Finance."

Lavín, Joaquín. 1988. *Chile, Revolución Silenciosa.* 6th ed. Santiago: Zig-Zag.

Leff, Nathaniel H. 1968. *Economic Policy-Making and Development in Brazil, 1947–1964.* New York: John Wiley and Sons, Inc.

Léniz, Fernando. 1992. Interview of August 3 with the former minister of the economy.

Lewis, Paul. 1992. *The Crisis of Argentine Capitalism.* Chapel Hill: University of North Carolina Press.

Little, Walter. 1984. "Civil-Military Relations in Contemporary Argentina." *Government and Opposition* 19 (2): 207–24.

Llambias, Joaquin. 1992. Interview of November 24 with the former subsecretary of the general economy.

Lohmann, Susanne, and Sharyn O'Halloran. 1994. "Divided Government and U. S. Trade Policy: Theory and Evidence." *International Organization* 48 (4): 595–632.

López Murphy, Ricardo. 1992. Interview of November 23 with the Argentine economist.

———. 1994. Interview of March 30 with the Argentine economist.

López Murphy, Ricardo, et al., 1988. *Un Ensayo sobre la Economía Uruguaya en la Decada de los 80.* Montevideo: Banco Central del Uruguay.

Loveman, Brian. 1998. "When You Wish upon the Stars: Why the Generals (and Admirals) Say Yes to Latin American 'Transitions' to Civilian Government." In Paul W. Drake and Mathew D. McCubbins, eds., *The Origins of Liberty: Political and Economic Liberalization in the Modern World*, 115–45. Princeton: Princeton University Press.

Loveman, Brian, and Thomas M. Davies, Jr., eds. 1989. *The Politics of Antipolitics: The Military in Latin America*. 2nd ed. Lincoln: University of Nebraska Press.

Lüders, Rolf. 1992a. Interview of August 24 with the former minister of finance.

———. 1992b. "El Estado Empresario en Chile: Las Bases de su Desarrollo hasta 1973, y la Privatización durante el Régimen Militar." In Daniel L. Wisecarver, ed., *El Modelo Económico Chileno*, 133–69. Santiago: Instituto de Económia de la Pontificia Universidad Católica de Chile.

Lusiardo Aznarez, Walter. 1981. *La Participación del Sector Público en la Economía*. Montevideo: Camara de Industrias del Uruguay Departmento de Estudios Economicas.

Macadar, Luis. 1982. *Uruguay, 1974–1980: ¿Un Nuevo Ensayo de Reajuste Economico?* Montevideo: CINVE.

Machiavelli, Niccolò. 1950. *The Prince and the Discourses*. New York: The Modern Library.

Mainhard, Edgar. 1992. "Derrota Política de Lacalle en el Plebiscito Uruguayo." *Diario Ambito Financiero* (December 14): 24.

Mainwaring, Scott, and Timothy R. Scully, eds. 1995. *Building Democratic Institutions: Party Systems in Latin America*. Stanford: Stanford University Press.

Mainwaring, Scott, and Matthew Soberg Shugart, eds. 1997. *Presidentialism and Democracy in Latin America*. New York: Cambridge University Press.

Mallon, Richard D., and Juan V. Sourrouille. 1975. *Economic Policymaking in a Conflict Society: The Argentine Case*. Cambridge: Harvard University Press.

Maravall, José María. 1995. "The Myth of the Authoritarian Advantage." In Larry Diamond and Marc F. Plattner, eds., *Economic Reform and Democracy*, 13–27. Baltimore: Johns Hopkins University Press.

Marsh, David. 1991. "Privatization under Mrs. Thatcher: A Review of the Literature." *Public Administration* 69 (4): 459–80.

Marsh, Robert. 1978. "Does Democracy Hinder Development in the Latecomer Developing Nations?" *Comparative Social Research* 2: 215–48.

Marshall, Jorge, and Felipe Monte. 1988. "Privatization in Chile." In Paul Cook and Colin Kirkpatrick, eds., *Privatization in Less Developed Countries*, 281–307. New York: Hanover Wheatsheaf.

Martínez, José. 1992. Interview of August 18 with the former director of normalization in CORFO.

Martínez de Hoz, José Alfredo. 1981. *Bases para una Argentina Moderna, 1976–80*. Buenos Aires: Emecé Editores.

———. 1990. "José Alfredo Martínez de Hoz." In Guido di Tella and Carlos Rodríguez Braun, eds., *Argentina, 1946–83: The Economic Ministers Speak,* 151–80. Oxford: Macmillan Press.

———. 1991. *15 Años Después.* Buenos Aires: Emecé Editores.

———. 1992. Interview of November 16 with the former minister of the economy.

Martins, Luciano. 1986. "The 'Liberalization' of Authoritarian Rule in Brazil." In Guillermo O'Donnell, Philippe C. Schmitter, and Laurence Whitehead, eds., *Transitions from Authoritarian Rule: Latin America,* 72–94. Baltimore: Johns Hopkins University Press.

Martz, John D. 1992. "Contemporary Colombian Politics: The Struggle over Democratization." In Alvin Cohen and Frank R. Gunter, eds., *The Colombian Economy: Issues of Trade and Development,* 21–46. Boulder: Westview Press.

Massad, Carlos. 1992. Interview of July 16 with the former IMF representative to Chile.

Massey, Andrew. 1992. "Managing Change: Politicians and Experts in the Age of Privatization." *Government and Opposition* 27 (4): 486–501.

Matthei, General Fernando. 1992. Interview of August 26 with the former air force junta leader.

Mayhew, David R. 1974. *Congress: The Electoral Connection.* New Haven: Yale University Press.

Maynard, Geoffrey. 1989. "Argentina: Macroeconomic Policy, 1966–73." In Guido di Tella and Rudiger Dornbusch, eds., *The Political Economy of Argentina, 1946–83,* 166–74. Oxford: Macmillan Press.

McClintock, Cynthia. 1983. "Velasco, Officers, and Citizens: The Politics of Stealth." In Cynthia McClintock and Abraham F. Lowenthal, eds., *The Peruvian Experience Reconsidered,* 275–308. Princeton: Princeton University Press.

———. 1989. "Peru: Precarious Regimes, Authoritarian and Democratic." In Larry Diamond, Juan J. Linz, and Seymour Martin Lipset, eds., *Democracy in Developing Countries: Latin America,* 335–86. Boulder: Lynne Rienner Publishers.

McDonald, Ronald H. 1975. "The Rise of Military Politics in Uruguay." *Inter-American Economic Affairs* 28 (4): 25–43.

McDonald, Ronald H., and J. Mark Ruhl. 1989. *Party Politics and Elections in Latin America.* Boulder: Westview Press.

McGuire, James W. 1995. "Political Parties and Democracy in Argentina." In Scott Mainwaring and Timothy R. Scully, eds., *Building Democratic Institutions: Party Systems in Latin America,* 200–248. Stanford: Stanford University Press.

Medina, General Luis. 1992. Interviews of August 14 and September 3 with the former minister of health.

Meller, Patricio. 1984. "Los Chicago Boys y el Modelo Económico Chileno, 1973–1983." *CIEPLAN* 43 (January).

———. 1992. Interview of September 9 with the director of CIEPLAN.

———. 1993. "A Review of Chilean Privatization Experience." *The Quarterly Review of Economics and Finance* 33 (special issue): 95–112.

Méndez, Juan Carlos. 1992. Interview of July 24 with the former budget director.

Milner, Helen V. 1997. *Interests, Institutions, and Information: Domestic Politics and International Relations.* Princeton: Princeton University Press.

Ministerio de Economía. 1981. *Memoria.* Buenos Aires: Ministerio de Economía.

Mitchell, Christopher. 1967. "The Role of Technocrats in Latin American Integration." *Inter-American Economic Affairs* 21 (1): 3–29.

Montecinos, Veronica. 1988. "Economics and Power: Chilean Economists in Government, 1958–1985." Ph. D. dissertation, University of Pittsburgh.

Montecinos, Veronica, and John Markoff. 2001. "From the Power of Economic Ideas to the Power of Economists." In Miguel Angel Centeno and Fernando Lopez-Alves, eds., *The Other Mirror: Grand Theory through the Lens of Latin America,* 105–50. Princeton: Princeton University Press.

Moore, Richard Kinney. 1978. "Soldiers, Politicians, and Reaction: The Etiology of Military Rule in Uruguay." Ph. D. dissertation, University of Arizona.

Muñoz, Oscar. 1992. Interview of July 24 with the CIEPLAN economist.

Myers, Scott L. 1988. "Uruguay: The Traumatic Years, 1967–1987." Ph. D. dissertation, Washington University, St. Louis.

Naím, Moisés. 1993. *Paper Tigers and Minotaurs: The Politics of Venezuela's Economic Reforms.* Washington, D. C.: The Carnegie Endowment for International Peace.

Nelson, Joan. 1988. "The Political Economy of Stabilization: Commitment, Capacity, and Public Response." In Robert H. Bates, ed., *Toward a Political Economy of Development: A Rational Choice Perspective,* 80–130. Berkeley: University of California Press.

———. 1990. "Introduction: The Politics of Economic Adjustment in Developing Countries." In Joan Nelson, ed., *Economic Crisis and Policy Choice: The Politics of Adjustment in the Third World,* 3–32. Princeton: Princeton University Press.

Nogues, Julio J. 1988. "La Economía Política de Proteccionismo y la Liberalización en la Argentina." *Desarrollo Económico* 28 (110): 159–82.

North, Liisa. 1983. "Ideological Orientation of Peru's Military Rulers." In Cynthia McClintock and Abraham F. Lowenthal, eds., *The Peruvian Experience Reconsidered,* 254–74. Princeton: Princeton University Press.

O'Brien, Philip J. 1982. *The New Leviathan: The Chicago School and the Chilean Regime 1973–1980.* Glasgow: University of Glasgow, Institute of Latin American Studies Occasional Papers No. 38.

———. 1983. *Chile: The Pinochet Decade: The Rise and Fall of the Chicago Boys.* London: Latin American Bureau.

———. 1985. "Authoritarianism and the New Economic Orthodoxy: The Political Economy of the Chilean Regime, 1975–1983." In Philip O'Brien and Paul

Cammack, eds., *Generals in Retreat: The Crisis of Military Rule in Latin America*, 144–83. Manchester, N. H.: Manchester University Press.

O'Donnell, Guillermo A. 1973. *Modernization and Bureaucratic Authoritarianism: Studies in South American Politics*. Berkeley: Institute of International Studies, University of California.

————. 1976. "Modernization and Military Coup Theories, Comparisons, and the Argentine Case." In Abraham F. Lowenthal, ed., *Armies and Politics in Latin America*, 197–243. New York: Holmes and Meier.

————. 1978. "Reflections on the Patterns of Change in the Bureaucratic Authoritarian State." *Latin American Research Review* 13 (1): 3–38.

————. 1981. "Las Fuerzas Armadas y el Estado Autoritario del Cono Sur de América Latina." In Norbert Lechner, ed., *Estado y Política en América Latina*, 199–235. Madrid: Siglo XXI Editores, S. A.

————. 1988. *Bureaucratic Authoritarianism: Argentina, 1966–73 in Comparative Perspective*. Berkeley: University of California Press.

Olson, Mancur. 1965. *The Logic of Collective Action: Public Goods and the Theory of Groups*. Cambridge: Harvard University Press.

————. 1982. *The Rise and Decline of Nations: Economic Growth, Stagflation, and Social Rigidities*. New Haven: Yale University Press.

Packenham, Robert A. 1973. *Liberal America and the Third World: Political Development Ideas in Foreign Aid and Social Science*. Princeton: Princeton University Press.

Palmer, David Scott. 1980. *Peru: The Authoritarian Tradition*. New York: Praeger Publishers.

Papageorgiou, Demetris, et al. 1991. *Liberalizing Foreign Trade: Argentina, Chile, and Uruguay*. Vol. 1. Cambridge: Basil Blackwell.

Paredes, Carlos Eduardo, with Alberto Pasco-Font. 1991. "The Behavior of the Public Sector in Peru: A Macroeconomic Approach." In Felipe Larraín and Marcelo Selowsky, eds., *The Public Sector and the Latin American Crisis*, 191–236. San Francisco: International Center for Economic Growth.

Patterson, Albion. 1995. Interview of February 27 and May 17 with the former director of AID's Point Four Program in Ojai, California.

Peirano, Ricardo. 1992. Interview of September 30 with the founder of *El Observador*.

Pekkarinen, Jukka. 1989. "Keynesianism and the Scandinavian Models of Economic Policy." In Peter A. Hall, ed., *The Political Power of Economic Ideas: Keynesianism across Nations*, 311–46. Princeton: Princeton University Press.

Pempel, T. J. 1999. "The Developmental Regime in a Changing World Economy." In Meredith Woo-Cummings, ed., *The Developmental State*, 137–81. Ithaca: Cornell University Press.

Perelli, Carina. 1990. "The Legacies of Transitions to Democracy." In Louis W. Goodman, Johanna S. R. Mendelson, and Juan Rial, eds., *The Military and*

Democracy: The Future of Civil-Military Relations in Latin America, 39–53. Lexington, Mass.: Lexington Books.

Pérez de Arce, Hermogenes. 1992. Interview of August 19 with the former member of the legislative commission.

Pessino, Captain Salvador. 1992. Interview of December 12 with the former naval captain.

Pessino, Carola. 1994. Interview of March 30 with the Argentine economist.

Peterson, M. J. 1992. "Whalers, Ceteologists, Environmentalists and the International Management of Whaling." In Peter Haas, ed., "Knowledge, Power and International Policy Coordination." *International Organization* 46 (1): 147–86.

Piñera, José. 1991a. "Political Economy of Chilean Reform." *International Economic Insights* 2 (4): 6–9.

———. 1991b. *El Cascabel al Gato: La Batalla por la Reforma Previsional.* Santiago: Zig-Zag.

———. 2000. "A Chilean Model for Russia." *Foreign Affairs* 79 (5): 62–73.

Pinochet Ugarte, Augusto. 1974. *Geopolitica.* 2nd ed. Santiago: Editorial Andres Bello.

Pinto, Aníbal, and Oswaldo Sunkel. 1966. "Latin American Economists in the United States." *Economic Development and Cultural Change* 15 (1): 79–86.

Pion-Berlin, David. 1985. "The Fall of Military Rule in Argentina: 1976–1983." *Journal of Interamerican Studies and World Affairs* 27 (2): 55–76.

———. 1986. "The Defiant State: Chile in the Post-Coup Era." In Abraham F. Lowenthal and J. Samuel Fitch, eds., *Armies and Politics in Latin America,* 317–34. Rev. ed. New York: Holmes and Meier.

———. 1989. *The Ideology of State Terror: Economic Doctrine and Political Repression in Argentina.* Boulder: Lynne Rienner Publishers.

Poggi, Victor. 1992. Interview of November 16 with the former subsecretary of the ministry of economy.

Portales, Carlos, and Augusto Varas. 1983. "The Role of Military Expenditure in the Development Process. Chile 1952–1973 and 1973–1980: Two Contrasting Cases." *Ibero-Americana* 12 (1–2): 21–50.

Potash, Robert A. 1969. *The Army and Politics in Argentina, 1928–1945: Yrigoyen to Perón.* Stanford: Stanford University Press.

———. 1980. *The Army and Politics in Argentina.* Stanford: Stanford University Press.

Prebisch, Raúl. 1947. *Introducción a Keynes.* México: Fondo de Cultura Económica.

Protasi, Juan Carlos. 1992. Interview of September 22 with the former director of the central bank in Uruguay.

Przeworski, Adam. 1991. *Democracy and the Market: Political and Economic Reforms in Eastern Europe and Latin America.* New York: Cambridge University Press.

Puryear, Jeffrey M. 1994. *Thinking Politics: Intellectuals and Democracy in Chile, 1973–1988*. Baltimore: Johns Hopkins University Press.

Rabello de Castro, Paulo, and Marcio Ronci. 1991. "Sixty Years of Populism in Brazil." In Rudiger Dornbusch and Sebastian Edwards, eds., *The Macroeconomics of Populism in Latin America*, 151–74. Chicago: The University of Chicago Press.

Rabkin, Rhoda. 1993. "How Ideas Become Influential." *World Affairs* 156 (1): 3–25.

Ramamurti, Ravi. 1992. "The Impact of Privatization on the Latin American Debt Problem." *Journal of Interamerican Studies and World Affairs* 34 (2): 93–125.

———. 1996. "The New Frontier of Privatization." In Ravi Ramamurti, ed., *Privatizing Monopolies: Lessons from the Telecommunications and Transport Sectors in Latin America*, 1–45. Baltimore: Johns Hopkins University Press.

Ramanadham, V.V., ed. 1993. *Privatization: A Global Perspective*. New York: Routledge.

———. 1994. *Privatization and After: Monitoring and Regulation*. New York: Routledge.

Ramos, Joseph. 1986. *Neoconservative Economics in the Southern Cone of Latin America, 1973–1983*. Baltimore: Johns Hopkins University Press.

Remmer, Karen L. 1986. "The Politics of Economic Stabilization: IMF Standby Programs in Latin America, 1954–1984." *Comparative Politics* 19 (1): 1–24.

———. 1988. *The Chilean Military under Authoritarian Rule, 1973–1987*. Albuquerque: University of New Mexico, Occasional Paper Series No. 1, Latin American Institute.

———. 1989. "State Change in Chile, 1973–1988." *Studies in Comparative International Development* 24 (3): 5–29.

———. 1990. "Democracy and Economic Crisis: The Latin American Experience." *World Politics* 42 (3): 315–35.

———. 1991. *Military Rule in Latin America*. Boulder: Westview Press.

Reyes, General Luis. 1992. Interview of September 9 with the general.

Rial, Juan. 1984. *Elecciones: Reglas de Juego y Tendencias*. Montevideo: CIEP.

———. 1986. *Las Fuerzas Armadas: ¿Soldados-Políticos Garantes de la Democracia?* Montevideo: CIESU.

———. 1989. "The Military in the Role of Substitute Political Party and Redemocratization in Uruguay." In Augusto Varas, ed., *Democracy under Siege: New Military Power in Latin America*, 97–114. New York: Greenwood Press.

Ricci, María Susan, and J. Samuel Fitch. 1990. "Ending Military Regimes in Argentina: 1966–73 and 1976–83." In Louis W. Goodman, Johanna S. R. Mendelson, and Juan Rial, eds., *The Military and Democracy: The Future of Civil-Military Relations in Latin America*, 55–74. Lexington, Mass.: Lexington Books.

Rock, David. 1987. *Argentina, 1516–1987: From Spanish Colonization to Alfonsín.* Berkeley: University of California Press.

———. 1989. "The Military in Politics in Argentina, 1973–83." In Brian Loveman and Thomas M. Davies Jr., eds., *The Politics of Antipolitics: The Military in Latin America,* 321–34. 2nd ed. Lincoln: University of Nebraska Press.

Rodríguez, Carlos. 1994. Interview of March 28 with the director of CEMA.

Rodríguez, Ernesto, and Pablo da Silveira. 1984. "Apogeo y Crisis de la Educación Uruguaya." In *El Proceso Educativo Uruguayo: Dos Enfoques.* Montevideo: Fundación de Cultura Universitaria.

Roett, Rordan. 1972. *Brazil: Politics in a Patrimonial Society.* Boston: Allyn and Bacon, Inc.

Rosanvallon, Pierre. 1989. "The Development of Keynesianism in France." In Peter A. Hall, ed., *The Political Power of Economic Ideas: Keynesianism across Nations,* 171–94. Princeton: Princeton University Press.

Rosenberg, Emily, and Norman Rosenberg. 1994. "From Colonialism to Professionalism: The Public-Private Dynamic in United States Foreign Policy Advising." In Paul W. Drake, ed., *Money Doctors, Foreign Debts, and Economic Reforms in Latin America from the 1890s to the Present,* 59–84. Wilmington, Del.: Scholarly Resources, Inc., Jaguar Books on Latin America, number 3.

Roth, Roberto. 1980. *Los Años de Onganía: Retato de un Testigo.* Buenos Aires: Ediciones la Campana.

Rouquié, Alain. 1981. *Poder Militar y Sociedad Política en la Argentina.* Buenos Aires: Emecé Editores.

———. 1987. *The Military and the State in Latin America.* Translated by Paul E. Sigmund. Berkeley: University of California Press.

Rueschemeyer, Dietrich, and Peter B. Evans. 1985. "The State and Economic Transformation: Toward an Analysis of the Conditions Underlying Effective Intervention." In Peter B. Evans, Dietrich Rueschemeyer, and Theda Skocpol, eds., *Bringing the State Back In,* 44–77. Cambridge: Cambridge University Press.

Salant, Walter S. 1989. "The Spread of Keynesian Doctrines and Practices in the United States." In Peter A. Hall, ed., *The Political Power of Economic Ideas: Keynesianism across Nations,* 27–52. Princeton: Princeton University Press.

Sanders, Thomas G. 1981. "The New Institutionality and the Constitution." In Howard Handelman and Thomas G. Sanders, eds., *Military Government and the Movement toward Democracy in South America,* 346–77. Bloomington: Indiana University Press.

Santo, Michele. 1992. Interview of September 15 with the Uruguayan economist.

Scheetz, Thomas. 1991. "The Macroeconomic Impact of Defence Expenditures: Some Econometric Evidence for Argentina, Chile, Paraguay and Peru." *Defence Economics* 3: 65–81.

———. 1992. "The Evolution of Public Sector Expenditures: Changing Political Priorities in Argentina, Chile, Paraguay and Peru." *Journal of Peace Research* 29 (2): 175–90.

Schenone, Osvaldo H. 1991. "Public Sector Behavior in Argentina." In Felipe Larraín and Marcelo Selowsky, eds., *The Public Sector and the Latin American Crisis*, 11–52. San Francisco: International Center for Economic Growth.

Schneider, Ben Ross. 1987. "Politics within the State: Elite Bureaucrats and Industrial Policy in Authoritarian Brazil." Ph.D. dissertation, University of California, Berkeley.

———. 1991. *Politics within the State: Elite Bureaucrats and Industrial Policy in Authoritarian Brazil*. Pittsburgh: University of Pittsburgh Press.

———. 1999. "The Desarrollista State in Brazil and Mexico." In Meredith Woo-Cummings, ed., *The Developmental State*, 276–305. Ithaca: Cornell University Press.

Schvarzer, Jorge. 1979. "Empresas Públicas y Desarrollo Industrial en Argentina." In *Economia de America Latina: Estado y Proceso de Acumulación*. Buenos Aires: CIDE 3: 45–68.

———. 1981. *Expansión Económica del Estado Subsidiario, 1976–1981*. Buenos Aires: CISEA.

———. 1983. *Martínez de Hoz: La Lógica Política de la Política Económica*. Buenos Aires: CISEA.

Schydlowsky, Daniel. 1989. "Comment." In Guido di Tella and Rudiger Dornbusch, eds., *The Political Economy of Argentina, 1946–83*, 175–88. Oxford: Macmillan Press.

Schydlowsky, Daniel, and Juan J. Wicht. 1983. "The Anatomy of an Economic Failure." In Cynthia McClintock and Abraham F. Lowenthal, eds., *The Peruvian Experience Reconsidered*, 94–143. Princeton: Princeton University Press.

Seguel, General Enrique. 1992. Interview of August 11 with the former president of the central bank.

Seidel, Robert N. 1994. "American Reformers Abroad: The Kemmerer Missions in South America, 1923–1931." In Paul W. Drake, ed., *Money Doctors, Foreign Debts, and Economic Reforms in Latin America from the 1890s to the Present*, 86–109. Wilmington, Del.: Scholarly Resources, Inc., Jaguar Books on Latin America, number 3.

Sheahan, John. 1980. "Market-Oriented Economic Policies and Political Repression in Latin America." *Economic Development and Cultural Change* 28: 267–91.

Shugart, Matthew Soberg, and John M. Carey. 1992. *Presidents and Assemblies: Constitutional Design and Electoral Dynamics*. Cambridge: Cambridge University Press.

Sigmund, Paul E. 1982. "The Military in Chile." In Robert Wesson, ed., *New Military Politics in Latin America*, 97–116. New York: Praeger.

———. 1990. "Chile: Privatization, Reprivatization, Hyperprivatization." In Ezra Suleiman and John Waterbury, eds., *The Political Economy of Public Sector Reform and Privatization*, 346–63. Boulder: Westview Press.

Sikkink, Kathryn. 1991. *Ideas and Institutions: Developmentalism in Brazil and Argentina.* Ithaca: Cornell University Press.

Silva, Eduardo. 1991. "The Political Economy of Chile's Regime Transition: From Radical to 'Pragmatic' Neoliberal Policies." In Paul W. Drake and Iván Jaksic, eds., *The Struggle for Democracy in Chile, 1982–1990,* 98–127. Lincoln: University of Nebraska Press.

———. 1993. "Capitalist Coalitions, the State, and Neoliberal Economic Restructuring: Chile, 1973–88." *World Politics* 45 (July): 526–59.

Silva, Ernesto. 1992. Interview of September 8 with a former member of ODEPLAN, of the Chilean Copper Commission, and ENAP.

Silva, Patricio. 1991. "Technocrats and Politics in Chile: From the Chicago Boys to the CIEPLAN Monks." *Journal of Latin American Studies* 23 (2): 385–410.

Simone, Dante. 1992. Interview of October 28 with the former national director under Martínez de Hoz.

Sjaastad, Larry A. 1989. "Argentine Economic Policy, 1976–81." In Guido di Tella and Rudiger Dornbusch, eds., *The Political Economy of Argentina, 1946–83,* 254–75. Oxford: Macmillan Press.

Skidmore, Thomas E. 1973. "Politics and Economic Policy Making in Authoritarian Brazil, 1937–71." In Alfred Stepan, ed., *Authoritarian Brazil: Origins, Policies, and Future,* 3–46. New Haven: Yale University Press.

———. 1977. "The Politics of Economic Stabilization in Post War Latin America." In James Malloy, ed., *Authoritarianism and Corporatism in Latin America,* 249–90. Pittsburgh: University of Pittsburgh Press.

———. 1988. *The Politics of Military Rule in Brazil, 1964–85.* Oxford: Oxford University Press.

Skidmore, Thomas E., and Peter H. Smith. 1989. *Modern Latin America.* 2nd ed. Oxford: Oxford University Press.

Skocpol, Theda, and Margaret Weir. 1985. "State Structures and the Possibilities for 'Keynesian' Responses to the Great Depression in Sweden, Britain, and the United States." In Peter B. Evans, Dietrich Rueschemeyer, and Theda Skocpol, eds., *Bringing the State Back In,* 107–68. Cambridge: Cambridge University Press.

Smith, Peter H. 1980. "Argentina: The Uncertain Warriors." *Current History* (February): 62–86.

Smith, William C. 1991. "State, Market, and Neoliberalism in Post-Transition Argentina: The Menem Experience." *Journal of Interamerican Studies and World Affairs* 33 (4): 45–82.

Snow, Peter G. 1979. *Political Forces in Argentina.* New York: Praeger.

Solanet, Manuel. 1992. Interview of November 19 with the former minister of finance.

Spooner, Mary Helen. 1999. *Soldiers in a Narrow Land: The Pinochet Regime in Chile.* Berkeley: University of California Press.

Stallings, Barbara. 1983. "International Capitalism and the Peruvian Military Government." In Cynthia McClintock and Abraham F. Lowenthal, eds., *The Peruvian Experience Reconsidered*, 144–80. Princeton: Princeton University Press.

———. 1990. "Politics and Economic Crisis: A Comparative Study of Chile, Peru, and Colombia." In Joan Nelson, ed., *Economic Crisis and Policy Choice: The Politics of Adjustment in the Third World*, 113–68. Princeton: Princeton University Press.

———. 1992. "International Influence on Economic Policy: Debt, Stabilization, and Structural Reform." In Stephan Haggard and Robert R. Kaufman, eds., *The Politics of Economic Adjustment: International Constraints, Distributive Conflicts, and the State*, 44–88. Princeton: Princeton University Press.

Stallings, Barbara, and Robert R. Kaufman. 1989. "Debt and Democracy in the 1980s: The Latin American Experience." In Barbara Stallings and Robert Kaufman, eds., *Debt and Democracy in Latin America*, 201–23. Boulder: Westview Press.

Stenzel, Konrad. 1988. "Markets against Politics in the Chilean Dictatorship: The Role of Professional Economists." *Vierteljahresberichte* 113: 325–34.

Stepan, Alfred. 1971. *The Military in Politics: Changing Patterns in Brazil.* Princeton: Princeton University Press.

———. 1973. "The New Professionalism of Internal Warfare and Military Role Expansion." In Alfred Stepan, ed., *Authoritarian Brazil: Origins Policies, and Future*, 47–68. New Haven: Yale University Press.

———. 1978. *The State and Society: Peru in Comparative Perspective.* Princeton: Princeton University Press.

———. 1985. "State Power and the Strength of Civil Society in the Southern Cone of Latin America." In Peter B. Evans, Dietrich Rueschemeyer, and Theda Skocpol, eds., *Bringing the State Back In*, 317–46. Cambridge: Cambridge University Press.

———. 1988. *Rethinking Military Politics: Brazil and the Southern Cone.* Princeton: Princeton University Press.

Stigler, George J. 1975. *The Citizen and the State: Essays on Regulation.* Chicago: The University of Chicago Press.

Sturzenegger, Adolfo. 1994. Interview of March 29 with the Argentine economist.

Teijeiro, Mario. 1992. Interview of October 29 with the former director of research for the treasury.

Thorp, Rosemary, ed. 1984. *Latin America in the 1930s: The Role of the Periphery in the World Crisis.* New York: St. Martin's Press.

Tiribocchi, Colonel Amilcar. 1992. Interview of September 24 with the former director of the institute of military education.

Tixe Morales, Ana Maria. 1990. "Relaciones Universidad-Gobierno: Uruguay, 1958–1985." Ph. D. dissertation, UCLA.

Tocqueville, Alexis de. 1945. *Democracy in America.* Vol. 1. New York: Random House, Vintage Books.

Tullock, Gordon. 1990. "The Costs of Special Privilege." In James E. Alt and Kenneth A. Shepsle, eds., *Perspectives on Positive Political Economy,* 195–211. Cambridge: Cambridge University Press.

Unión Panamericana. 1972. *América en Cifras; Situación Económica.* Washington, D.C.: Unión Panamericana.

Urrutia, Miguel. 1994. "Colombia." In John Williamson, ed., *The Political Economy of Policy Reform,* 285–315. Washington, D.C.: Institute for International Economics.

Valdés, Juan Gabriel. 1989. *La Escuela de Chicago: Operación Chile.* Buenos Aires: Grupo Editorial Zeta, S.A.

———. 1995. *Pinochet's Economists: The Chicago School in Chile.* Cambridge: Cambridge University Press.

Valenzuela, Arturo. 1978. *The Breakdown of Democratic Regimes: Chile.* Baltimore: Johns Hopkins University Press.

———. 1989. "Chile: Origins, Consolidation, and Breakdown of a Democratic Regime." In Larry Diamond, Juan J. Linz, and Seymour Martin Lipset, eds., *Democracy in Developing Countries: Latin America,* 159–206. Boulder: Lynne Rienner Publishers.

———. 1991. "The Military in Power: The Consolidation of One-Man Rule." In Paul W. Drake and Iván Jaksic, eds., *The Struggle for Democracy in Chile, 1982–1990,* 21–72. Lincoln: University of Nebraska Press.

Valenzuela, J. Samuel, and Arturo Valenzuela, eds. 1986. *Military Rule in Chile: Dictatorship and Oppositions.* Baltimore: Johns Hopkins University Press.

Van Niekerk, A.E. 1974. *Populism and Political Development in Latin America.* Rotterdam: Rotterdam University Press.

Varas, Augusto. 1987. *Las Fuerzas Armada en la Transición Consolidación Democratica en Chile.* Santiago: Centro de Estudios del Desarrollo.

———. 1992. Interview of August 21 with the FLACSO political scientist.

Varas, Florencia. 1979. *Gustavo Leigh: El General Disidente.* Santiago: Editorial Aconcagua.

Vaz, Daniel. 1992. Interview of September 11 and 14 with the general manager of the central bank in Uruguay.

———. 1994. Interview of March 18 with the general manager of the central bank in Uruguay.

———. 1995. Written communication of June 21 with the general manager of the central bank in Uruguay.

Végh Villegas, Alejandro. 1975. "Política Económica: Sus Fundamentos y sus Objetivos." *Búsqueda* (34): 12–16.

———. 1977. *Economía Política: Teoría y Acción.* Montevideo: Ediciones Polo Ltda.

———. 1992a. Interview of December 17 with the former minister of finance.

———. 1992b. "Reflections on Some Experiences in Economic Policymaking." Unpublished manuscript.

Venezian, Eduardo. 1982. "The Economic Sciences in Latin America." In Laurence D. Stifel, et al., eds., *Social Sciences and Public Policy in the Developing World*, 189–210. Lexington, Mass.: Lexington Books.

Vergara, Pilar. 1985. *Auge y Caída del Neoliberalismo en Chile*. Santiago: Facultad Latinoamericana de Ciencias Sociales.

———. 1986. "Changes in the Functions of the Chilean State under the Military Regime." In J. Samuel Valenzuela and Arturo Valenzuela, eds., *Military Rule in Chile: Dictatorship and Oppositions*, 85–116. Baltimore: Johns Hopkins University Press.

Vernon, Raymond, ed. 1988. *The Promise of Privatization: A Challenge for U.S. Policy*. New York: Council on Foreign Relations.

Viana, Luis. 1992. Interview of September 18 with the Uruguayan economist.

Videla, Jorge. 1992. Interview of November 25 with the former Argentine junta leader from 1976 to 1981.

Waisbord, Silvio. 1991. "Politics and Identity in the Argentine Army: Cleavages and the Generational Factor." *Latin American Research Review* 26 (2): 157–70.

Waisman, Carlos A. 1989. "Argentina: Autarkic Industrialization and Illegitimacy." In Larry Diamond, Juan J. Linz, and Seymour Martin Lipset, eds., *Democracy in Developing Countries: Latin America*, 59–110. Boulder: Lynne Rienner Publishers.

Walker, Ignacio. 1992. Interview of September 9 with the former secretary general of the Chilean government.

Weede, Erich. 1983. "The Impact of Democracy on Economic Growth: Some Evidence from Cross-National Studies." *Kyklos* 36: 21–39.

Wehbe, Jorge. 1992. Interview of December 9 with the former minister of finance.

Werneck, Rogério F. 1991. "Public Sector Adjustment to External Shocks and Domestic Pressures in Brazil." In Felipe Larraín and Marcelo Selowsky, eds., *The Public Sector and the Latin American Crisis*, 53–88. San Francisco: International Center for Economic Growth.

Weyland, Kurt. 1994. "Neo-populism and Neo-liberalism in Latin America: Unexpected Affinities." Presented at the annual meeting of the American Political Science Association, the New York Hilton.

Whitaker, Arthur P. 1968. "Flourish of Trumpets: Enter the Military, 1930–1943." In Joseph R. Barager, ed., *Why Perón Came to Power: The Background of Peronism in Argentina*, 138–50. New York: Alfred A. Knopf.

Wilkie, J., et al., eds. 1993. *Statistical Abstract of Latin America*. Vol. 30. Los Angeles: UCLA Latin American Center Publications, University of California.

Williamson, John, ed. 1994. *The Political Economy of Policy Reform*. Washington, D. C.: Institute for International Economics.

Williamson, John, and Stephan Haggard. 1994. "The Political Conditions for Economic Reform." In John Williamson, ed., *The Political Economy of Policy Reform*, 527–96. Washington, D. C.: Institute for International Economics.

Wilson, James Q., ed. 1980. *The Politics of Regulation*. New York: Basic Books.

Wise, Carol. 1990. "Peru Post-1968: The Political Limits to State-Led Economic Development." Ph. D. dissertation, Columbia University.

Woo-Cummings, Meredith. 1999. "Introduction: Chalmers Johnson and the Politics of Nationalism and Development." In Meredith Woo-Cummings, ed., *The Developmental State*, 1–31. Ithaca: Cornell University Press.

World Bank. 1978. *Report No. 2241-UR Economic Memorandum on Uruguay*. Washington, D. C.: World Bank (Latin America and the Caribbean Region Country Programs Department II).

———. 1990. *Uruguay: Trade Reform and Economic Efficiency*. Washington D. C.: World Bank.

———. 1995. *Bureaucrats in Business: The Economics and Politics of Government Ownership*. Washington, D. C.: World Bank.

Wynia, Gary W. 1978. *Argentina in the Postwar Era: Politics and Economic Policymaking in a Divided Society*. Albuquerque: University of New Mexico Press.

———. 1982. "The Argentine Revolution Falters." *Current History* (February): 74–77.

———. 1986. *Illusions and Realities*. New York: Holmes and Meier.

INDEX

Agency for International Development (AID), 144, 146–48, 150, 152–53, 155–56, 158
Alemann, Roberto, 36
Alfonsín, Raúl, 176–77
Allende, Salvador, 26–27, 53, 64, 120, 122, 192n.17, 193n.26
Ames, Barry, 9–10, 55–56
appointments: possible strategies of government officials, 8, 56–57, 116–17, 163–64, 186n.16; strategies chosen under democratic rule, 163–79, 182–83; strategies chosen under military rule, 9–11, 13–15, 17, 58–63, 94–95, 117–19, 123, 126–27, 129–36, 160
Argentina: appointment strategies in, 72–77, 102–4, 129–32, 160–61, 164–68, 176–78; control over promotions and retirements in, 73; economic policies during democratic years (post-military rule), 161, 164, 166–68, 176–77; economic policies during military period, 31–37, 127–32; employment prospects for economists in, 151–53; governing institutions in, 71–76, 160–61, 164–68; history of economic policies

before military era, 22–24, 30–31, 34, 112–13, 127; history of economics profession in, 143–45, 151–54; interest group lobbying in, 73–74, 76, 104–6, 131–32; inter-service rivalries in, 70–71, 129–30; military factionalism in, 70–77; privatization in, 127–32. *See also* appointments; governing institutions; military; military regimes
Ascher, William, 149
azules, 71

Banco Nacional de Desenvolvimento Econômico e Social (BNDES), 84
Barco, Virgilio, 19, 168–70, 177, 179
Batlle y Ordóñez, José, 23, 38, 54, 113, 132
Bessone, General Díaz, 75
Betancur, Belisario, 178
Blanco Party (PN), 38, 174–75, 189n.10
Bordaberry, Juan María, 19, 39, 55, 77–80, 106–7, 179, 198n.31
Brazil: appointment strategies in, 82–83, 161; economic policies during military period, 82–86; governing institutions in, 80–86, 161; history of military in, 80–81; influence in other countries, 78; interest